Praise for *Escape from Overshoot*

Uses sound economics to map a path out of overshoot. Highly recommended.

—Herman Daly

An excellent primer
economics
from a celebrated pi

r, *Less is More*

Peter Victor provides for the economic rocket humanity needs for a safe landing on Spaceship Earth. In our turbulent times, with multiple planetary boundaries breached and tipping points approaching fast, *Escape from Overshoot* provides the perfect launch pad for new economic thinking that reconnects the world with planet Earth.

—Johan Rockström, Professor, Earth System Science; Director of the Potsdam Institute for Climate Impact Research; and co-author, *Earth for All*

The title of Peter Victor's important book says it all: the planet is in peril and a major factor is a global economy too big for nature to flourish. Human beings are animals and thus, like all other species, constrained by nature and nature's laws. An economy unfettered by the needs and limits of nature and propelled by a fool's goal of endless growth has created the twin ecological crises of climate change and biodiversity loss. All who care about the kind of world we are leaving to our grandchildren and what we can do to bring the economy into harmony with nature must read this vital book.

—David Suzuki, emeritus professor and grandfather

What a *tour de force*. I simply love this book. Peter Victor makes it clear that economic activity has overshot, putting the future of human society in peril. But, beyond evidence and analysis, Victor offers ideas about what governments, society, and organizations can do. This is a must-read for anyone concerned about our collective future.

—Pratima (Tima) Bansal, Canada Research Chair in Business Sustainability, Ivey Business School, University of Western Ontario

The biggest challenge facing humanity today is building a future that is both sustainable and desirable to most people and the rest of nature. Peter Victor's *Escape from Overshoot* plots a detailed yet feasible course to that future, based on a post-growth, ecological economic vision and new systems-dynamics modelling. Victor shows how escaping our addiction to the current economic paradigm (and the overshoot and collapse that portends) can result in the better, fairer, more prosperous world we all want. A must-read for the rapidly growing movement we need to make that happen.

—Robert Costanza, Institute for Global Prosperity, University College London

Dr. Peter Victor skilfully shows us that indeed we are in overshoot and time is not on our side. There is no doubt that we could have avoided overshoot if we had listened both to the warnings in *Limits to Growth* and many subsequent publications by prominent scientists and ecological economists over the last 50 years. If we are to finally find an exit route from our own human folly—our addiction to growth—we need Peter Victor's book and many others to draw a vision of the future that is both hopeful andreal. Victor draws a plausible pathway that nicely intertwines with a growing body of evidence and proposals for new economic models from across the globe. This book is timely and gives cause for hope!

—Sandrine Dixson-Declève, co-president, the Club of Rome,
and co-author, *Earth for All*

Peter Victor has consistently been a leading general in the Paul Revere Brigade, presciently warning us for decades of the interconnected ecological and economic crises now unfolding before our eyes. He has also been an always courageous, clear thinkerand rigorous analyst illuminating sensible rather than fanciful pathways out of our predicament. Stop what you are doing and read this important book!

—John B. Fullerton, founder and president, Capital Institute

Overdue, but not too late. I can't think of anyone who shouldn't read *Escape from Overshoot*. Victor provides essential insights into the economic thinking that led to social and environmental disaster and draws critically important policy implications from the new models that will facilitate our escape.

—Richard B. Norgaard, Professor Emeritus of Energy and Resources,
University of California, Berkeley

Global civilization is in ecological overshoot, depleting and polluting the biophysical basis of its own existence. Untreated, overshoot is a fatal condition. Erudite and lavishly illustrated, Peter Victor's *Escape from Overshoot* is a sweeping analysis of the flawed economic mindset that has pushed us to the brink and an inspired prescription for the new economics needed to help pull us back.

—William Rees, professor emeritus, University of British Columbia,
former director of the School of Community and Regional Planning (SCARP),
and co-author, *Our Ecological Footprint*

In this ambitious, deeply humanistic, and very accessible volume, Peter Victor explains the origins of the current global predicament of ecological overshoot, and points to a path toward diminishing it. In the process, he takes a reader on a grand tour of ecological and earth systems science, economics, history, demography, energy and technology studies, and contemporary debates about post-growth wellbeing economics. It is a must-read for all who like complexity made comprehensible, and who reach beyond headlines, doomsday predictions, and simplistic solutions. This is a terrific book! I wish I had it when I was teaching and it should be a required text for all university students, regardless of specialization.

—Halina Szejnwald Brown, Professor Emerita of Environmental Science
and Policy Clark University, and co-founder, Sustainable Consumption
Research and Action Initiative (SCORAI)

Whether you're a reformer or a revolutionary, this compelling and provocative work is a critical resource as we grapple with the climate crisis, planetary health, and reversing biodiversity loss. The book explores alternatives and sustainable paths moving forward in plain terms and I highly recommend it to anyone in the sustainability field.

—Paul Bubelis, Executive Director, Sustainability Network

An intriguing book for troubled times. Peter Victor brilliantly weaves together the history of economic thought, economic and social development, and the path to the current ecological overshoot. He brings realism to proposed solutions by exposing myths, for example with regard to green GDP, and then highlights a plausible way forward. If you want to understand the past, the present, and potential economic and ecological futures, this book is for you.

—Brynhildur Davidsdottir, Professor of Environment
and Natural Resources, University of Iceland

The scale of our economy is driving overshoot and resulting in overlapping ecological crises. Peter Victor provides a clearly written introduction to the links between economic growth and ecological impact, and offers tools and policy pathways for avoiding disaster. *Escape from Overshoot* is a must-read for the next generation of economists.

—Brett Dolter, Assistant Professor,
Department of Economics, University of Regina

If human history is our guide, then overshoot is our destiny. Yet Peter Victor's comprehensive review of the evidence, debates, and alternatives also provides a credible escape plan from planetary disaster. I wish our leaders had this balanced sensibility between reality and imagination.

—Jon D. Erickson, professor, University of Vermont,
and author, *The Progress Illusion*

I own hundreds of books, all carefully curated. But I reserve one short shelf for books that I think everybody needs to read right away in order to grasp the human condition and what needs to be done. Peter Victor's *Escape from Overshoot* is now at the front of that shelf. It is clearly and entertainingly written and elicits an aha! on every page. *Escape from Overshoot* would be a great book on those merits alone, even if it weren't the key to our collective fate.

—Richard Heinberg, Senior Fellow, Post Carbon Institute, and author, *Power*

An engaging and learned discussion that brings to a wide audience the fruits of several decades of research and public policy experience of Dr. Victor. The book describes and explains succinctly humanity's predicament and develops an escape strategy from overshoot towards a more attractive future than what we are facing if current trends continue.

—Aitf Kubursi, Ph.D., Professor Emeritus of Economics, McMaster University

Escape from Overshoot is a timely reminder that humankind's predicament is not just about how we do individual things, but also about the scale at which we do everything. Victor offers a nuanced approach to thinking about and designing plausible escape paths from overshoot that everyone should be cognizant of and seriously consider. A very important and accessible book.

—Professor Philip Lawn, Torrens University, Adelaide

Peter Victor is a world expert on the clash between the economy and the environment. His fifty-year career in university and public administration reached the top with his "ecological macroeconomics," developed in the last decades in the pursuit of a paradigm of "post-growth." In *Escape from Overshoot*, he writes with authority on the main themes considered in this guidebook for the future: social metabolism and energy, macroeconomics, demography, consumption, food, technology, wage-work, robots, and advertising. This is a unique book illustrated with many graphics and drawings like a (deadly serious) comic. It is not a long treatise, it is a short, well-informed book with crucial proposals written in easy-to-read language.

—Joan Martínez Alier, emeritus professor,
ICTA-Universitat Autònoma de Barcelona

An absolute must read—I could not put it down and read it in one sitting. Peter Victor masterfully ties the threads of economic thought together to demonstrate why—and how—we can collectively do our best to avoid climate and ecological breakdown.

—David Miller, managing director, C40 Centre
for City Climate Policy and Economy

Escape from Overshoot is a tour de force of the latest research in ecological economics from one of the top researchers in the field. In a highly accessible style, with a helpful figure or illustration on almost every page, Peter Victor explains how the current economic system works, how it has pushed us to the precipice of environmental collapse, and how a post-growth economy could pull us back from the edge.

—Dan O'Neill, Associate Professor in Ecological Economics,
University of Leeds, and president,
European Society for Ecological Economics

Peter Victor shares his perspectives from a lifetime of environmental analysis and activism in this wide-ranging take on the most pressing world challenges. He is a genial, progressive, knowledgeable guide through reams of information, and this book opens many doors for new strategizing about ways to escape overshoot trends.

—Ellie Perkins, professor, Faculty of Environmental
and Urban Change, York University

It is increasingly clear that our current system is dangerously dysfunctional—inequality, oppression, and ecological devastation are coming at us fast and furious. Victor, always proficient in making complex ideas and models accessible, has written a superb account of the economic ideas which helped lead us here, and the rich menu of post-growth options currently available. Highly recommended for anyone looking for an escape from a doomed future.

> —Juliet Schor, economist and sociologist,
> and author, *Plenitude: The New Economics of True Wealth*

No one pulls it all together as well as Peter Victor. His *Escape from Overshoot* covers climate and other key issues with a compelling clarity. I highly recommend this book.

> —James Gustave Speth, former Dean, Yale School of the Environment,
> and author, *America the Possible*

Peter Victor is a scholar our world needs more of, and this book is indicative of the breadth of his analysis, the rigor with which he dismantles the flimsy assumptions on which so much policy is unfortunately built, and the hope his ideas and recommendations are infused with. The more people that read, digest, and take note of this book, the better prospects our world has for tackling the crises we currently face.

> —Dr. Katherine Trebeck, University of Edinburgh, and co-founder, WEAll

Peter Victor is the ultimate doctor in economics: he diagnoses not only the 21st century's most debilitating disease, but also explores therapeutic options. His fabulous book reveals the symptoms of persistent overshoot, delivers myriad options for curing the disease, and assures us that the gains outweigh by far the therapeutic pains. If you want to enable the next generation to build a successful future, ditch the textbooks from the past and get this one instead.

> —Mathis Wackernagel, Ph.D., founder and president,
> Global Footprint Network, and author, *Ecological Footprint*

Escape from Overshoot

ESCAPE
FROM
OVERSHOOT

ECONOMICS FOR
A PLANET IN PERIL

PETER A. VICTOR

new society
PUBLISHERS

Cover design by Diane McIntosh. Cover image © iStock

All images © Peter Victor unless otherwise noted.
Page 1 © Julia/ Adobe Stock.

Printed in Canada. First printing March 2023.

Inquiries regarding requests to reprint all or part of *Escape from Overshoot* should be addressed to New Society Publishers at the address below. To order directly from the publishers, please call 250-247-9737 or order online at www.newsociety.com.

Any other inquiries can be directed by mail to:

New Society Publishers
P.O. Box 189, Gabriola Island, BC V0R 1X0, Canada
(250) 247-9737

LIBRARY AND ARCHIVES CANADA CATALOGUING IN PUBLICATION

Title: Escape from overshoot : economics for a planet in peril / Peter A. Victor.

Names: Victor, Peter A., 1946– author.

Description: Includes bibliographical references and index.

Identifiers: Canadiana (print) 20220493820 | Canadiana (ebook) 2022049388X | ISBN 9780865719750 (softcover) | ISBN 9781550927696 (PDF) | ISBN 9781771423656 (EPUB)

Subjects: LCSH: Environmental economics. | LCSH: Sustainable development.

Classification: LCC HC79.E5 V53 2023 | DDC 333.7—dc23

Funded by the Government of Canada

Financé par le gouvernement du Canada

Canada

New Society Publishers' mission is to publish books that contribute in fundamental ways to building an ecologically sustainable and just society, and to do so with the least possible impact on the environment, in a manner that models this vision.

new society PUBLISHERS

Certified
B Corporation

FSC MIX Paper from responsible sources www.fsc.org FSC® C016245

Contents

Acknowledgments

Normally, when authors thank their editor, they do so after thanking everyone else who helped them bring their idea for a book to fruition. In this instance that would be inappropriate, since the idea for this book was Rob West's, the Acquisitions Editor at New Society Publishers, not mine. Early in February 2021 Rob contacted me. He had watched the online Gideon Rosenbluth Memorial Lecture I had just given and suggested that I write a future-oriented book, based on my many decades of work on economy and environment. It would be heavily illustrated, with a sparse text, written for a wide audience. This book is the result, not only of Rob's original suggestion, but of the generous assistance he and his colleagues provided throughout the project. I particularly want to thank Murray Reiss for his excellent copyediting. I am extremely grateful to them all.

It is with great pleasure and deep gratitude that I thank Herman Daly, Martin Sers, and Peter Timmerman for their learned help in writing this book. They commented on drafts of each chapter, and their suggestions, criticisms and support are reflected on every page. Sadly, after the book was completed, Herman passed away surrounded by his family. I and so many others, miss him dearly.

I also thank Ed Hanna who has, for so many years, helped me understand the natural sciences and engineering, and did so once again when I wanted to express complicated scientific ideas in simple terms.

This book would not exist were it not for all those who wrote the many reports, books, and papers on which I drew, especially for the 170 images that it contains. Two contributors to the literature on overshoot that stand out are William Catton Jr., whose book *Overshoot, The Ecological Basis of Revolutionary Change*, published in 1982, explained how today's profligate use of what the Earth provides comes at the expense of our descendants, and William Rees, originator and co-developer of the ecological footprint, who has written several recent, influential scientific papers on overshoot. I am especially appreciative to all those who made their images available through a Creative Commons licence and to those who granted me permission to reproduce their work. I have tried to name all of them in the book and apologise if I have missed anyone.

The book is dedicated to my three friends from undergraduate days at Birmingham University: David Franks, Tony Klug, and Lance Blackstone. I have never forgotten how supportive they were as I plunged myself into the study of economics all those years ago. I'm so glad we have remained friends despite living so far apart. Many years later, I befriended Tim Jackson, a man whose range and depth of knowledge and remarkable talents have few equals, and with whom I have written many papers and reports of which I am very proud. I was delighted when Tim agreed to write the foreword to this book and thank him for doing so.

Finally, to Maria, my brilliant, loving, principled, tenacious wife of 50 years—without her encouragement and patience, this book would never have been written. I hope that you, dear reader, will find that it was worth the effort.

Foreword

Escape is in our blood. It's probably in our DNA. Our ancestors survived by learning to escape from predators, from famine and from each other. When our lives are bleak, dangerous, and exhausting—or even just mildly boring—we dream of escaping to more exciting, more convivial, kinder places.

These aspirations have driven humanity towards extraordinary achievements. Nobody can deny that, for the lucky few at least, life has become richer in material terms. More comfortable. Less dangerous on a day-to-day level. It's not improbable to assume that we've achieved this degree of progress, in part, by dreaming of escape.

But today our challenge is massively different. Our escape from drudgery came at the expense of devastating climate change. Our escape from poverty imposed poverty on others. Our escape from biological scarcity inflicted extinction on other species. Our escape from boredom was built on a massive expansion in technological complexity that now threatens our humanity. Today we must fashion an escape from the damage we ourselves have wreaked on the planet—and on each other.

How to achieve that is the most vital question of our age. It's the question at the heart of Peter Victor's wide-ranging, ambitious, and highly accessible tour through several decades of ecological science and economics. It's a question that has been, as *Escape from Overshoot* makes clear, at the forefront of intellectual thinking for more than half a century. Ever since we could see the loneliness of this planet for ourselves.

When the former Soviet Union sent the very first orbital satellite, Sputnik 1, into space in October 1957, an American newspaper celebrated the launch as the first "step toward escape from [our] imprisonment to the earth." Reading that comment, the social philosopher Hannah Arendt expressed amazement at the extent to which our dreams of endless expansion had found their way from "non-respectable" science fiction into a mainstream newspaper—and aired her dismay at the implications of this.

Should the "emancipation" of the secular age, which had begun with a turning away from "God the father," end with "an even more fateful repudiation of an Earth who was the Mother of all living creatures under the sky?" she asked, in the opening chapter of her 1958 masterpiece *The Human Condition*. "The earth is the very quintessence of the human condition," she declared. And our "rebellion" against its confines can only be "self-defeating."

Fast forward to the early 2020s, and Arendt would have been unsurprised perhaps but even more dismayed to find several of the richest men in the world vying to win a kind of billionaires' space race. As most of the rest of humanity struggled with a lockdown even more pernicious than our planetary confinement, their immediate goal was to outdo each other in reaching the Karman line—the place where the earth's atmosphere ends and outer space begins. Their eventual dream: a science-fiction-fuelled fantasy of human life reaching out across (and one day perhaps even beyond) the galaxy.

SpaceX founder and serial entrepreneur Elon Musk was one of these new rocket men. When asked by TED curator Chris Anderson what drove his vision of reaching space and eventually colonizing Mars, Musk said: "I'm just trying to think about the future—and not be sad." Those who attack the space race, he insisted, "maybe don't realize that space represents hope for so many people."

That may be true in a world where huge inequalities of wealth and privilege strip hope from the lives of billions of people. But it obscures the extraordinary demands associated with escaping the earth's gravity: the energy, the materials, the people, the time. Resources that could achieve considerably more in terms of human prosperity if they were directed towards the pressing global problems of today.

It also neglects the immensely slim odds of finding anywhere a habitat as convivial as this one. Mars may be the least uninhabitable planet in the solar system, outside Earth. But it's still a very far cry from the beauty of home—whose fragility, ironically, we only truly learned to appreciate from the images sent back to us from space.

Nature photographer Galen Rowell once called William Anders' iconic photo *Earthrise*, taken from the Apollo 8 module in lunar orbit, "the most influential environmental photograph ever taken." *Earthrise* brought home to us, in one astonishing image, the stark reality that this shining orb was—and still is—humanity's best chance for anything that might meaningfully be called the "good life." It may well be "unique in the universe in providing human beings with a habitat in which they can move and breathe without effort and without artifice," wrote Arendt.

If we are to do justice to that insight, if we are to protect this precious life support system, if there is an escape to be had from the damage inflicted on the planet by two centuries of industrial expansion, then it seems we must begin by looking inwards rather than outwards. We must correct the inner workings of our own dysfunctional economy before exporting its influence into space. We must get our own house in order before we set our sights on the stars.

This other journey—something we could legitimately call an escape from overshoot—may not be so ostentatiously bold as a confrontation with the final frontier. But it is still in many respects a formidable venture. An excursion into the unknown. Not without its excitements and rewards. But undoubtedly beset with obstacles that challenge our ingenuity and demand our courage.

It's definitely the kind of expedition on which it's wise to choose an experienced and sympathetic guide. A companion willing to share with you their knowledge of the terrain and their insights on the world. Someone wise enough to avoid the pitfalls of hubris and creative enough to bring the "dismal science" of economics alive. It's no surprise to find that guide in these pages.

When Peter Victor and I first met, almost fifteen years ago, we had been working separately for some time on a common problem.

Virtually unrecognized by mainstream economists, the discipline of ecological economics shines an inquiring light on the sheer scale of economic activity on a finite planet. Like many ecological economists, we were both already wary of the mantra of eternal economic growth. At one point we were (probably) the only two economists in the world to have written books with the inflammatory words "without growth" in the title.

In a climate of academic competition, that unlikely qualification might easily have divided us. The decision instead to pool our resources was due in no small part to Peter's open-hearted approach to scientific endeavour. For more than a decade now we have worked closely together to try and understand what an economy looks like when it's no longer fixated on growth but rather seeks to improve people's wellbeing within planetary boundaries. That project to build a "post-growth economics" now also attracts some of the brightest young economists in the world. No doubt they will boldly go where Peter and I have only begun to tread.

In the meantime, I see it as an enormous privilege that some of our shared work has found its way into this timely and critical book. More than that, I am delighted to recommend as a guide on this other journey a man whose decency, integrity, and kindness made our own collaboration much more than an intellectual adventure. Whether we are searching inwards or gazing outwards, the one thing we should never forget is our own humanity. Any escape from overshoot must ultimately return us to ourselves.

— Tim Jackson

Prologue: A Planet in Peril

Homo sapiens became established on planet Earth at least 200,000 years ago, and perhaps well before.[1] It took until the year 1800 or thereabouts for the human population to reach one billion. A second billion was added in only 124 years, with successive billions added at intervals of thirty-three, fifteen, twelve, twelve, twelve, and thirteen years,[2] surpassing eight billion in total in 2022. Most of the one billion humans living at the beginning of the 19th century had a very low material standard of living. Billions still do today, but for billions more living standards have increased by leaps and bounds, faster even than the increase in population. Meanwhile, the planet has not increased in size at all. Essentially the same amount of sunlight is intercepted by the Earth each year, providing life-giving energy which, through photosynthesis, supports virtually all life on Earth, including humans.

The combination of billions of people and the gargantuan quantities of materials we use to enrich our lives is imposing a burden on the Earth's ecological systems that cannot be sustained. It is in this sense that the planet is in peril. Earth itself is not in danger. It will be here long after humans have come and gone, but we are imperiling it as a home for our species and that of many others not because we want to, but because so far have been unable to stop depleting and degrading the capacity of the planet to sustain us all.

There is overwhelming evidence that human impacts on the zone of life on Earth—the biosphere—have surpassed sustainable levels in several crucial respects. We are in Earth overshoot. Of course, there are huge differences in how much different people and nations have contributed to overshoot and its effects, both historically and now. There is also a disturbing disconnect between those primarily responsible for overshoot and those most vulnerable to its consequences, and the situation is getting worse.

None of this is to deny the remarkable improvements in many aspects of people's lives experienced by the most recent generations. Material living standards have reached unprecedented levels for literally billions of people, though billions more still languish in abject poverty, still hoping for a better future for themselves and their children. Many believe that the technological advances, fuelled by cheap fossil fuel energy, that led from the steam age to the widespread, innovative uses of electricity, computerization, and remarkable achievements in the life sciences, will overcome any and all obstacles. But these advances have come at a cost. Great damage has been done and continues to be done to our Earthly home, and to the other species with which we share it. There have been occasional gains such as the reduction in acid rain in the 1980s and 90s in the USA and Canada, and the partial recovery of the stratospheric ozone layer, though not without strong corporate opposition and government hesitancy. However, despite the seemingly endless succession of international commitments and well-intended plans for reducing greenhouse gas emissions, protecting biodiversity and endangered species, and addressing numerous other aspects of overshoot, we are figuratively and literally losing ground. What is to be done?

There is no simple solution to such an entanglement of complex problems. But there are ways of thinking and acting that can help. Some of these come from economics, which has a rich stock of ideas and insights developed over the past two centuries as well as from more contemporary sources, from which we can draw. The aim of this book is to bring to a wide audience the fruits of several decades of research that describes and explains humanity's predicament and points towards a more attractive future than if current trends continue. The emphasis is on economics because the economic activities of production and consumption are so intimately related to overshoot, and as an economist, it is what I know best. But just as fire, police, and ambulance are routinely called to emergencies, we will need all the best ideas that humanity has to offer, not just from economics, to find an escape from overshoot. And the escape plan, to the extent that one can be synthesized by a single author, is intended primarily for high-income countries which, as a matter of justice and efficacy, should take the lead in reducing their impacts on planet Earth.

The book begins with an account of overshoot drawing on peer-reviewed and government sources. It tells a very disturbing story. Since we are concerned about the future, evidence for overshoot is followed by a discussion of the difficulty—impossibility even—of predicting the future. But prediction as normally understood is not the objective of this book. Any prediction of the future is contingent on what we decide and do today. This book is intended to help us make better decisions, informed by careful, systematic consideration of their possible and probable consequences. This is our best chance of finding an escape from overshoot and a better future for all.

The immediate cause of overshoot is the combination of the massive increase in the number of people and what we produce made possible by the rapid and grossly uneven experience of economic growth of the past two hundred years. In many parts of the world, economic growth has become virtually synonymous with the idea of progress. This did not happen without critical commentary, including some from influential economists, which was, however, largely ignored. In this book we will hear their voices once again and maybe this time we will listen more closely.

It is common in academic disciplines for members to coalesce around a few key ideas or principles, giving rise to different schools of thought. In mainstream, neo-classical economics, environmental problems have generally been seen as a problem in *microeconomics*—the economics of individuals and markets. The same is true of issues relating to the depletion of natural resources. From this comes useful insights about the failure of markets—where they exist at all—to register environmental damages and excessive rates of resource use. Policy proposals that flow from this microeconomic analysis emphasize the use of various types of emission charges such as a carbon tax, grounded in the belief that if we "get the prices right" markets will automatically yield the right quantities of polluting emissions and rates of resource utilization. An alternative approach arising from this neo-classical perspective, is to establish markets where none exist—say of permits to emit pollutants or to catch fish—and allow the permits to be traded with their price determined by demand and supply.

These microeconomic approaches to environmental and resource issues have a place in the menu of policy options, but they fall short of what is required to escape from overshoot. The reason for this is that emission charges and tradable permits are designed to make markets more efficient—to assign inputs of all kinds to their best uses. But overshoot is less a problem of efficiency in this sense than one of *scale*, of the physical size of the economy in relation to the physical size of the Earth and its ecological systems on which economies depend. Overshoot is first and foremost a problem of *macroeconomics*, of the whole economy. So, for this reason, most of the economics used to address overshoot in this book comes from macroeconomics, with its scope expanded to encompass this essential dependency of economies on the environment.

The predominant economic system in today's world is some form of capitalism and so we will compare, at a macro level, how several of these schools of thought analyze capitalism. We will see that they differ greatly in the different features of capitalism that they highlight, suggesting different obstacles to and possibilities for an escape from overshoot, though this was not their originators' main concern. However, it is the concern of several current proposals for more sustainable economies, such as steady-state economics, doughnut economics, and degrowth, from which we can draw elements of an escape plan. These proposals all draw on ecological economics, a new branch of economics founded on the understanding that economies are sub-systems of the biosphere, entirely dependent on Earthly supplies of materials (including fossil fuels), air, land, and water.[3] Ecological economics recognizes that inputs to the economy are transformed and degraded through production and consumption, which, when excessive, upset the balance between humans and the rest of nature.

One way of delineating future possibilities is to draw a conceptual map of the terrain based on key topics. The map of the future sketched in this book consists of points of interest such as consumption, technology, work, and equity but, like an ordinary printed map, it does not prescribe a particular route. Some routes—green growth and the circular economy for example—are promoted based on the questionable belief that economic growth can be permanently decoupled from resources and wastes. An alternative is to look forward to a post-growth future and the various forms that it might take, starting in high-income economies. Simulation of various scenarios are featured, culminating in a list of what needs to change to get the future we choose, rather than the one that ignorance, vested interests, and complacency will otherwise oblige us and those who follow to take. Examples of positive change are not hard to find, and we look at a few. Their very existence gives grounds for hope. The challenge is to ramp them up quickly to a level sufficient to escape from overshoot, and this book helps point the way.

FIGURE 1.1.
The Earth from
space 1972.

Credit: NASA.

1

OVERSHOOT:
A LOOK AT THE EVIDENCE

The first photographs of Earth from space were taken in 1946 from a sub-orbital V-2 rocket and only showed a small section of the planet, just enough to reveal its curvature. In the 1960s, when the space race between the USA and the USSR was in full swing, people saw for the very first time the entire planet in color. It was an astonishing sight. Seeing the Earth, bounded on all sides by space, brought home the fact that we live on a finite planet. Life on Earth is totally dependent on the materials carried on board spaceship Earth and the influx of solar energy that makes life possible, just like the capsules that took animals then humans into space and sent back mind-bending images.

Economist Henry George is thought to be the first person to liken Earth to a spaceship. Nearly 150 years ago he described the Earth as "a well-provisioned ship, this on which we sail through space."[4] In 1965, the year he died, Adlai Stevenson, U.S. Ambassador to the United Nations said, "We travel together, passengers on a little spaceship, dependent on its vulnerable reserves of air and soil; all committed for our safety to its security and peace; preserved from annihilation only by the care, the work, and, I will say, the love we give our fragile craft. We cannot maintain it half fortunate, half miserable, half confident, half despairing, half slave to the ancient enemies of man, half free in a liberation of resources undreamed of until this day. No craft, no crew can travel safely with such vast contradictions. On their resolution depends the survival of us all."[5] It was true then and is even truer today.

1

The need to resolve the contradictions that Stevenson spoke of is more pressing than ever.

In the more than half a century since Stevenson spoke those words, world population has increased by over 230 percent and world GDP, which measures the market value of final goods and services, by over 960 percent. The size of planet Earth remains unchanged while the on-board stocks of easily accessible materials have diminished, lands and water have been degraded, species extinction has accelerated while many more have become threatened, and the climate is heating up. Advances in science and technology have also been amazing. Equip-

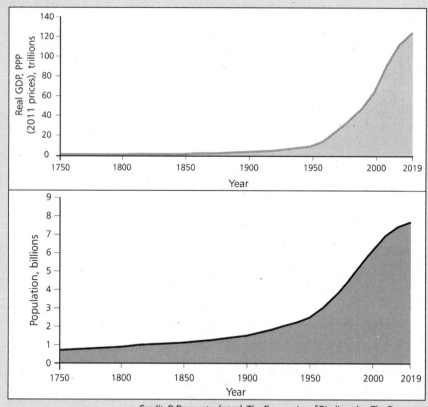

FIGURE 1.2.
Global population and economic output 1750 to 2019.

Credit: P. Dasgupta, (2021), The Economics of Biodiversity: The Dasgupta Review. Abridged Version. (London: H.M. Treasury).

ment has become more efficient, and new technologies such as nuclear power, genetic modification, and smart phones have been invented. The list is a long one. Innovation on all fronts continues such that many people pin their hopes for the future on developments in science and technology. But will it be enough to escape from overshoot?

Overshoot

Let's look a little deeper into the meaning of overshoot. When any organism exceeds the capacity of its environment to sustain it, it is in overshoot. This can be true of bacteria growing in a Petri dish with a limited food supply. It can also be true of humans when our use of what nature provides is greater than nature's capacity to regenerate. The accumulation of greenhouse gases in the atmosphere that could be irreversibly changing the climate means we are in overshoot. If more fish are caught than are reproduced by the remaining stock, we have overshot. Overshoot can happen to ecosystems at all scales from a single pond to the entire planet and to any species. Humans are no exception.

When a population exceeds the carrying capacity of its environment a combination of three things happens: (1) the death rate in the population increases, (2) the birth rate may change positively but usually negatively, and (3) habitat productivity may be degraded which reduces the habitat's carrying capacity. Many outcomes are possible. One is population collapse. Another is a combination of a reduction in the population and consumption levels until a smaller population consuming less is once again living within the depleted carrying capacity. Yet another possibility specific to humans is that carrying capacity can be and has been increased through massive growth in materials extraction, extensive land transformation, and increased access to energy, all made possible by developments in science and technology, but too often at the expense of disadvantaged communities and other species. This ability of humans to change carrying capacity to their benefit is a major reason why there is such a wide range of estimates of the Earth's human carrying capacity. A survey of 65 estimates in 2012

twenty studies say, $\leq$ 8 billion people is the limit

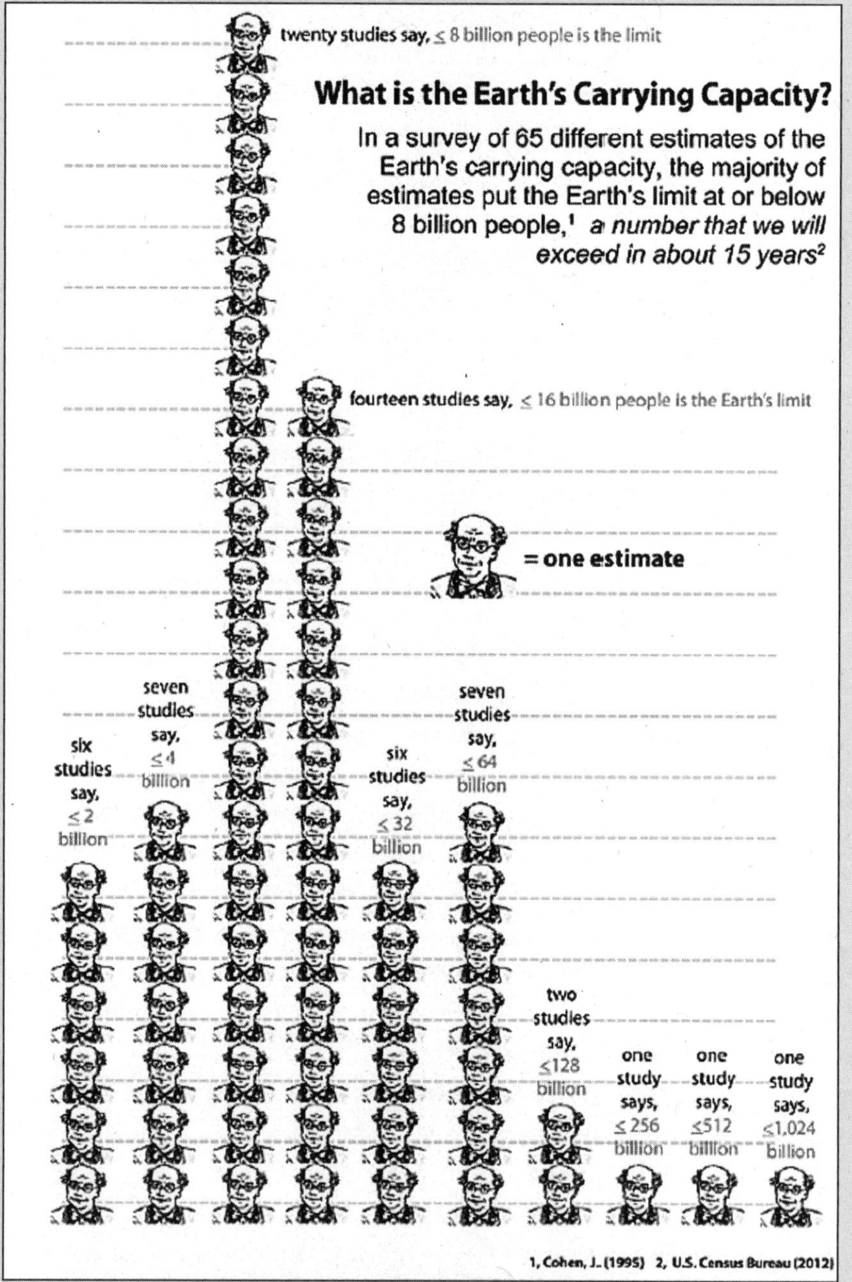

What is the Earth's Carrying Capacity?

In a survey of 65 different estimates of the Earth's carrying capacity, the majority of estimates put the Earth's limit at or below 8 billion people,[1] *a number that we will exceed in about 15 years*[2]

fourteen studies say, $\leq$ 16 billion people is the Earth's limit

= one estimate

seven studies say, $\leq$ 4 billion

six studies say, $\leq$ 2 billion

seven studies say, $\leq$ 64 billion

six studies say, $\leq$ 32 billion

two studies say, $\leq$ 128 billion

one study says, $\leq$ 256 billion

one study says, $\leq$ 512 billion

one study says, $\leq$ 1,024 billion

1, Cohen, J. (1995) 2, U.S. Census Bureau (2012)

FIGURE 1.3. Estimates of Earth's carrying capacity.

Credit: B. Pengra, One Planet, How Many People? A Review of Earth's Carrying Capacity, UNEP 2012.

showed most estimates at or below 8 billion, which is about where we are now, and rising.

To put these estimates of human carrying capacity in historical context, it is useful to look at population growth further back than the start of industrialization, all the way to the end of the last ice age around 10,000 BCE. At that time about five million people are estimated to have been living on Earth, which is about the same as the number living today in the Washington metropolitan area in the USA, making it only the 77th largest city in the world, less than one seventh the size of Tokyo. It took some twelve thousand years for the human population to reach one billion around the year 1800, but only 220 years since then to add another seven billion. The rate of population growth has begun to slow, but we are still adding a billion more people every 14 years.

A population cannot remain in overshoot indefinitely. The population and the carrying capacity of its environment eventually must rebalance, unless, as some technological optimists believe, human ingenuity can keep expanding carrying capacity faster than growth in the human population. But even then, who would want to live in an increasingly crowded planet, unless those holding this belief that technology will save us are counting on the rapid colonization of space?

FIGURE 1.4. Historical world population since 10,000 BCE.

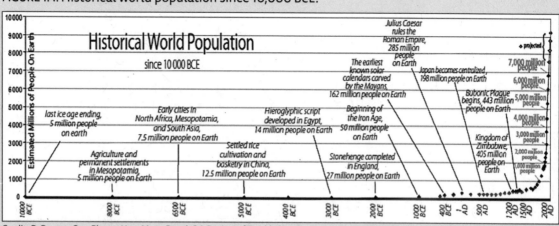

Credit: B. Pengra, One Planet, How Many People? A Review of Earth's Carrying Capacity, UNEP 2012.

There are many paths that can bring population back into balance with carrying capacity. One possibility is that overshoot leads to increased deaths, reducing the population below carrying capacity, and possibly reducing carrying capacity as well. If this leads to increased births the system may return to overshoot and if it continues with diminishing fluctuations and declining carrying capacity a new balance can be reached.

Other possibilities are that overshoot leads to a relatively smooth process of adjustment, such as the one described in Chapter Seven, or to chaotic and catastrophic changes from which recovery is difficult, painful, even impossible, and these changes can happen locally, regionally, and globally, particularly where humans are involved. A lack of food, for example, which used to be a local phenomenon for isolated groups of hunter gatherers, and later for small, largely separate communities, has, with the increase in human mobility and numbers of people, become regional and potentially global. At the same time, increasing connections among humans, especially through the international movement of goods and much better communications, has made it possible for many nations to import food from others to fill

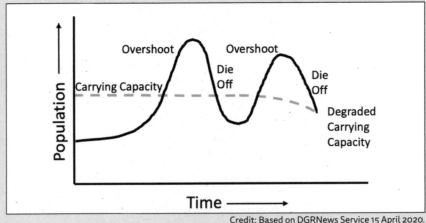

FIGURE 1.5.
Exponential growth of population with overshoot.

Credit: Based on DGRNews Service 15 April 2020.

gaps in what they produce themselves, providing they have something to export and can pay. Otherwise, they must depend on foreign aid which is not always forthcoming. But global integration has its downsides too. The rapid spread of COVID-19 around the world, in its original and mutating varieties, is the most obvious recent example of what in earlier times might have been contained locally, simply because of a smaller population living with less human interaction.

In the early 1990s Professor William Rees and his doctoral student Mathis Wackernagel turned carrying capacity on its head. Instead of asking what size of population can be supported by a given carrying capacity, they asked how much of the regenerative capacity of the biosphere—its biocapacity—was being used to support human activities.[6] They called this the ecological footprint. To measure the ecological footprint of individuals and groups, Rees and Wackernagel converted different types of land to a common spatial unit—global hectares (gha)—taking account of differences in the biological productivity of different land uses (e.g., forests compared to pasture) and in yields within the same land use (e.g., tropical forests compared to boreal forests). They used global hectares to measure the biocapacity of the planet (and regions within it) and the demand placed on biocapacity for materials and the absorption of excess emissions of carbon dioxide globally, regionally, and individually. This demand is measured by the ecological footprint. Biocapacity and ecological footprints have been estimated for over two hundred countries going back to 1961, based on databases from the United Nations and UN-affiliated organizations and from peer-reviewed science publications and reports.[7]

The data reveal a startling fact. Around 1970 the global ecological footprint began to exceed global biocapacity, marking the beginning of global overshoot. What humans were demanding from the biosphere had begun to exceed what the biosphere could provide through its capacity to regenerate. By 2018 the global ecological footprint was exceeding global biocapacity by 75 percent. In other words, the human population in 2018 required the biocapacity of 1.75 Earths to sustain it, but with only one Earth available something must give. Individual

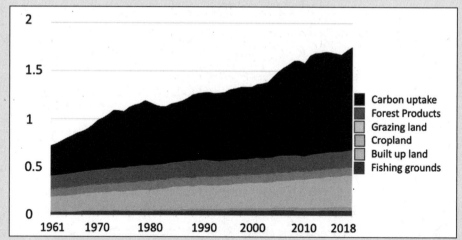

FIGURE 1.6.
World ecological footprint divided by biocapacity.

Credit: York University Ecological Footprint Initiative & Global Footprint Network. National Footprint and Biocapacity Accounts, 2022 edition, https://www.footprintnetwork.org/footprint-initiative-york/

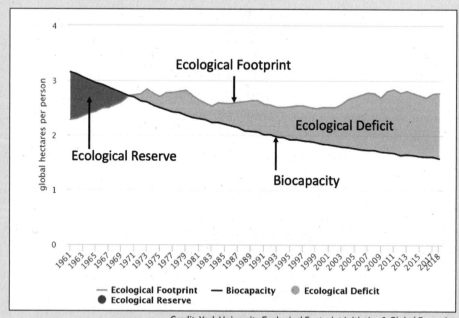

FIGURE 1.7.
World ecological footprint and biocapacity per capita.

Credit: York University Ecological Footprint Initiative & Global Footprint Network. National Footprint and Biocapacity Accounts, 2022 edition.

nations with an ecological footprint greater than their domestic bio-capacity can make up the difference through imports, but this is not an option for the entire planet. Temporarily, an ecological deficit can be maintained by further depleting stocks of timber, fish, and soil nutrients but this reduces biocapacity and sooner or later the demands being placed on the biosphere can no longer be met. Biocapacity can also be increased through human actions such as irrigation and intensive management to increase agricultural output, or the more ambitious approach to food production of agroecology in which ecological concepts and principles are applied to farming.[8] Such increases as have happened in the past are reflected in the National Footprint and Biocapacity Accounts which records the ecological footprint and biocapacity of nations and the world for past years.

The data can also be displayed in terms of the average ecological footprint and biocapacity per capita, with the decline in biocapacity per capita being due largely to the increasing population.

Another way of thinking about overshoot is to recognize that each year global biocapacity—the regenerative capacity of the planet—is fully used before the year is over. The day on which this happens is Earth Overshoot Day. From 1970 to 2019 Earth Overshoot Day arrived earlier each year. In 2020 the downturn in economic activity caused by the COVID-19 pandemic postponed Earth Overshoot Day by about three weeks but it returned to its pre-Covid level in 2021 as the economy picked up. This connection between economic output and human impacts on the biosphere is a theme we will return to many times.

As noted, the ecological footprint and biocapacity are estimated for countries and for smaller regions as well. Some municipalities such as Athens, Cairo, and Barcelona have used estimates of their ecological footprints for planning purposes.[9] Many people have estimated their own individual ecological footprint using an online calculator.[10] There is a tremendous difference in individual ecological footprints at all levels. In 2018 the average ecological footprint worldwide was 2.8 gha per capita, found simply by dividing the global ecological footprint by the global population. This compares with the average ecological

FIGURE 1.8. World Overshoot Day 1970–2021.

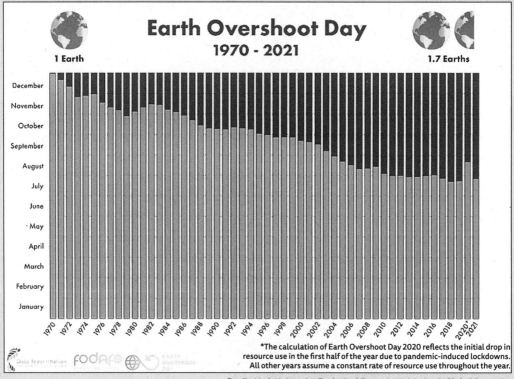

Credit: York University Ecological Footprint Initiative & Global Footprint Network. National Footprint and Biocapacity Accounts, 2022 edition.

footprint of someone living in the United States of 8.1 gha, in China 3.8 gha, 0.9 gha in Bangladesh, and a global average of per capita biocapacity of 1.6 gha. There are also very substantial differences in the ecological footprints of people living within the same country, reflecting the large differences in incomes and consumption levels and in patterns of consumption. For example, a family living in an apartment, relying on walking, cycling and public transport, eating a vegetarian or vegan diet, and vacationing locally, has a much smaller ecological footprint than a family of similar size living in a large, detached house, with two or three cars, eating meat frequently, and enjoying trips to far-off places. This does not mean that a high living standard cannot be maintained with a much-reduced ecological footprint. For example, in 2018 the average German had an ecological footprint about 40 percent less than the average person in the USA while enjoying similar living standards. The ecological footprints of the average person in France and the UK were lower still.

These differences among the ecological footprints of people living in high-income countries pale in comparison to the differences in average ecological footprints of people in countries grouped by income levels. Using the World Bank's classification of countries— high-income, upper-middle income, lower-middle income, and low-income—in 2020 15 percent of the global population lived in high-income countries, yet because of their high levels of consumption, they accounted for 33 percent of the global ecological footprint. Meanwhile, with 35 percent of global population, upper middle-income countries accounted for 43 percent of the global ecological footprint. The 37 percent of global population living in lower middle-income countries accounted for only 19 percent of the global ecological footprint, and

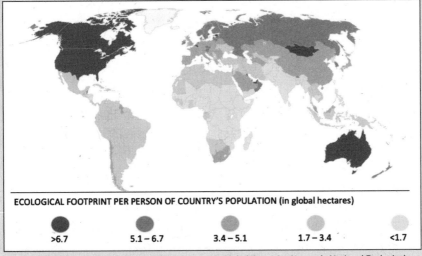

ECOLOGICAL FOOTPRINT PER PERSON OF COUNTRY'S POPULATION (in global hectares)

| >6.7 | 5.1 – 6.7 | 3.4 – 5.1 | 1.7 – 3.4 | <1.7 |

FIGURE 1.9. Mapping the Ecological Footprint 2020.

Credit: York University Ecological Footprint Initiative & Global Footprint Network. National Ecological Footprint and Biocapacity Accounts, 2022 Edition. Produced for the Footprint Data Foundation.

the 12 percent of the global population living in low-income countries accounted for just five percent.

Changes in the ecological footprint of nations or regions over time can be attributed to a combination of changes in population and average per capita footprint. The ecological footprint of a country or

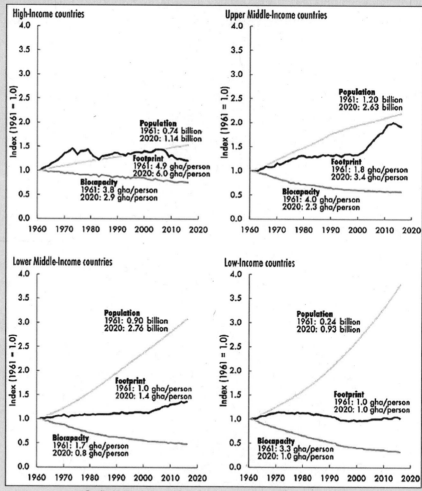

FIGURE 1.10.
Ecological footprint, biocapacity and population for high-income, upper-middle income, lower-middle income and low-income countries, 1961–2016.

Credit: M. Wackernagel (2021), "Shifting the Population Debate: Ending Overshoot, by Design & not Disaster," August 5, Global Footprint Network, https://www.overshootday .org/content/uploads/2021/08/Population-Perspective-M-Wackernagel-2021.pdf

region equals the population of the country or region multiplied by its average per capita footprint. Over time this allows an assessment of the separate contributions of changes in population and changes in average per capita footprint. We see that from 1961 to 2016 the increase in population in each group of countries contributed more to the group's total ecological footprint than the increase in their average per capita ecological footprints. Population is a very sensitive issue and is often downplayed for that reason, yet it remains an important consideration in the context of overshoot.

The ecological footprint tells us that we are in planetary overshoot, but it does not say what the effects of overshoot are on the planetary systems that are affected. In 2009 Johan Rockström and twenty-eight other scientists introduced the concept of planetary boundaries.[11] They were concerned that human pressures on the fundamental physical, chemical and biological processes which make up the Earth's systems had reached a level where abrupt global environmental change had become a very real possibility. In their widely read work, they presented data covering nine interrelated issues that are global or continental in scope: climate change, ocean acidification, stratospheric ozone depletion, interference with the global phosphorous and nitrogen cycles, the rate of biodiversity loss, global freshwater use, land-system change, aerosol loading, and chemical pollution. Some of these issues, such as climate change and ocean acidification, have thresholds or tipping points that if transgressed are very likely to change the behavior of the climate and oceanic systems suddenly and irreversibly. Climate change is already bringing more frequent wildfires, longer periods of drought, and an increase in the number, duration, and intensity of tropical storms.[12] Ocean acidification affects many marine organisms, especially those that build their shells and skeletons from calcium carbonate, such as corals, oysters, clams, mussels, snails, and phytoplankton and zooplankton, the tiny plants and animals that form the base of the marine food web.[13]

Other issues, such as a lack of fresh water and a high rate of biodiversity loss, have no identifiable thresholds but they can cause disproportionate impacts and, if severe enough, force masses of people to migrate. They can also be globally significant when they are widespread, as is increasingly the case.

Faced with considerable uncertainty about these thresholds and about the relationships between deteriorating conditions and their consequences, Rockström and his colleagues proposed a set of boundaries below which they deemed the risk of catastrophe to be low. This was a judgment call on their part, a precautionary approach in the face of uncertain, highly adverse consequences.

The combination of these boundaries give what the Rockström team called a "safe operating space for humanity." Where there were sufficient data, they proposed numerical values for these boundaries, such as 350 ppm for atmospheric carbon dioxide, and global freshwater use of 4,000 cubic kilometers per year. For others, such as atmospheric aerosol loading and chemical pollution they acknowledged that the data were too limited to set quantitative boundaries, though subsequent researchers have proposed boundaries for all but one of the original set of nine.

In 2015 an expanded research team published a follow-up study

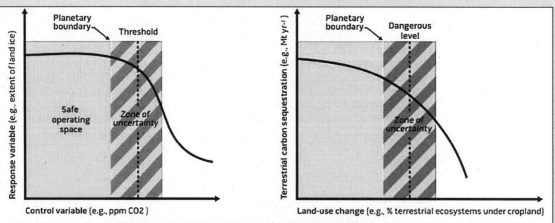

FIGURE 1.11. Conceptual diagram of planetary boundary, threshold, and zone of uncertainty.

Credit: Designed by Azote for Stockholm Resilience Centre, based on analysis in Persson et al., 2022 and Steffen et al., 2015.

which further advanced the concept and quantification of planetary boundaries, for example by replacing "chemical pollution" with "novel entities" covering new substances, new forms of existing substances, and modified life forms that have the potential for unwanted geophysical and/or biological effects. Six years later Rockström and colleagues were featured in *Breaking Boundaries*, a deeply disturbing Netflix documentary on the planetary boundaries presented by David Attenborough who described the precarious state of the Earth systems.

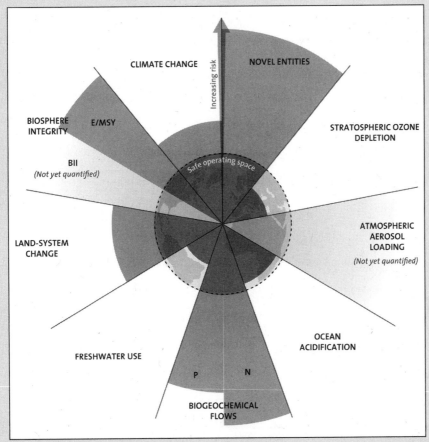

FIGURE 1.12.

Planetary boundaries.

Credit: Designed by Azote for Stockholm Resilience Centre, based on analysis in Persson et al., 2022 and Steffen et al., 2015.[14] Note: E/MSY is extinctions per million species-years and BII is biodiversity intactness index.

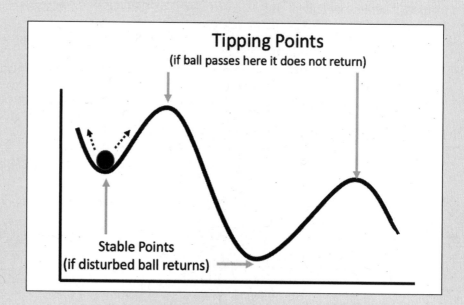

FIGURE 1.13.
Tipping points.

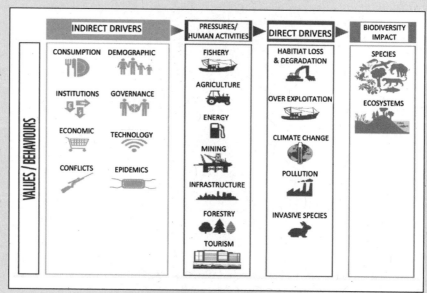

FIGURE 1.14.
Threats to
nature and
the pressures
behind them.

Credit: WWF (2020), *Living Planet Report 2020—Bending the curve of biodiversity loss.* R. E. A. Almond, M. Grooten and T. Petersen, (eds). WWF, Gland, Switzerland.

Closely associated with the idea of boundaries is the concept of tipping points. Tipping points are most easily understood in relation to climate change but can apply to many natural, social, and economic systems. There is an increasing likelihood that the accumulation of greenhouse gases in the atmosphere will reach a tipping point, pushing the climate irreversibly out of the relatively stable 12,000-year Holocene epoch which made agriculture feasible and, for a while at least, capable of supporting the 8+ billion people alive today. The global consequences of such a shift from a stable climate, to which humans and other species have adapted, to another one far less suitable for humans at least, hardly bears thinking about, but think about them we must if we are to plan an escape. A good place to start is with the economy.

The Economy as a Sub-System of the Planet

The message from looking at the ecological footprint and planetary boundaries is clear. We are living in an unprecedented time of global overshoot. The causes and consequences of overshoot vary from place to place and between rich and poor, but even for the very rich there is no escape. We are not all in this together equally by any means, but we are in it together and should look for solutions that work well for us all. An element of that search is an improved understanding of the relationships between economies and the Earth systems on which they depend. This is essential since overshoot is fundamentally related to economic activity:

- to what is produced and how
- how it is transported and distributed
- the levels and patterns of consumption
- the materials and energy that are used
- the land that is transformed
- the waste products that are released back to the environment.

The economy is usually discussed as if it were independent of these Earth systems, a serious mistake that blinds some economists from appreciating the inescapable fact that the economy is a subsystem of the biosphere. Economies are open systems which means that their structure and functions depend on a continual "throughput" of materials and energy from and to the environment. They require resource inputs and produce waste outputs just like any other open system. All forms of life are open systems including you and me. We eat and excrete. Our lives depend upon it. Machines are open systems too. They require energy to operate, they are made of materials that must be replaced when they wear out, and depending on their purpose, they process materials and generate products and waste. Likewise, economies require ongoing inputs of materials and energy which eventually become wastes which must be removed. Reuse and recycling can extend the useful life of materials in an economy, but as they degrade they reach a point where they can be used no more and become waste.

The economy's fundamental dependency on the environment is all too often overlooked in discussions of the economy. The neglect of this dependency underlies the belief that economic growth can continue indefinitely. Take, for example, the simplest model of an economy,

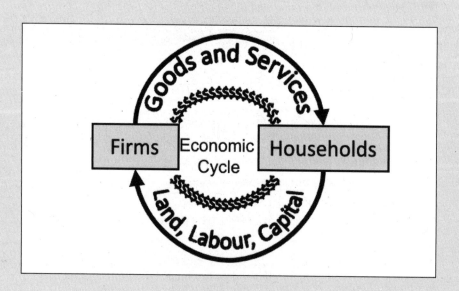

FIGURE 1.15.
The circular flow of income.

one that appears in most introductory economics textbooks. It consists only of households and firms. The households are the ultimate owners of the land, labor and capital, the so-called "factors of production." They make these available to firms in return for rent, wages, and profits. All households are assumed to own their labor; only some own land and capital. The firms make the goods and services which are sold to the households who pay for them from their incomes. The factors of production and goods and services flow in one direction, and money flows in the other. Once absorbed by students, an image of this sort, showing the circular flow of income, becomes their frame of reference with little or no appreciation of the environmental dependency of the economy and its consequences.

Much is missing from this image of the circular flow of income. Government is one, banks are another. More importantly for our purposes is the omission of the environment and the material and energy flows on which all economic activity depends. Without the life-giving energy from the sun, the Earth would be a desolate, cold, and dark place. Apart from a tiny amount of material from outer space that survives passage through the Earth's atmosphere, all that enters spaceship Earth is energy from the sun and virtually all that leaves is heat. Let's see what the economy looks like when we take these facts of economic life into account.

In terms of flows within the planet we can start with the natural resources extracted from the Earth's crust for use in the economy. These are shown with lines coming from an open pit mine and a forest. The resources go primarily to firms which process them into goods and services for sale to each other and to households. Included in these natural resources are fossil fuels which are used to supply energy to firms and households, as well as biomass, other minerals, and non-metallic minerals. Some of the resources used in the economy remain there for considerable periods of time in infrastructure, buildings, and equipment. Other resources are disposed of back into the environment almost immediately upon use. This includes energy (as waste heat), food, and disposable consumer products. Reuse, recovery and

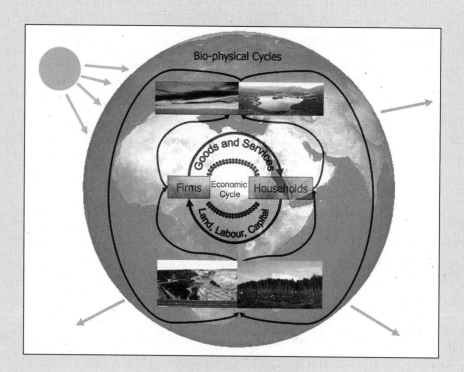

FIGURE 1.16.
Spaceship Earth.

recycling can reduce throughput, but as materials are degraded with repeated use they too are eventually returned to the environment as waste. The same is true of energy which can be used more efficiently but cannot be recycled since its capacity to do work is always diminished with use.

The lines linking firms and households to the images of the atmosphere and a lake represent the flows of waste materials and energy back to the environment. Overshoot occurs when these flows exceed the capacity of the environment to absorb them without causing significant damage. When the bio-physical-chemical cycles in the Earth system are disrupted, it can, through feedback, reduce the supply of natural resources. In conjunction with the transformation of land to suit human purposes, this disruption of biophysical cycles can be devastating to other species living on planet Earth.

Material Flows

Now that we have in our minds an image of the economy embedded in the environment we can probe further into overshoot. Let's start with the increasingly rapid rise in global materials extraction from 1900 onwards. In the first fifty years of the twentieth century, the global extraction of materials increased exponentially so that by 1950 global materials extraction per year was more than double what it had been in 1900. Each of its four main components—biomass, fossil fuels, ores and industrial minerals, and construction materials—increased. This growth in materials extraction was due largely to economic growth in the United States, Western Europe, and the USSR. In the second half of the century global materials extraction accelerated so that by the year 2000 it approached four times its level in 1950. In this period, economic growth spread to more countries, most notably Japan, China and other Asian countries, all requiring increasing quantities of materials. During the first fifteen years of the twenty-first century, the rate of increase in global materials extraction accelerated again. By 2015 it was 60 percent higher than in the year 2000 with China being the dominant contributor followed at a distance by India and Brazil.[15]

This phenomenal increase in global materials extraction is a crucial factor in planetary overshoot. A large proportion of these materials is disposed of back into the environment very quickly, often exceeding its regenerative capacity. This may be because the dumped quantity of an otherwise unproblematic substance such as carbon dioxide is excessive, or because the extracted materials were used in the manufacture of non-biodegradable products. But even when the waste materials are not themselves particularly harmful, the massive mining and forestry operations to extract them at the outset can be extraordinarily damaging.

Recently, new light has been thrown on the question of what happens to the extracted materials after they have entered the global economy. We now talk about the "metabolism" of economies, borrowing from the biological sciences which use the term to describe the process by which living organisms obtain energy from food to sustain life and in doing so create degraded waste products that must be removed. The

FIGURE 1.17. Evolution of the world's material footprint between 1970 and 2019 (Gt).

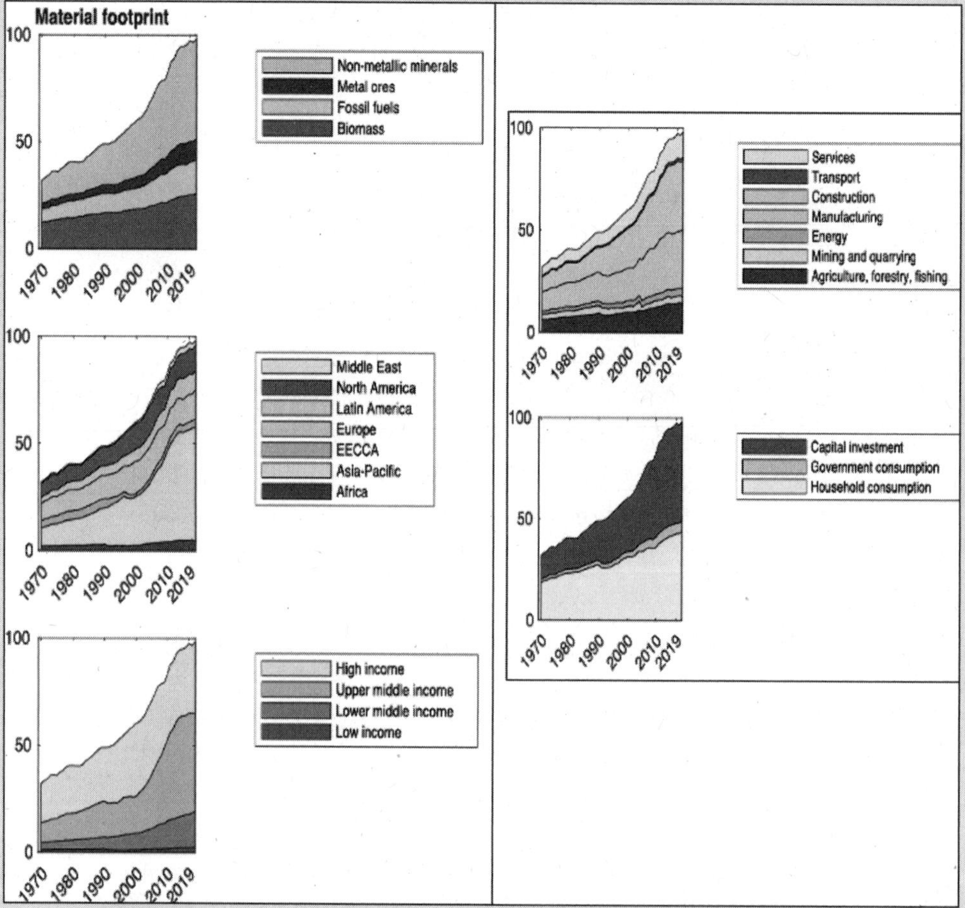

Credit: M. Lenzen et al., (2020), "Implementing the material footprint to measure progress towards Sustainable Development Goals 8 and 12," *Nature Sustainability*, 5, 157–166, https://doi.org/10.10138/s41893-021-008111-6

material metabolism of the global economy is conveniently illustrated with a Sankey diagram, first devised by Irish Captain Henry Phineas Riall Sankey in 1898. In a Sankey diagram, the width of the arrows is proportional to the flow rate. When applied to the material metabolism of economies, a Sankey diagram traces the flow of materials from extraction through processing, where it is divided between those used as materials and those used for energy. Some of the extracted materials

FIGURE 1.18. Mining devastation.

Credit: Sebastian Pilcher on Unsplash.

are accumulated in stocks of infrastructure, buildings, equipment, and consumer durables which remain in the economy for years, decades, and centuries. From 1900 to 2010 global material stocks increased a remarkable 23-fold requiring further material inflows for maintenance, repair, and energy.[16]

Other components of extracted materials, including energy, are used as interim outputs (i.e., goods and services), and become final outputs returned to the environment as water vapor, emissions to air, and solid and liquid wastes. Recycling and downcycling (i.e., reuse) are also included for a complete accounting of material flows.

Sankey diagrams for global material flows for 1973 and 2015 show the phenomenal increase in these flows in just over four decades. Global materials extraction increased from 35 gigatons in 1973 to 88.9 gigatons in 2015. Recycling and downcycling more than tripled as a percentage of all processed materials between 1973 and 2015, reducing the requirement for virgin materials, but even in 2015 they were still only 6.4 percent of all processed materials.

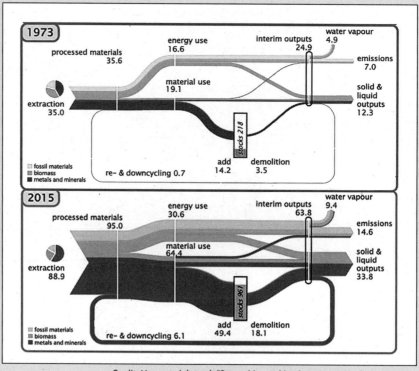

FIGURE 1.19.
Material flows
on planet Earth
(Gt/yr) 1973 and
2015. Stocks are
in Gt.

Credit: Haas, et al, (2020), "Spaceship earth's odyssey to a circular economy—
a century long perspective", *Resources, Conservation & Recycling*, 163, 1–10.

Forests

Increasing requirements for biomass have had very significant impacts
on the forests of the world. After many decades of exploitation beyond
the rate of regeneration, forests still cover almost one third of global
land area and provide habitat for most of the Earth's terrestrial biodiversity. This includes 80 percent of amphibian species, 75 percent of
bird species, 68 percent of mammal species, and more than 60 percent
of all vascular plants, such as grass, coniferous trees, and flowering
plants, that have special tissues that carry water and food throughout
the plant. Global efforts to reduce the rates of deforestation and degradation have had some success but both continue at alarming rates
and are significant contributors to the ongoing loss of biodiversity. An

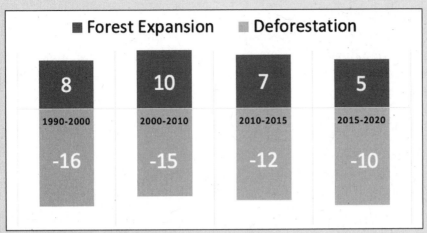

FIGURE 1.20.
Global forest expansion and deforestation 1990–2020 (million hectares per year).

FIGURE 1.21. Humanity's destruction of forests by expanding agricultural land.

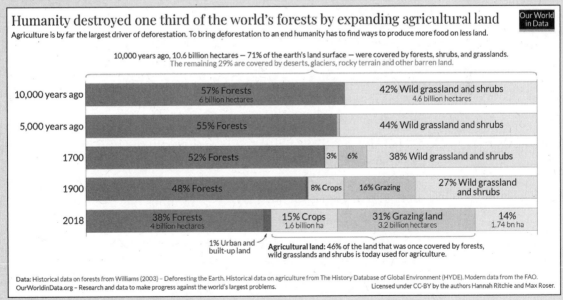

estimated 420 million hectares of forests were lost to deforestation between 1990 and 2020 although this was partially offset by natural expansion and the establishment of new forests. The net result was a reduction in global forest area of 178 million hectares, an area about the same as the combined area of Texas, California, Montana, and New Mexico.[17]

Agriculture

The main cause of deforestation is the expansion of agriculture to feed the growing global population and to accommodate changes in diet that have accompanied increases in income. Between 2000 and 2010, cattle ranching and soya bean and oil palm cultivation by large commercial operations accounted for 40 percent of tropical deforestation. The increase in local subsistence farming accounted for another 33 percent. When forests and grasslands are converted to farm fields and pastures, valuable topsoil can be lost. It is estimated that half of the planet's topsoil has disappeared through erosion in the past 150 years. Agriculture land suffers from other pressures too, such as compaction from heavy farm equipment, impaired soil structure, loss of nutrients, and increasing salinity. Runoff of phosphorous, nitrogen, and other chemicals added to agricultural soils to enhance their productivity contaminates rivers and lakes, which also suffer from increased sedimentation from eroded soils, harming aquatic life.[18]

For the past two centuries global food production has more than kept pace with population growth, allaying fears of widespread famine famously described by Thomas Malthus in the late eighteenth century. In fact, the incidence and severity of famines has declined considerably since the middle decades of the twentieth century, as have deaths from malnutrition. Many factors have contributed to this: food production increased faster than population largely due to increased yields from improved breeding, extensive use of synthetic fertilizers, genetic modification, more irrigation, mechanization powered by fossil fuels, and beneficial changes in other factors such as reduced conflict and poverty, greater access to markets and healthcare, and improved politi-

FIGURE 1.22. Famine victims worldwide since the 1860s.

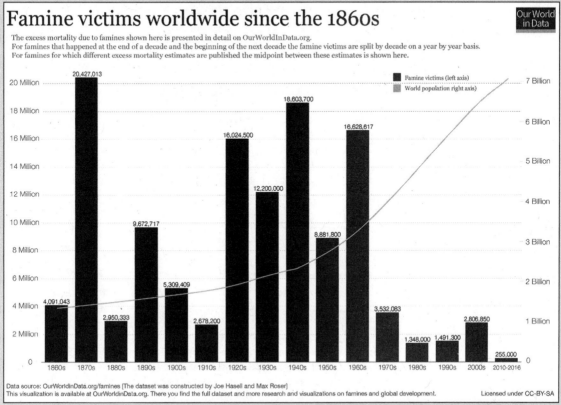

Credit: Joe Hasell and Max Roser (2013), "Famines." https://ourworldindata.org/famines.

cal institutions.[19] Yet, in light of the ongoing degradation of agricultural land, the depletion of groundwater, and the climate-driven need to reduce the high dependence of farming on fossil fuels, the underlying situation of overshoot may well show itself in the years to come through disruption to and reductions in the food supply. David Beasley, head of the UN World Food Program, said its latest analysis shows that "a record 345 million acutely hungry people are marching to the brink of starvation"—a 25% increase from 276 million at the start of 2022 before Russia invaded Ukraine on February 24. The number stood at 135 million before the COVID-19 pandemic in early 2020.[20]

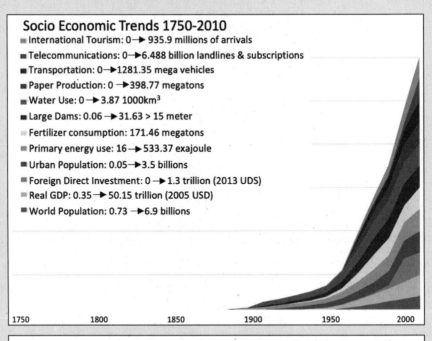

Socio Economic Trends 1750-2010

- International Tourism: 0 → 935.9 millions of arrivals
- Telecommunications: 0 → 6.488 billion landlines & subscriptions
- Transportation: 0 → 1281.35 mega vehicles
- Paper Production: 0 → 398.77 megatons
- Water Use: 0 → 3.87 1000km³
- Large Dams: 0.06 → 31.63 > 15 meter
- Fertilizer consumption: 171.46 megatons
- Primary energy use: 16 → 533.37 exajoule
- Urban Population: 0.05 → 3.5 billions
- Foreign Direct Investment: 0 → 1.3 trillion (2013 UDS)
- Real GDP: 0.35 → 50.15 trillion (2005 USD)
- World Population: 0.73 → 6.9 billions

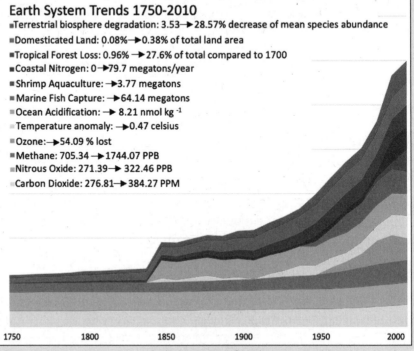

Earth System Trends 1750-2010

- Terrestrial biosphere degradation: 3.53 → 28.57% decrease of mean species abundance
- Domesticated Land: 0.08% → 0.38% of total land area
- Tropical Forest Loss: 0.96% → 27.6% of total compared to 1700
- Coastal Nitrogen: 0 → 79.7 megatons/year
- Shrimp Aquaculture: → 3.77 megatons
- Marine Fish Capture: → 64.14 megatons
- Ocean Acidification: → 8.21 nmol kg⁻¹
- Temperature anomaly: → 0.47 celsius
- Ozone: → 54.09 % lost
- Methane: 705.34 → 1744.07 PPB
- Nitrous Oxide: 271.39 → 322.46 PPB
- Carbon Dioxide: 276.81 → 384.27 PPM

FIGURE 1.23. Global socio-economic and Earth system trends 1750 to 2010.

Credit: Source data is from the International Geosphere-Biosphere Programme www.igbp.net, Created by Bryan MacKinnon.

Forestry, fishing, and farming are the three main sectors of the economy that extract biomass from the Earth to feed, literally and figuratively, the world's economies. Non-living materials are extracted by the mining sector. Because minerals are non-living and do not regenerate naturally, or exceedingly slowly like oil, the concept of overshoot does not apply in the same way. The extraction of minerals depletes deposits in the Earth's crust. This becomes problematic if the rate of extraction is high relative to known reserves and readily accessible deposits. New extraction technologies, combined with more efficient use, recovery, and recycling induced by higher prices, regulation, and better management, can alleviate these problems, at least temporarily. However, mining puts pressure on the Earth's biological systems through erosion, sinkholes, and the chemical contamination of soil, groundwater, and surface water, so excessive exploitation of mineral deposits can reduce biological regeneration, exacerbating overshoot.

The Great Acceleration

Earlier we saw the very rapid increase in the human population and global economic output since 1750. This period is sometimes referred to as the Great Acceleration in recognition of the rapid increase in a wide variety of interrelated socio-economic and Earth-systems. Extensive research and many reports and scientific papers have been written about each of these accelerating changes in the systems. They are indicative of the Anthropocene—the unofficial name given to the current era in the Earth's geological history—signifying the extraordinary impact of human activity on the planet's climate and ecosystems.

Biodiversity

One of most devastating impacts of these trends is the dramatic decline in the populations of numerous non-human species and the reduction in biodiversity on planet Earth. We have reached the point where humans and their livestock together account for 96 percent of the mass of all mammals on the planet. Wild animals account for the remaining four percent and their populations are declining as they lose habitat.[21]

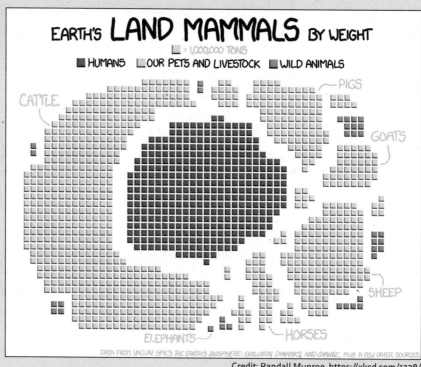

FIGURE 1.24.
Earth's land
mammals by
weight.

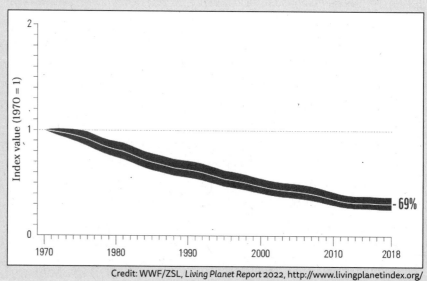

FIGURE 1.25.
The global
Living Planet
Index.

The Living Planet Index, published annually by the World Wildlife Fund, shows a steady reduction of 69 percent between 1970 and 2018 in the average percent change in the populations of mammals, birds, fish, reptiles, and amphibians. 'This estimate is based on monitoring data for nearly 32,000 populations around the world covering more than 5,200 different species, and is a measure of the state of the world's biodiversity. An even greater reduction averaging 84 percent occurred in the more than 900 species that make up the Freshwater Living Planet Index of freshwater populations.

Marine fisheries are also in decline largely because of overfishing. In 1974 90 percent of fish stocks were within biologically sustainable levels, falling to 65.8 percent in 2017.

FIGURE 1.26. Status of the world's fish stocks.

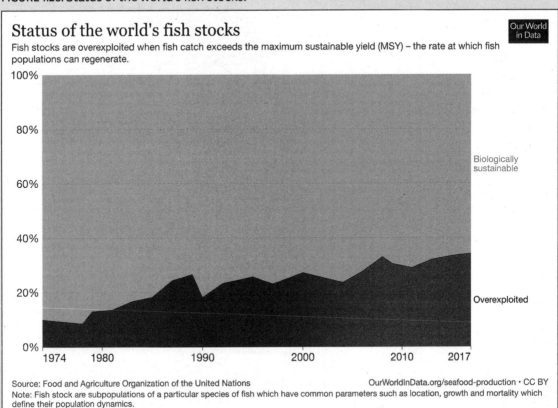

Credit: Hannah Ritchie and Max Roser, 2021, "Biodiversity." https://ourworldindata.org/biodiversity

'**Human actions threaten more species with global extinction now than ever before**. An average of around 25% of species in assessed animal and plant groups are threatened, suggesting that around 1 million species already face extinction, many within decades, unless action is taken to reduce the intensity of drivers of biodiversity loss. Without such action, there will be a further acceleration in the global rate of species extinction, which is already at least 10s to hundreds of times higher than it has averaged over the past 10 million years. the Intergovernmental.

Globally, local varieties and breeds of domesticated plants and animals are disappearing. This loss of diversity, including genetic diversity, poses a serious risk to food security by undermining the resilience of many agricultural systems to threats such as pests, pathogens and climate change.' (IPBES 2019)

FIGURE 1.27.
Scientists warn of threatened species.

Credit: S. Díaz et al., (2019), "Summary for policymakers of the global assessment report on biodiversity and ecosystem services of the Intergovernmental Science-Policy Platform on Biodiversity and Ecosystem Services," IPBES secretariat, Bonn, Germany

These reductions in populations on land and sea have been accompanied by an acceleration in the rate of species extinction. The warnings to policy makers of the 2019 Global Assessment Report on Biodiversity and Ecosystem Services are chilling.

This anticipated increase in the already high rate of extinction is only to be expected as wild animals are forced to survive in disappearing and degraded habitat. It is making some scientists think that we are on the verge of—or already in—the Sixth Great Extinction, the last one being 65 million years ago when all dinosaurs unable to fly became extinct. About half of the Earth's population was killed when a meteor

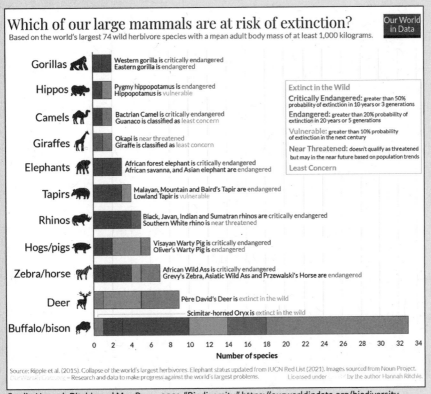

FIGURE 1.28.
Large mammals at risk of extinction.

Credit: Hannah Ritchie and Max Roser, 2021, "Biodiversity." https://ourworldindata.org/biodiversity

fell into the Gulf of Mexico. Combined with high volcanic activity, it released vast quantities of carbon dioxide, dramatically changing the conditions under which so many species, dinosaurs among them, had evolved and thrived. The Sixth Extinction has a totally different set of causes, all traceable to overshoot.[22]

The International Union for Conservation introduced Nature's Red List of Threatened Species in 1964. It is a critical indicator of the health of the world's biodiversity. As of 2022, 142,500 species have been assessed for the Red List. More than 40,000 species are threatened with extinction ranging from 13 percent of birds to 63 percent of cycads (tropical palm-like evergreen plants). The increasing risk of extinction

FIGURE 1.29.
More than 40,000
species threatened
with extinction.

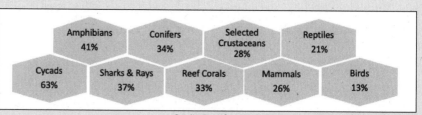

Credit: Data from IUCN Red List https://www.iucnredlist.org/

FIGURE 1.30. Five globally threatened bird species and underlying drivers.

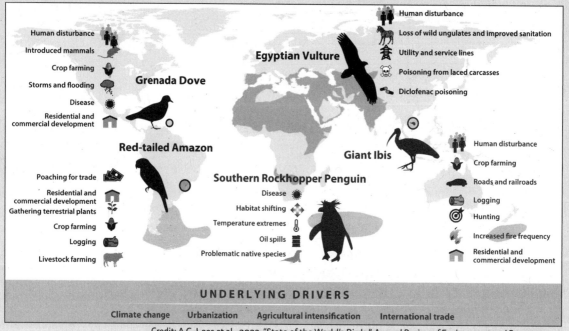

Credit: A.C. Lees et al., 2022, "State of the World's Birds," *Annual Review of Environment and Resources*, 47.

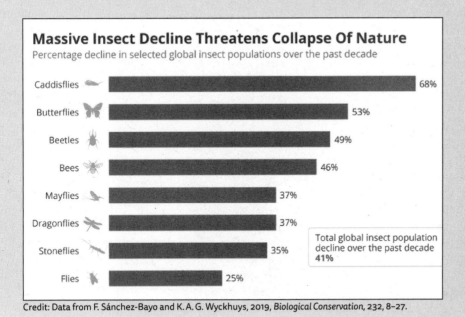

FIGURE 1.31. Massive insect decline threatens collapse of nature. (Percentage decline in selected global insect populations 2010–2019.)

to birds is typical of the situation faced by all categories of species on the Red List.

It is not only mammals, birds, fish, reptiles, and amphibians that are in decline but also insects on which many of these populations further up the food chain depend, including humans who rely on pollination for about a third of global crop production.[23] The causes of the decline in insect populations are many and varied, with human demands on the biosphere the common denominator, as with all the other examples of overshoot given in this chapter. Ultimately, it is these demands that will have to be reduced if we are to escape from overshoot. Whether and how this can be done equitably and effectively, is the theme that runs through all the chapters that follow.

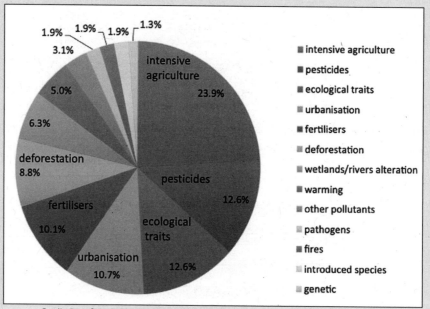

FIGURE 1.32.
Main factors
associated with
insect declines.

Credit: Data from F. Sánchez-Bayo and K.A.G. Wyckhuys, 2019, *Biological Conservation*, 232, 8–27.

2

HOW TO THINK
ABOUT THE FUTURE

Thinking about what the future might hold and how we might influence it has been a preoccupation of human beings for a very long
time. If we are to find an escape from overshoot, we too must engage
in future thinking and we will lay the groundwork for doing so in this
chapter.

In contemporary Western culture when we think about the future
we assume that the past lies behind us and that the future lies ahead.
We talk about "facing" the future, but it has not always been this way.
For the ancient Mesopotamians, it was the past that lay before them
and which they faced. At their back was the future, something which
could not be seen. They thought of themselves as backing into the
future with their eyes fixed on the past, blind to what might lay ahead.
Perhaps we are not so different. The only knowledge we have is of the
past and only momentarily of the present. It's how we use that knowledge that differentiates us from the Mesopotamians and their like. Our
impulse is to extrapolate from the past into the future and, if we don't
like what we see, we think about what we can do to improve it. That's
not to say that we are very good at this but it's far better than a fatalistic
outlook that says nothing can be done, so why bother?

No one said this better than Charles Dickens in *A Christmas Carol*.
Dickens tells the story of the miser, Ebenezer Scrooge, who one Christmas Eve dreamed of meeting three ghosts: the ghosts of Christmas
past, Christmas present, and Christmas yet to come. To the ghost of

FIGURE 2.1.
August Rodin's
"The Thinker"

Credit: Mustang Joe, www.flickr.com/photos/mustangjoe/5966894496

FIGURE 2.2.
The ghost of
Christmas yet
to come.

Credit: John Leech and Charles Dickens.

Christmas yet to come Scrooge says, "Answer me one question. Are these the shadows of the things that Will be, or are they shadows of things that May be, only?" The ghost shows Scrooge what lies ahead if he doesn't change his ways. On waking from his dream Scrooge, having seen the future that awaits him, becomes a generous, loving person much celebrated by family, friends, and the community. The point of the story that Dickens tells so well is that we can learn from the past, examine the present, and change what we do to create a better future.

These days, much of the discussion about the future focuses on technology, which is not surprising given the ever more rapid rate at which technology has been changing since the Industrial Revolution. It is as if technology has a life of its own. We experience it, but we think it is beyond our control. It is progress and we can't stop that even if we wanted to, or so we are led to believe. Or perhaps we could if we understood better the forces that lie behind new technologies—who owns them and whose interests they serve—and thought more carefully about what their consequences might be.

Forecasting technology is notoriously difficult. In 1899, the French artist Jean-Marc Côté produced a set of images to show what life would be like in the year 2000. Some were absurdly wrong, such as one of people underwater in diving gear fishing for seagulls with bait floating on the surface attached to fishing lines. The image shows a seagull going for the bait and being dragged under by the hook and line, to be summarily dispatched for who knows what purpose. Another image shows winged firemen high in the sky circling a burning tower, trying to douse a fire with their hoses. Several fanciful images are of novel forms of transportation: an underwater whale-drawn bus, a variety of flying machines quite unlike the one that the Wright brothers used in the powered flight at Kitty Hawk just four years later in 1903. Some of Côté's images of the future were more far-sighted, such as one of a school where books are being fed to students via electric signals through headphones. Just how the machine at the front of the class turns the books into audio messages is a mystery, maybe it was only

FIGURE 2.3. High-tech education in 2000 as seen in 1900.

Credit: Jean-Marc Côté, https://publicdomainreview.org
/collection/a-19th-century-vision-of-the-year-2000

symbolic, but the main idea is not so far off from today's ebooks and the internet.

A striking feature of Côté's speculations about life in the year 2000 was his lack of imagination about what society, not just technology, might be like a hundred years on. A maid aided by a cleaning machine cleans her employer's house. At the opera, a man looks on with binoculars next to a lady dressed in 19th-century style. Only the absence of musicians playing the mechanized instruments is different. The social scene is just the same as in 1900. In all the many images, people are wearing clothes from late nineteenth century France and the relationships between men and women appear to be from that time as well.

Some of the most interesting and imaginative views of the future come from science fiction writers. In the middle of the twentieth century Arthur C. Clarke, one of the best known of these, published his

Chart of the Future in which he extrapolated "the time-scale of past scientific achievement into the future." As a well-trained physicist with wartime experience as a radar specialist Clarke was well equipped to do this though he did tell us not to take his chart too seriously. He also said that "the quick summary of what has happened in the *last* 150 years should convince anyone that no present-day imagination can hope to look beyond the year 2100." In his chart Clarke listed the main developments in transportation, communication/information, materials manufacture, biology/chemistry, and physics from 1800 to 1960. Then he continued the chart into the future to 2100.[24]

If we look at Clarke's predictions from 1960 to 2020, his expectations for space exploration were in the right direction—a moon landing, space lab, interstellar probes—though less rapidly than he anticipated. For example, there has been no colonization of other planets by the year 2000 as he predicted. His predictions for communication and information were more accurate. In 1945 Clarke proposed that stationary satellites around the Earth could be used for communications, something that was realized nearly 20 years later. All the other communication and information technologies that he predicted by 2020 are in place: translating machines, personal radio, artificial intelligence, a global library, telesensory devices and logical languages. Clarke was less successful in his predictions about materials manufacture—fusion power has not been mastered and neither has weather control—but there have been significant advances in efficient electric storage (though not in the 1970s as he predicted), wireless energy, and sea mining.

When it comes to the natural sciences, it is more difficult to assess Clarke's predictions since they were less precise than his predictions about technology. Still, there is plenty of evidence that cetaceans (marine mammals) use language though we have yet to decode it for human understanding; work is well underway on exobiology (the study of life in the universe); and while there are no cyborgs there is increasing use of cyborg technology to enhance specific functions in humans (e.g., heart pacemakers and implanted defibrillators). Time and perception enhancement is in widespread use in video games and through computers more generally, and prenatal gene therapy is used to prevent diseases in babies before they are born. In the category of physics, gravity waves have been detected though more than two decades after Clarke predicted, whereas progress in understanding subnuclear structure has come more rapidly; and recently, depleted uranium from nuclear power has been used as a catalyst for converting water into oxygen and hydrogen. All told, this is not a bad track record for someone who did not want his predictions to be taken too seriously.

Of course, the future is about much more than science and technology. It is about the state of the planet and the conditions for life—not just human life, but the life of all species—and about how we organize ourselves and how we relate to each other. It is about power, political and economic, and about the influence of education, religion, advertising, social media, and much more. There is so much to think about when it comes to the future that it can be overwhelming. Perhaps we can learn from theologian Reinhold Niebuhr who prayed for "the serenity to accept the things I cannot change, courage to change the things I can, and wisdom to know the difference." This is not easy but it is worth a try.

One way of contemplating the future it is to use what Joseph Voros calls a futures cone. Starting from the present, Voros distinguishes among several types of alternative futures that are judgments both about what might come to be and what is preferable. These judgments can change as time passes, so that something once considered preposterous, such as flying machines or human-induced climate change, becomes possible, then plausible, then probable, until actually realized. Likewise, what was considered preferable (to men at least), such as the exclusion of women from the professions or denying them the right to vote, could later be rejected as contrary to human rights. As Voros explains, "The cone metaphor can be likened to a spotlight or car headlight: bright in the centre and diffusing to darkness at the edge." It is a way of thinking about the future, but as Voros cautions, "Just because we cannot imagine a future does not mean it cannot happen..."[25]

Still, the futures cone offers a systematic framework for taking

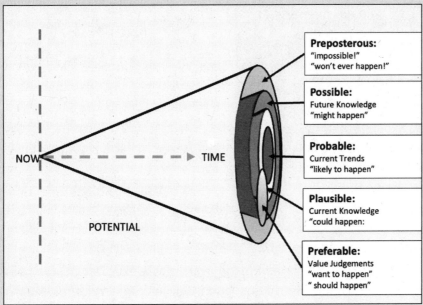

Preposterous:
"impossible!"
"won't ever happen!"

Possible:
Future Knowledge
"might happen"

Probable:
Current Trends
"likely to happen"

Plausible:
Current Knowledge
"could happen:

Preferable:
Value Judgements
"want to happen"
" should happen"

NOW
TIME
POTENTIAL

Credit: Author, based on J. Voros, "The Futures Cone, use and history," *The Voroscope*, 24 February.

FIGURE 2.4.
The futures cone.

stock of possible futures, including some preposterous ones, and invites us to discuss, debate, and decide which futures are preferable and to be sought, and which are undesirable and to be avoided. The critical element is the relationship between the future we want and the decisions we take today that will increase the likelihood of something like it coming to pass. We will be reminded of Voros's futures cone throughout this book as we attempt to chart a way to a more desirable future than the one that current circumstances and recent trends would indicate.

There are many ways of thinking about the future. Different cultures and religions have developed their own ways. Storytellers, poets, artists, astrologers, philosophers, and scientists have developed theirs. Modes of expression differ as well, encompassing oral and written, meditative and ritualistic. With the invention of the electronic computer in the 1940s, new possibilities for exploring the future became

FIGURE 2.5. Simulation modeling: what you see and what you get.

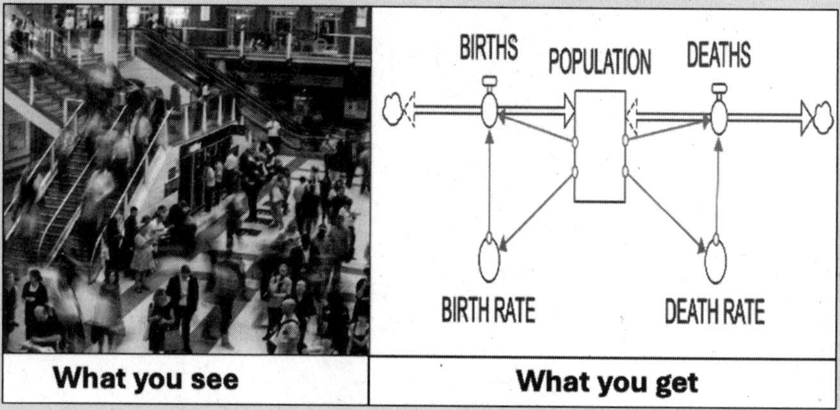

Credit: Photo from https://pxhere.com/en/photo/99109

available. An early use relating to overshoot was by Dennis Meadows and his colleagues who, in 1972, published *Limits to Growth*.[26] Meadows appeared on television to explain the possible futures that his team at MIT foresaw using a computer model of the "world system." He stood beside a large printer from which emerged, line by line, graphs showing the world system collapsing in the first half of the twenty-first century, if trends prevailing in the 1960s continued. According to the computer model, other more appealing futures were possible, but they required major changes in the direction in which the world was headed. Decades later, Graham Turner compared several of these possible futures with what had occurred in the intervening years in terms of population, industrial output, food supply, services, global pollution, and the availability of non-renewable resources. He discovered that the so-called Standard Run—the business-as-usual scenario—that Meadows described in 1972 was uncomfortably close to the path the world was actually on.[27] Others reached similar conclusions, though finding that persistent pollution rather than resource shortages may be more limiting to continued growth.[28]

Computer simulations of the future are not magic. They are simply a convenient way of projecting past trends and changes in those trends. These projections are not predictions of what will happen in the sense that fortune tellers make them, but only what *may* happen should certain circumstances arise. They are sometimes expressed as probabilities, rather like a weather forecast where computer simulations are run many times and the outcomes, such as snow, rain, and sunshine, are tabulated in terms of percentages, like when it says there is a 60 percent probability of precipitation.

Computers cannot decide what kind of world we want to live in, but they can systematically process a much wider range of interactions among variables such as food, population, energy, economic production and consumption, and environmental impacts, than the human brain is able to do. And they can draw on and analyze vast quantities of data extremely rapidly. Most striking of all is that some computer models can display "emergent behavior"—behavior that is not built into the model or anticipated by the model designers, but from which a great deal can be learned.

What this means in terms of Voros's futures cone, is that our capacity to act on the distinction among the different types of alternative futures has increased enormously in the past 70 years and it looks like it will continue to do so—a statement that itself is a prediction. At the same time, the need to think about the future and to find ways of changing direction has never been greater. As we approach the first quarter-century mark of the third millennium, we are being swamped by an avalanche of evidence that humanity is exceeding the capacity of the planet to support us. The climate crisis and the loss of biodiversity are beginning to get the recognition they deserve in the corridors of power, but the trends have yet to turn around. Overfishing, mineral scarcities, and the pressing need to make a rapid transition away from fossil fuels are beginning to command attention. Meanwhile, there is concern that the COVID-19 pandemic will at best be managed, but will linger, and new pandemics may be quick to follow in such a globally integrated world. And the human population, already exceeding eight billion people, continues to grow despite signs that this may cease by the end of the century or even before.

In the previous chapter we looked at the accumulating evidence that, from a planetary perspective, we are in overshoot—that we are living beyond the planet's ability to provide, not only for the lives of more than eight billion humans, many living in extreme poverty, but for the lives of many other species as well. Any escape route from overshoot raises the question of whether the economic system(s) that led to overshoot can find their way out of it. In the next chapter we will meet economists from the past who warned of the situation we are now facing. Their words ring even more true today than when they wrote them. They certainly didn't have all the answers, but had their warnings been listened to, we would not be facing overshoot to the same degree as we are today, and maybe not at all.

3

VOICES FROM THE PAST:
ECONOMIC GROWTH AND ITS CRITICS

Until recently it was assumed that with age came learning, and with learning came wisdom to be passed on to younger generations. In the 1960s this began to change. Bob Dylan's "The Times They Are A-Changin'" became an anthem for the young, with a message directed at their parents. Dylan said that changing times called for new ideas, and if parents do not understand or can't help, they should step aside and let the next generation lead the way.

Times changed but not in quite the way that Dylan and the generation he spoke for envisaged. For one thing, it was the widespread adoption of digital technologies that reversed the traditional relationships between the generations. Now it is the young who teach the old how to operate their smart phones, computers, and other electronic equipment. It is the young who are the expert video game players and users of social media. It is the young, now more than ever, who question the relevance of what they are taught in school to lives so different from those of their parents and grandparents. Led and inspired by Greta Thunberg and her Fridays for Future climate movement, they point an accusatory finger at the older generations who, they say, are leaving them a world in a far worse state than they inherited, a world in overshoot.

One outcome of these changes is the all too easy assumption that there is nothing much to be learned from those who came before,

FIGURE 3.1. Bob Dylan.

Credit: doddis77/Shutterstock.com

especially long dead, largely white, mainly European, male econo-mists. But that would be a mistake, and a painful one, because as we shall see in this chapter, there are more than a few economic voices from the past from whom important, highly relevant lessons can still be learned. This will also lay the foundation for understanding the eco-nomic system as it is today, which we explore in the next chapter.

From Progress to Economic Growth

Since the time of Adam Smith, some 250 years ago, most economists have been interested in improving the human condition through eco-nomic progress, so a good place to start is with the idea of progress itself. It is an idea that is much more recent than is commonly realized.

Fundamental to the modern idea of progress is the belief that time is linear, running from a worse past, through the present, to a better future. In terms of human history, this linear notion of time is quite recent, perhaps no more than 700 years old, when mechanical clocks began to become commonplace and the passage of time could be easily measured. Far more common historically, and still in evidence in some

FIGURE 3.2. The idea of progress.

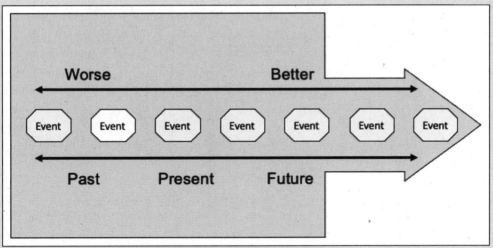

cultures today, is the idea that patterns repeat themselves, the seasons return, and time, if thought about at all, simply tallies recurring experience.

In addition to the linear notion of time, a second element of the modern idea of progress is a means for judging whether human well-being is improving over time. This can be a single criterion such as happiness or utility (in the language of economics), or the fulfillment of human capabilities, or it can be a wider set of values not combined in a single measure but taken together to indicate progress. Progress can have an ethical dimension. It can be about a movement towards a more egalitarian society, a more resilient society, a more peaceful society, a society where freedom from discrimination and ill-health prevails as well as freedom to speak and do. Progress conceived in these ways is multifaceted, ethical, social, and political as well as economic. Only after the Second World War did the meaning of progress become so tightly bound to economic growth. How did this happen?

In the 1930s, economists were at a loss to account for the depth and longevity of the Great Depression. The lasting achievement of British

FIGURE 3.3. From progress to economic growth.

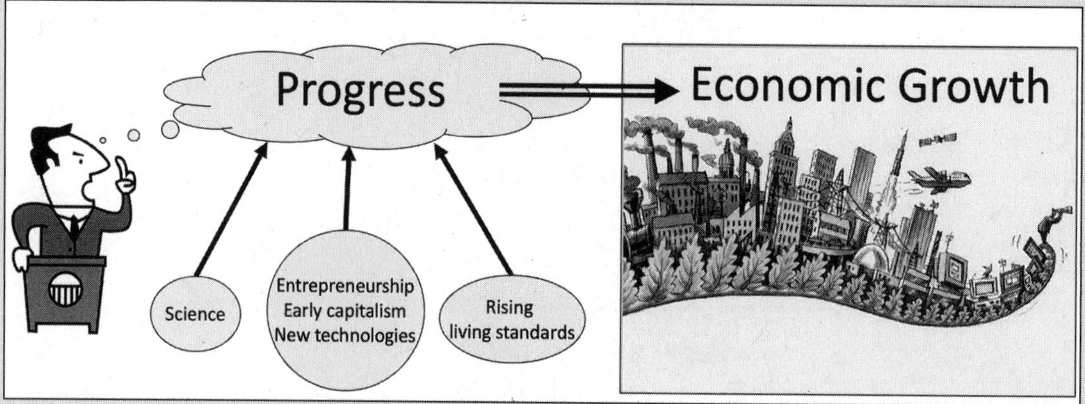

Credit: Author and Ingram Pinn.

economist John Maynard Keynes was to explain that the main reason for sustained unemployment, especially of labor but also capital (buildings, equipment, infrastructure), was insufficient expenditure.[29] His views were validated in the Second World War when governments spent unprecedented sums on armaments, and unemployment was essentially eliminated. Once governments understood that they had the means to increase employment through their expenditures and taxes as Keynes had said, many passed legislation making government responsible for achieving and maintaining full employment.

Keynes, who died in 1946, was interested in avoiding another Great Depression. His was a theory for the short term. He did not concern himself with what happens over the long term, when investment in new capital by businesses and governments expands the productive capacity of the economy. In the immediate post-war period economists turned their attention to this question. They concluded that the total level of expenditure on goods and services in the economy would have to keep increasing if full employment is to be maintained when the capital stock and labor force were expanding. In other words, economic growth was essential for full employment.

As the Cold War between the USA and USSR became more intense in the 1950s, the two superpowers began to compete to see whose economy would grow faster. Very soon economic growth displaced full employment as the measure of economic success by which governments sought to be judged. The idea of progress, which had been multidimensional, was reduced to economic growth. Producing and consuming more and more with each passing year became the objective for other rich countries and most poor countries, who were in the slipstream of the superpowers.

It is this identification of progress with economic growth, or, at least, the assumption that progress depends on economic growth, that gives the ideas of economists a certain cachet. Their forecasts of economic growth are regularly featured in the media. Politicians justify their policies and programs with claims about what they will do to stimulate growth. Without economic growth it is feared that unemployment will rise, public services will suffer, and the national debt will be an unbearable burden on future generations. With economic growth all things are possible, or so we are led to believe, so it may be sobering to discover that some of the most famous economists from the nineteenth and twentieth centuries took a different view.

Unsurprisingly, the field of economics co-evolved with the economic systems that economists set out to describe, analyze, and make forecasts for. The early economists wrote about, interpreted, and prescribed for the capitalism that was emerging in eighteenth-century Britain. As capitalism evolved and spread, later economists developed different theories, more in keeping with the times. Alternatives to capitalism, such as socialism and communism, were also proposed in response to capitalism's evident shortcomings. This process of continuous back and forth between actual economies and the ideas of economists continues to this day. Problems arise when the economic theories developed for one set of historical, geographical, and cultural circumstances are used to explain and prescribe for another set of circumstances. For example, many mainstream economists today seem oblivious to overshoot, and they fail to appreciate the fundamental role of energy in economic growth, especially the one-time anomaly of cheap and highly concentrated fossil fuels on which the economic growth of the past two centuries is based. This allows them to promote endless economic growth, comfortable in the idea that it can continue indefinitely based on human ingenuity and enterprise, its physical dimensions being of little or no consequence.

Classical Economics and Economic Growth

Some notable economists, from the Frenchman François Quesnay, who preceded Adam Smith, through John Stuart Mill and Karl Marx, to John Maynard Keynes and others, had rather different ideas which we can draw on to help understand our situation and to consider what can be done to improve our prospects. Let's begin with Adam Smith, who is sometimes referred to as the father of economics, and whose influence can still be seen today in the way economies are understood and in prescriptions offered for the problems they encounter.

Born in Kircaldy, Scotland, in 1723, Smith rose to the position of professor of moral philosophy at the University of Glasgow. In 1764 he resigned his position to become tutor to the young Duke of Buccleuch at a greatly increased salary. They spent several years touring Europe which allowed Smith to meet many influential scholars. One of these was François Quesnay, a leader in the physiocratic school of economics. Smith was much taken by the emphasis that the physiocrats gave to individual liberty, in sharp contrast to the mercantilists who stressed government control and were the target of much of Smith's criticisms. At that time, France was still largely a society built on agriculture, whereas Britain had already begun the process of industrialization and commerce which was thriving and was the focus of Smith's interest. In retrospect, it is unfortunate that Smith did not see the value of Quesnay's attempt to trace all output of the French economy back to agriculture and the land through his Tableau Économique. Had he done so he might have advanced the invention of the ecological footprint by a couple of centuries and alerted economists to the potential for overshoot.

FIGURE 3.4. Quesnay's Tableau Économique.

François Quesnay
1694-1774

Credit: François Quesnay.

In Quesnay's diagram there are three economic sectors: on the left-hand side is the Proprietary class of landowners who produce nothing but buy from the other classes using the rent paid for land; in the middle, the Productive class of agricultural workers who produce food from land leased from the landowners and who buy products from artisans and merchants; and on the right-hand side the Sterile class of artisans and merchants who buy food from the farmers and other goods from merchants abroad. In the physiocrat account of the economy, only agriculture is truly productive and there are no capitalists and no economic growth. This was a different world from that which Smith and the other classical economists such as Malthus and Ricardo sought to describe. They were living in Britain where the Industrial Revolution was already under way and where economic growth could be witnessed, even though it was not being measured as it is today.

Smith, Malthus, and Ricardo established the foundations of classical economics. Others contributed, of course, but these were the three most responsible for what became the main principles of economics, especially in Britain, well into the nineteenth century. They agreed on many things. One was that economic growth would not last, but their reasoning was different. Smith saw the accumulation of capital as the main source of economic growth. Capital accumulation, he said, was made possible by the profits of manufacturing from expanding output and the division of labor into specialized tasks. Since, according to Smith, the division of labor is limited by the extent of the market, opportunities for increasing profits and the accumulation of capital would eventually cease as markets could not expand forever. Smith's ideas about capital accumulation and economic growth are relevant to an escape from overshoot in ways he could not have anticipated. As explained in Chapter 6, escaping from overshoot will involve a diversion of investment away from the expansion of productive capacity to investment in costly mitigation measures, e.g., to reduce greenhouse gas emissions, paying for expensive natural and engineered sequestration measures to reach net zero, incurring costs of damages from extreme weather, and funding adaptation to climate heating. Quite separate from this is the diversion of investment away from investment in real capital as investors become increasingly attracted by investments in purely financial instruments, which contribute very little to economic output.

Smith made an interesting observation about the longevity of economic growth. He commented that "the course of human prosperity" usually endures for two hundred years, a length of time already passed in his time since the reign of Elizabeth I. He thought that rising wages would eventually limit the capacity of capitalists to invest, leading eventually to a "stationary state" with no further increase in wages, along with a stable population and capital stock, a situation Smith described as "dull". Now we find ourselves in a situation where the prospects for long-term economic growth faces additional obstacles of a different kind, more akin to the concerns of Smith's contemporaries, Malthus and Ricardo.

For Malthus, economic growth would be temporary because he believed the food supply could not keep up with the increase in population. Wages could only rise above subsistence level for a time, resulting in further increases in population that would bring wages back to subsistence level, though he did allow the possibility that "moral restraint" could raise the living standards of the poor. In retrospect, Malthus failed to see that rising living standards would help reduce the birth rate, but his fundamental concern, that the human population threatened to out-run the capacity of the planet to support it, continues to ring true in the face of overshoot.

Ricardo agreed with Smith that economic growth depends on capital accumulation, but he thought it would be limited, not by a lack of markets, but by the diminishing productivity of farm workers as land of decreasing fertility is brought into use, forcing food prices to rise. Ricardo, like Malthus, did not foresee the dramatic increase in food production made possible by new farming practices, technologies, chemicals, and fossil fuels, more than sufficient, for two centuries, to compensate for losses in the natural fertility of soil. But in the twenty-first century, as the world strives to reach net zero greenhouse gas (GHG) emissions by mid-century by ending dependency on fossil fuels, we face the enormous task of simultaneously increasing food production, which requires a transition to food-producing methods and technologies that are less dependent on fossil fuels than current methods, and ensuring that people everywhere have enough to eat, while dramatically reducing the use of fossil fuels for transportation in a world where very few countries are self-sufficient in food supply and depend on imports.[30]

Although Smith, Malthus, and Ricardo were writing in the days when economic growth had taken root in just one country, Britain, they had reasons to doubt its longevity. Their gloomy outlooks, especially those of Malthus and Ricardo, earned economics the epithet "The Dismal Science," bestowed upon it by the historian Thomas Carlyle.

These founders of classical economics provided much of the narra-

FIGURE 3.5. Malthusian Theory of Population and Food.

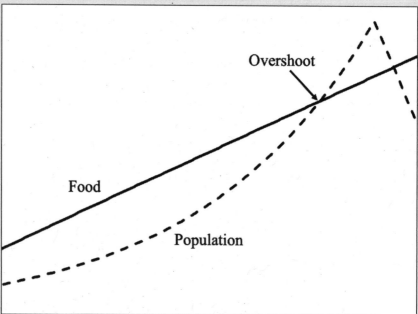

tive of economics, especially about economic growth, at least until the mid-nineteenth century in Britain. Indeed, more recent scholars still look to the classical economists when developing their own ideas about development and economic growth. One example is W. Arthur Lewis from Saint Lucia, who received the Nobel Memorial Prize in Economic Sciences in 1979. He based his own influential theory of economic growth on the ideas of Smith, Malthus, and Ricardo, finding them still relevant to countries with "surplus labor," by which Lewis meant, people living in rural areas at subsistence level who could move into the "modern" sector as wage labor, forestalling the need to increase wages and thus allowing the accumulation of capital.[31]

In 1848, John Stuart Mill published the first of seven editions of the *Principles of Political Economy*.[32] It soon became the standard account of classical economics in the second half of the nineteenth century. Mill took a markedly different view of the stationary state from the bleak outlook of Malthus, Smith, and Ricardo. It is no exaggeration to say that Mill looked forward to the stationary state. He devoted an entire chapter to it in his *Principles*, expressing his distaste for the hustle, bustle, and struggle of "industrial progress," overcrowding and

FIGURE 3.6. The classical economists: growth will end badly.

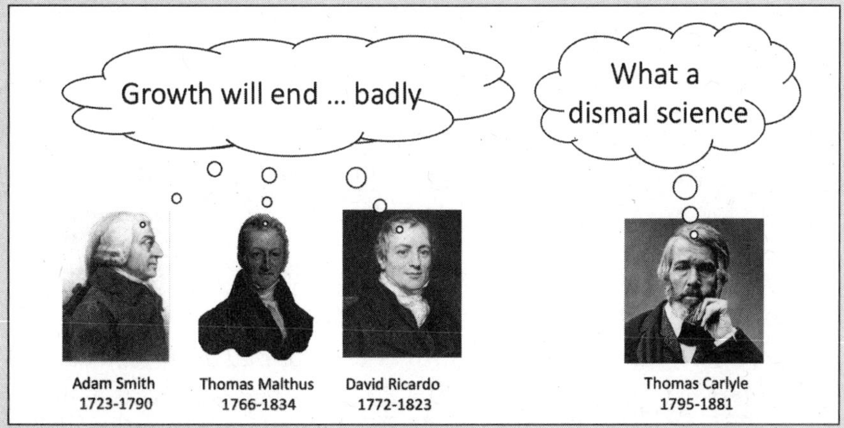

FIGURE 3.7. John Stuart Mill on the stationary state.

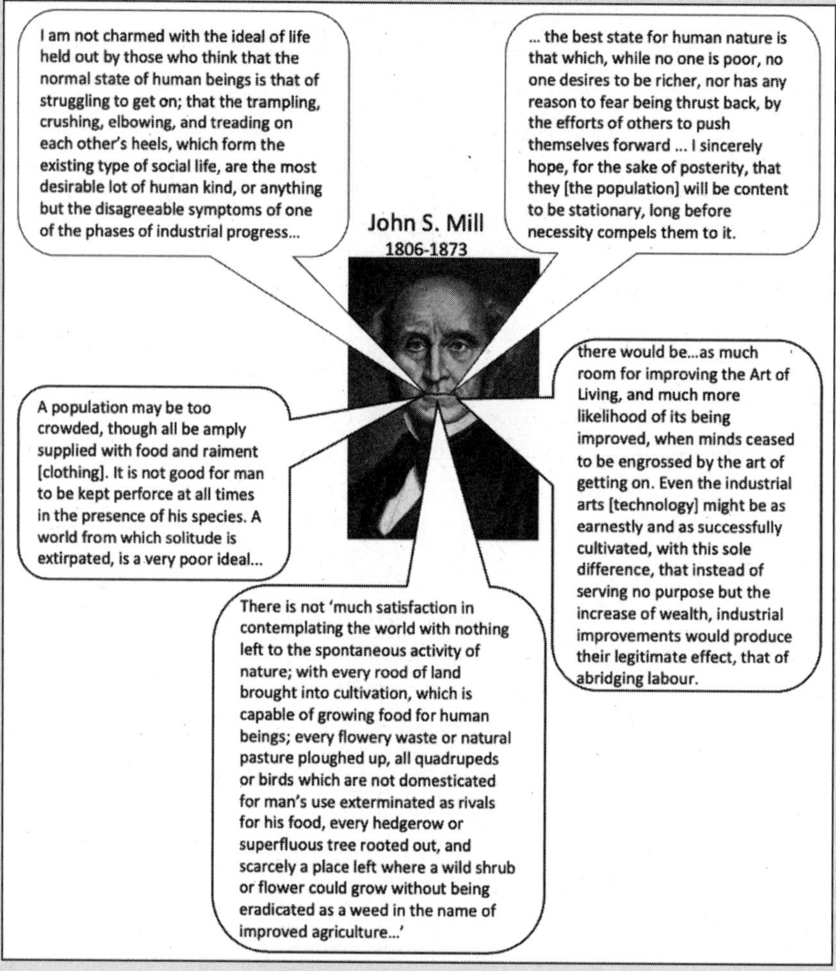

I am not charmed with the ideal of life held out by those who think that the normal state of human beings is that of struggling to get on; that the trampling, crushing, elbowing, and treading on each other's heels, which form the existing type of social life, are the most desirable lot of human kind, or anything but the disagreeable symptoms of one of the phases of industrial progress...

... the best state for human nature is that which, while no one is poor, no one desires to be richer, nor has any reason to fear being thrust back, by the efforts of others to push themselves forward ... I sincerely hope, for the sake of posterity, that they [the population] will be content to be stationary, long before necessity compels them to it.

John S. Mill
1806-1873

A population may be too crowded, though all be amply supplied with food and raiment [clothing]. It is not good for man to be kept perforce at all times in the presence of his species. A world from which solitude is extirpated, is a very poor ideal...

there would be...as much room for improving the Art of Living, and much more likelihood of its being improved, when minds ceased to be engrossed by the art of getting on. Even the industrial arts [technology] might be as earnestly and as successfully cultivated, with this sole difference, that instead of serving no purpose but the increase of wealth, industrial improvements would produce their legitimate effect, that of abridging labour.

There is not 'much satisfaction in contemplating the world with nothing left to the spontaneous activity of nature; with every rood of land brought into cultivation, which is capable of growing food for human beings; every flowery waste or natural pasture ploughed up, all quadrupeds or birds which are not domesticated for man's use exterminated as rivals for his food, every hedgerow or superfluous tree rooted out, and scarcely a place left where a wild shrub or flower could grow without being eradicated as a weed in the name of improved agriculture...'

the lack of needed solitude, and the destruction of natural habitat by agriculture. Were he alive today, Mill's distaste would likely turn to disgust at how his nineteenth-century concerns had magnified beyond his wildest imagination. In his own day, Mill saw possibilities in the stationary state for eliminating poverty and reducing inequality, and for technology to improve life and reduce the burden of work—ideas which in our own time have been most forcibly and consistently expressed by Herman Daly (see chapter four).

One of the defining features of classical economics was the labor theory of value. Classical economists distinguished between value in use and value in exchange. Value in use could vary from commodity to commodity and from person to person. Value in exchange—the rate at which one commodity could be traded for another (its price, in other words) which is the same for everyone—was primarily determined by the amount of labor required for its production. Marx adopted the labor theory of value from the classical economists, principally Ricardo, but used it for a different purpose which was to explain the source of profit in a capitalist economy (see chapter four). What is often overlooked in discussions of Marx's economics is that, along with the exploitation of labor, he argued that capitalism depended on the exploitation of nature. This exploitation entailed a transformation in the way nature was regarded; it came to be seen exclusively as an object in the service of humans, with no intrinsic value. The current fashion of renaming nature "natural capital" and theorizing about how best humans can use it, exemplifies this concern.

Marx observed that "all progress in increasing fertility of the soil for a given time is a progress toward ruining the lasting sources of that fertility...Capitalist production therefore develops technology, and the combining together of various processes into a social whole, only by sapping the original sources of all wealth: soil and labourer." He was also well aware that the concentration of people in towns and cities "disturbs the metabolism of man and the earth," which anticipated by a century or more the modern study of social metabolism—the flows of materials and energy between economies and nature and within and between different societies.[33]

Like Marx, English economist W. Stanley Jevons also had an appreciation of the physical basis of an economy. His interest was in coal, which provided the energy for industrialization, rather than in land as with Smith, Malthus, Ricardo, and Marx. Jevons was concerned that Britain's supremacy as a manufacturing nation in the second half of the nineteenth century would be eroded when, as he correctly forecast, coal production in Britain would become more costly than in other countries as Britain's best deposits were mined out. Jevons considered coal to be part of Britain's wealth or capital and contrasted its depletion with living off the reproductive capacity of land. He is remembered to this day for the "Jevons effect": when improvements in the efficiency of machines reduce both the energy costs of running them and the price of their output, leading to increased sales. As a result, total energy use can increase, despite increased efficiency, as more machines are re- quired to meet the increase in overall production required to satisfy the increase in the quantity demanded brought about by lower prices. Allowing for the Jevons effect, or rebound effect as it is also known, is critical when forecasting the contribution that technological advances can make to reducing and avoiding overshoot.[34]

Jevons was also one of the key contributors to the "marginal revo- lution" in economics in the fourth quarter of the nineteenth century. It began with the proposition that market prices are determined by the utility or value of the marginal (incremental) unit of any good or ser- vice, rather than the labor used in its production as the classical econo- mists and Marx believed. The basic idea is that the price people will pay for, say, an apple depends on how much utility they expect to derive from that one apple, which in turn, depends on how many apples they already have, and not on the utility they derive from all their apples or on the labor that went into supplying the apple. This marginal analysis was offered as a solution to the "diamond-water paradox." The value (or usefulness) of water is obviously greater than that of diamonds, but the price of diamonds is much higher than the price of water. Since water is relatively abundant and diamonds are relatively scarce, the *marginal* value of water—the value of a small increment—is much lower than that of diamonds, so water commands a much lower price. The adop- tion of marginal analysis to explain prices largely displaced the labor theory of value and signaled the end of the era of classical economics. It also undermined the political and ethical question of the distribution of wealth, which had been tied (in Marx particularly) to the production of actual goods and services. The marginal revolution eliminated any direct connection to the real, physical world, replacing it with subjective utility or value and—in the capitalist system—mediated through a signaling process called the market. This disconnect is part of why we are in overshoot: all too often market-determined prices fail as a signaling system of what is happening in the real, physical world.

Neoclassical Economics Takes Center Stage

Marginal analysis—the idea that decisions in an economy are based on consideration of small, incremental changes—was extended to many aspects of economics through the interaction of demand and supply. These simple but powerful concepts were applied to the labor, capital, and land used in production and to the goods and services that they produce forming the bedrock of neoclassical economics. This new approach to economics was developed and presented by Alfred Marshall in his highly influential *Principles of Economics*[35] which went through eight editions between 1890 and 1920. It was the standard economics textbook in English-speaking countries for several decades and was studied by generations of students including Arthur C. Pigou and John Maynard Keynes, Marshall's successors as professors of economics at the University of Cambridge. Much of what Marshall wrote a century or more ago remains in the economics curriculum that is taught today in high schools and universities. However, some of Marshall's ideas that are especially suited to a consideration of overshoot do not get the attention they deserve. These include his view that economics should be based on biological principles and that land, by which he presumably meant all of nature, should not be treated economically or ethically in the same way as labor and capital by governments, given their responsibilities towards future generations. Organizations such as the Intergovernmental Panel on Climate Change should take heed of these views when considering the kind of economic analysis put before them that all too often treats nature as just another form of capital and discounts the future. Such ideas are of questionable value for coming to terms with overshoot.

Critics of Economic Growth

E. F. Schumacher is best remembered for his short book *Small is Beautiful*,[36] which extols the virtues of small technologies and localized economies. Like Jevons before him, Schumacher bemoaned the practice of treating the depletion of natural resources, especially

FIGURE 3.8. Marx, Jevons, Marshall, and Schumacher on nature.

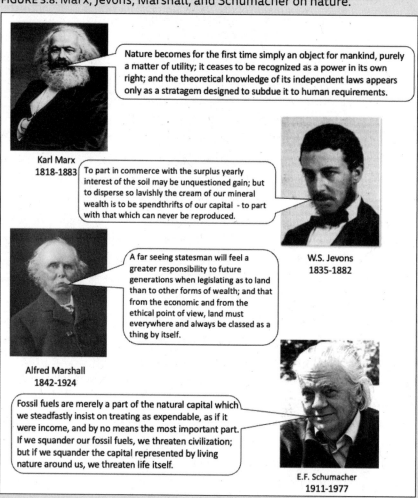

Karl Marx
1818-1883

Nature becomes for the first time simply an object for mankind, purely a matter of utility; it ceases to be recognized as a power in its own right; and the theoretical knowledge of its independent laws appears only as a stratagem designed to subdue it to human requirements.

W.S. Jevons
1835-1882

To part in commerce with the surplus yearly interest of the soil may be unquestioned gain; but to disperse so lavishly the cream of our mineral wealth is to be spendthrifts of our capital - to part with that which can never be reproduced.

Alfred Marshall
1842-1924

A far seeing statesman will feel a greater responsibility to future generations when legislating as to land than to other forms of wealth; and that from the economic and from the ethical point of view, land must everywhere and always be classed as a thing by itself.

Fossil fuels are merely a part of the natural capital which we steadfastly insist on treating as expendable, as if it were income, and by no means the most important part. If we squander our fossil fuels, we threaten civilization; but if we squander the capital represented by living nature around us, we threaten life itself.

E.F. Schumacher
1911-1977

fossil fuels, as if it is income when it is more akin to the dissolution of capital. He compared the over-exploitation of these resources to the difference between a person living off the interest from money in the bank, which can go on indefinitely, and spending more than the interest, which can only last until all the money in the bank has gone. This is how Schumacher saw the situation in the 1970s when global overshoot was beginning. The solution, he said, lay in using the technology

Conspicuous consumption of valuable goods is a means of reputability to the gentleman of leisure.

Thorstein Veblen
1857-1929

...the economic problem may be solved, or be at least in sight of solution, within a hundred years ... All kinds of social customs and economic practices, affecting the distribution of wealth and of economic rewards and penalties, which we now maintain at all costs, however distasteful and unjust they may be in themselves, because they are tremendously useful in promoting the accumulation of capital, we shall be free, at last to discard. In particular, The love of money as a possession – as distinguished from the love of money as a means to the enjoyments and realities of life – will be recognised for what it is, a somewhat disgusting morbidity, one of those semi-criminal, semi-pathological propensities which one hands over with a shudder to the specialists in mental disease.

J.M. Keynes
1883 -1946

The family which takes its mauve and cerise, airconditioned, power braked car out for a tour passes through cities that are badly paved, made hideous by litter, blighted buildings, billboards, and posts for wires that should long since have been put underground. They pass into a countryside that has been rendered largely invisible by commercial art...they picnic on exquisitely packaged food from a portable icebox by a polluted stream and go on to spend the night at a park which is a menace to public health and morals. Just before dozing off on an air-mattress, beneath a nylon tent, amid the stench of decaying refuse, they may reflect vaguely on the curious unevenness of their blessings.

John K. Galbraith
1908-2007

FIGURE 3.9.
Veblen, Keynes, and Galbraith on conspicuous consumption and status.

most appropriate to the task, which meant downscaling buildings and equipment and relying more and more on what could be regenerated naturally.

At the very start of the Industrial Revolution Adam Smith observed the prestige value of riches: "The rich man glories in his riches, because he feels that they naturally draw upon him the attention of the world..." In 1899 Thorstein Veblen coined the term "conspicuous consumption" to mean the display of one's wealth and social status through the purchase of goods and services which others cannot afford or only with difficulty.[37] Conspicuous consumption has been a common theme in advertising for quite some time where the social approval of friends, neighbors, workmates, and complete strangers is shown going to someone, anyone, if only they buy the advertised product. The deliberate cultivation of social media influencers to promote products is simply the latest iteration of conspicuous consumption, with no consideration of how it might generate overconsumption and contribute to overshoot. In 2021 the escapades of multi-billionaires Jeff Bezos of Amazon and Richard Branson of the Virgin Group to fly to the edge of space raised conspicuous consumption literally to new heights.

Writing just after the great stock market crash of 1929 at the start of the Great Depression, John Maynard Keynes turned his attention to possibilities for his grandchildren's generation, some hundred years in the future. He based his speculations on assumptions of "no important wars and no important increase in population," neither of which have stood the test of time, though his high hopes for continuing improvements in technology have been borne out. Nonetheless, we should heed Keynes' caution against the love of money as a possession, the endless pursuit of which is an obstacle to overcoming overshoot.[38]

The Canadian-American economist John Kenneth Galbraith adopted the Keynesian view of macroeconomics. In *The Affluent Society*[39] he offered a trenchant critique of the United States economy of the 1950s, one element being the imbalance between goods and services provided by the private sector and those provided by the public sector. He held out hope with a call to American society to invest in education that is no less relevant today: "Whether the problem be that of a burgeoning population and of space in which to live with peace and grace, or whether it be the depletion of the materials which nature has stocked in the earth's crust and which have been drawn upon more heavily in this century than in all previous time together, or whether it be that of occupying minds no longer committed to the stockpiling of consumer goods, the basic demand on America will be on its resources of intelligence and education." From Galbraith we learn that responding to overshoot requires collective action towards shared goals, not the exaggerated form of individualism that one finds in the current predominant ideology of the United States.

Environmental Economics

In the 1960s, when the modern environmental movement began to take shape, a few economists began to recommend that if there was a price on pollution, industrial and municipal polluters would have a financial incentive to reduce their emissions. This idea originated with Cambridge (UK) economist Arthur C. Pigou in 1920. His example of factory smoke causing losses to the community at large has since been extended to numerous unpaid environmental costs, most recently and perhaps most importantly to the emission of greenhouse gases that are causing climate change. Pigou's idea of imposing a charge on such emissions gave rise to the term "Pigovian tax."[40] Also in the 1960s, the creation of tradable emission allowances was proposed as an alternative to imposing a direct charge on emissions.[41] Both approaches are in use today with many different design features. The underlying theory can be traced back to the marginal revolution and the insights about how the price or cost of the incremental unit, in this case a tonne of GHG emissions, can influence behavior. But it will only do so in a significant way if the price is sufficiently high, something which is resisted when financial interests are threatened.

Where Pigou saw environmental externalities (the unpriced consequences of a transaction imposed on third parties) as the exception rather than the rule, others saw them as being the norm. K. William

Kapp was one of the first economists to see widespread environmental and social costs in market economies, the result, he said, of the cost-shifting intrinsic to capitalism, where companies strive to minimize their own, private costs.[42] Twenty years later, in 1970, Wassily Leontief explained that pollution is a by-product of all economic activities.[43] He adapted the method of input-output analysis, for which he had received the Nobel Memorial Prize in Economic Sciences, to estimate the effects on all prices in an economy of the costs of pollution abatement incurred by multiple sectors. Others went further than Leontief. They applied the physical principle of materials balance—tracing the flow of materials from the environment through an economy and back to

...marginal private net product falls short of marginal social net product (for)...resources devoted to the prevention of smoke from factory chimneys: for this smoke in large towns inflicts a heavy uncharged loss on the community.

Arthur C. Pigou
1877-1959

Pollution is a by-product of regular economic activities. In each of its many forms it is related in a measurable way to some particular consumption or production process: The quantity of carbon monoxide released in the air bears, for example, a definite relationship to the amount of fuel burned in various types of automotive engines; the discharge of polluted water into our streams and lakes is linked directly to the level of output of the steel, paper, the textile and all other water-using industries and its amount depends, in each instance, on the technological characteristics of the particular industry.

Wassily Leontief
1905-1999

FIGURE 3.10.
Pigou and Leontief
on pollution.

the environment so that nothing is lost—to the economic theory of multiple markets which underlies input-output analysis, and to what is now known as environmentally extended input-output analysis.[44]

Ecological Economics

A fundamental principle of physics is that the energy used in any process, including those of production and consumption in an economy,

FIGURE 3.11. Soddy, Boulding and Georgescu-Roegen on the second law of thermodynamics.

is conserved. This is the first law of thermodynamics. However, according to the second law of thermodynamics, while this energy can neither be created or destroyed, its form is altered such that its capacity to do work is reduced. In simple terms, the quantity of energy is always maintained but its quality diminishes. This accounts for the impossibility of perpetual motion machines. Some of the energy used to run such a machine is inevitably dissipated as low-temperature waste heat, which is incapable of being used to keep the machine running. Since energy cannot be recycled, though it can be used more efficiently, new inputs of energy are continually required to maintain any process. Similarly, even though materials, unlike energy, can be recycled, they are also degraded when used so that a complete closing of the production-consumption-recycle/reuse cycle in a "circular" economy is physically impossible. Even a steady-state economy, which as explained in Chapter One is an open system, requires ongoing inputs of virgin materials and energy.

Among the first to recognize the relevance of the laws of thermodynamics to economics was the Nobel prize-winning chemist Frederick Soddy whose highly readable accounts, written in the 1920s, were belittled or simply ignored by economists.[45] One who might have known about Soddy's foray into economics was Kenneth Boulding who, in 1966, wrote that thermodynamics should be included in the economic principles required to understand a spaceship economy.[46] As a student at Oxford University, Boulding had attended Soddy's lectures on chemistry before transferring to politics, philosophy, and economics. But either Soddy said nothing of his ideas on economics and thermodynamics or they only registered in Boulding's unconscious mind since, as he confessed years later, he slept through Soddy's lectures.

The person who did the most to explore the implications of the second law of thermodynamics for economics was Nicolas Georgescu-Roegen. Trained in mathematics, statistics, and economics, Georgescu-Roegen applied himself to the study of thermodynamics and from it drew conclusions about the inevitable decline in the capacity of the

Earth to sustain the human population and its economies.[47] Herman Daly, who was Georgescu-Roegen's student and later friend and colleague, has done much to popularize and promote his ideas about thermodynamics and economics, with Daly proposing a suitably scaled steady-state economy as the best way to avoid overshoot.[48]

Conclusion

As the world comes to terms with overshoot and tries to find a way forward that reduces humanity's impacts on the biosphere in ways that treat people everywhere equitably, there is much to be learned from these economists who were aware of the changing times and circumstances. There were many others too, such as Simon Kuznets who developed the system of national accounts in the 1930s now used by all countries to measure their GDP and national income (GDP plus net income from abroad which is also Gross National Product).[49] Kuznets warned against the misinterpretation of national income as a measure of well-being. Robert Kennedy said the same thing but more eloquently.[50] They followed in the path of many others from Adam Smith onwards, who sounded warnings that are still valid today. But it was not enough to steer humanity along a different path from the one that led to the situation we face now, with rampant inequality, ecological overshoot, and widespread insecurity. Neither was it sufficient to effectively challenge the pursuit of economic growth as the overarching priority of economic policy that still retains its grip on governments, even in rich countries with economies many times larger than when these critics were writing. There remains an abiding fear that without economic growth there will be recession, depression, mass unemployment, and despair. When defending the neoliberal version of capitalism—globalization, free markets and free trade—British Prime Minister Margaret Thatcher famously espoused the TINA principle: There is no alternative. Yet escape from overshoot requires that we find one. A better understanding of how capitalist economies function today will help, and that is what we turn to in the next chapter.

Simon Kuznets
1901-1985

The welfare of a nation can scarcely be inferred from a measurement of national income... Goals for "more" growth should specify of what and for what.

Too much and for too long, we seemed to have surrendered community excellence and community values in the mere accumulation of material things. Our gross national product ... if we should judge America by that - counts air pollution and cigarette advertising, and ambulances to clear our highways of carnage. It counts special locks for our doors and the jails for those who break them. It counts the destruction of our redwoods and the loss of our natural wonder in chaotic sprawl. It counts napalm and the cost of a nuclear warhead, and armored cars for police who fight riots in our streets. It counts Whitman's rifle and Speck's knife, and the television programs which glorify violence in order to sell toys to our children. Yet the gross national product does not allow for the health of our children, the quality of their education, or the joy of their play. It does not include the beauty of our poetry or the strength of our marriages; the intelligence of our public debate or the integrity of our public officials. It measures neither our wit nor our courage; neither our wisdom nor our learning; neither our compassion nor our devotion to our country; it measures everything, in short, except that which makes life worthwhile.

Robert Kennedy
1925-1968

FIGURE 3.12.
Kuznets and Kennedy on national income and gross national product.

4

THE ECONOMIC SYSTEM: HOW DOES IT WORK?

The story is told of an Englishman in a Welsh pub asking directions and being told, "If you want to get there I wouldn't start from here." One thing of which we can be certain is that whatever the future turns out to be, it must start from the present. In terms of the futures cone, the present is the point from which the cone is projected forward. What projections we make, and which ones we consider probable, plausible, possible, or preposterous depends on the forces that are propelling us into the future. Of primary interest in this book are the economic forces. In Chapter One we placed the economic cycle at the centre of the image of the Earth, with material and energy flows connecting the economy to the natural environment. Now it is time to describe the economic system most of us live under in a little more detail. How we understand the economic system is critical to how we think about the future.

To make this task manageable, we will confine ourselves to capitalism as represented by the member countries of the Organization for Economic Cooperation and Development (OECD), with only passing reference to other economic systems and non-member countries. Even with this limitation, there are major differences of opinion among economists about the nature of capitalism and how it functions, or even whether to name this economic system capitalism at all, preferring instead terms like "market" or "market-based" economies. The point is, different conceptions of the dominant economic system and how it works today lead to different ideas about tomorrow, where some forms of capitalism may still prevail, or may be displaced by forms of socialism, or by some other, unnamed economic system emerging from the escape from overshoot and other pressures.

The future of capitalism, the dominant economic system of the first decades of the twenty-first century, is highly uncertain. But we do know that capitalism, in its various forms, is where most countries are starting from today. How we think about the future of capitalism is greatly influenced by how we conceive it, and there are many ways of doing that. Three conceptions of capitalism that have long intellectual

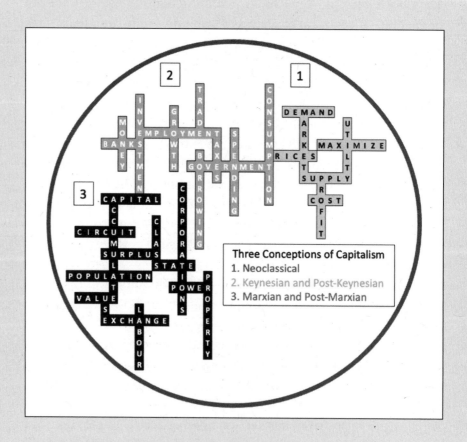

FIGURE 4.1.
Three conceptions of capitalism.

histories and many adherents are: (1) neoclassical economics with a strong emphasis on markets; (2) Keynesian and post-Keynesian economics, also supporting markets, but with an emphasis on aggregate demand and finance; and (3) Marxian and post-Marxian economics with an emphasis on capital accumulation and social class. Each conception represents a way of understanding capitalism that differs in the aspects and inter-relationships it emphasizes, and each has something to offer when we think about the likelihood of different futures. For our purposes, it is sufficient to focus on what differentiates these three conceptions of capitalism, rather than their similarities. Even then, we will only consider a few features of each, but enough to see there is something of value from them all in understanding different forms of capitalism.

The Neoclassical Capitalist Economy

The role of markets in organizing economic affairs is fundamental to the neoclassical conceptualization of capitalism. Neoclassical economics is the result of two centuries of work, advancing and refining the eighteenth-century insights of Adam Smith. It sees market prices as determined by the interaction of demand and supply. This applies to the prices of all commodities; that is, the goods and services purchased by households and by companies, and the land, labor, and capital used in their production. Government also buys goods and services, employs labor, and pays for land and capital through market transactions. Neoclassical economists are well aware that when a sector is dominated by a few large firms it can impede competition. Still, the basic theory is that households allocate their purchases so that they maximize their utility (the benefits they expect to obtain) and producers determine what they are going to produce, how, and in what quantities, to maximize their profits. Markets act as a mediator and signaling device for participants, guiding their choices and, at the same time, being affected by them. For example, if producers increase the price they charge for a commodity because their costs have increased, some customers can be expected to reduce the quantity they decide to buy.

This reduction in quantity demanded can result in a smaller price increase and lower sales than the producers intended.

One of the virtues claimed for markets is that they capture information held by buyers and sellers and known only to themselves. No central planning authority could possibly know about the tastes and preferences that guide the purchasing choices of millions of people, or about the processes and technologies available to producers as they respond to the ever-changing demands of their customers. The prices that emerge from this process balance demand and supply where, without direction from anyone, buyers and sellers settle on a combination of prices and quantities that no one wants to change, given prevailing incomes, preferences, and production and distribution costs.

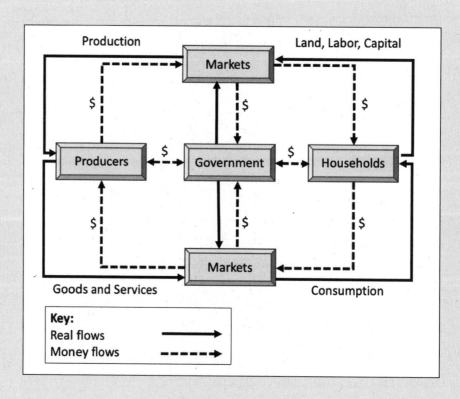

FIGURE 4.2.
Neoclassical
economics.

Markets, in the eyes of neoclassical economists, are an efficient, self-organizing system that functions best when left alone. This was an observation made by Adam Smith 250 years ago and has been repeated by classical and neoclassical economists ever since. But even Smith realized that government has important functions that are essential for an economic system based on markets to work. He mentioned national defense, law and order, and the provision of institutions and public works that are advantageous to society, but which by their nature cannot yield a profit if provided privately. Smith could well have included environmental protection—which is not profitable in most situations—but the environment was not a concern in Smith's time.

Today, we approach the question of when markets are both feasible and desirable for determining what should be produced in an economy by distinguishing two characteristics of commodities: *exclusion* and *rivalry*. Exclusion exists when there are enforceable property rights that entitle the owner to exclude others from using something. Of course, exclusion must also be technically feasible for property rights to have much effect. All the items found in supermarkets satisfy the requirement for exclusion, as anyone leaving a store without paying for something is likely to discover. Fish in the high seas, beyond the 200-mile exclusive economic zone claimed by each coastal country,[51] do not satisfy the conditions for exclusion since anyone can catch fish there. Even within exclusive economic zones there can be significant illegal fishing because monitoring and enforcement is technically challenging. Exclusion is both a matter of law and technology.

Rivalry has nothing to do with the law. It refers only to whether the use or consumption of an item by one person necessarily prevents its use or consumption by another. Food is an obvious example of rival items since one person's consumption prevents consumption by another. In contrast, when one person breathes clean air there is no less available for anyone else. Clean air is non-rival, as is information.

Exclusion and rivalry are often described in terms of either/or. Either those who do not pay can be excluded or they cannot. Either something is rival in consumption, or it is not. However, it is more accurate to think of exclusion and rivalry as matters of degree. Streaming services employ technology to exclude non-subscribers, but they work imperfectly. Roads are non-rival until they become congested, and their use becomes rival.

Of four possible combinations of exclusion and rivalry, the one for which markets work best is where there is high exclusion and high rivalry. Again, the items sold in supermarkets and other shops generally fall into this category. Even then, when markets work well in the sense that they result in quantities and prices that balance demand

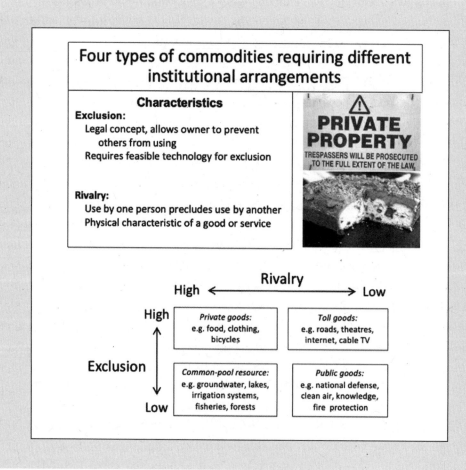

FIGURE 4.3.
Four types of commodities requiring different institutional arrangements.

and supply, it does not mean that the outcome is fair. Neoclassical economics holds that competitive markets are efficient, i.e., that mutual gains from transactions are maximized. For market outcomes to be equitable as well as efficient, the distribution of incomes and wealth must be judged to be fair, a judgment that neoclassical economists avoid, on the grounds that it requires a value judgment that is beyond the scope of economics.

Markets work less well, or not at all, for the other three possible combinations of rivalry and exclusion. Exclusion is a fundamental requirement for any market. If people cannot be excluded from obtaining a commodity unless they pay for it, producers cannot obtain revenue for their products and there will be no supply. However, even when exclusion is feasible, it may not be desirable from a broader social perspective for anything that is non-rival, since one person's consumption means no less for anyone else. Wi-Fi signals are a good example where exclusion is possible, but many people can use them without there being less for others. Why exclude someone when their consumption or use does not diminish availability to others, that is, when they are non-rival? And yet this is what provision through the market does. It excludes people from using or consuming anything for which they do not pay; even when allowing them to do so would mean no less for anyone else. The usual answer is that exclusion is necessary for a price to be charged, which is essential if the private sector is to have the necessary financial incentive and resources to provide a non-rival good or service. An alternative institutional arrangement is public provision with free access funded by taxation. Toll roads versus toll-free roads is one example. Public parks versus private fairgrounds, is another. Even where conditions of exclusion and rivalry obtain, some services are provided by the government when access is considered a right, as with the public provision of health care and education in many countries.

An important feature of capitalism is the powerful incentive it gives the private sector to practice exclusion wherever possible, and to develop technologies that facilitate it, whether a good or service is rival or non-rival. One example is the replacement of rooftop antennas which allowed anyone to pick up non-rival radio and TV signals free of charge, as opposed to cable and internet streaming where exclusion is practiced and fees are charged. Another example of market-based exclusion of non-rival services is the legal protection given to intellectual property. Information, knowledge, and ideas are non-rival and yet access to them is often restricted by a complex web of patent and copyright law, with the usual justification that the laws are required to secure the necessary financial returns. Yet universities around the world have an impressive record in undertaking research and making the findings freely available. Even in the private sector much of the innovative work is performed by salaried employees who do not share in company profits—profits that may be magnified by limiting access through high prices.

When exclusion is either illegal or technically infeasible, market-driven provision by the private sector cannot be relied upon, regardless of whether a good or service is rival in consumption. Environmental protection is an obvious example. People cannot be excluded from the benefits of reduced environmental contamination, so there is no specific market incentive for firms or individuals to reduce the pollution they cause. Consequently, governments the world over use a combination of regulation and direct public expenditures and subsidies to control pollution and protect natural areas.

Arising out of the neoclassical emphasis on markets, and the useful role played by prices in balancing what people want and can afford with what suppliers choose to provide, is the recommendation that prices be used as an instrument for environmental protection. Prices imposed by government can be an incentive for households, businesses, and other sources of air and water emissions and waste disposed on land to reduce the quantities they generate. This is the rationale for a carbon tax, which is an example of the Pigovian tax described in the previous chapter. If fossil fuel companies are required to pay a tax based on the carbon emissions from burning their fuels, the price of the fuels will be higher, and sales, and therefore emissions, will be reduced.

Another way of creating a price on pollution is through tradable emission allowances created by government, as in Europe and parts of

North America, for reducing greenhouse gas emissions. Under such a scheme, emission sources obtain by auction or are given freely, tradable emission allowances. Each source must have sufficient allowances to cover their emissions or be fined. If they have insufficient allowances, they can either reduce their emissions or buy additional allowances from other sources which have a surplus. Paying for carbon emission allowances has a similar incentive effect as a carbon tax by providing sources with a financial incentive to reduce emissions, though the administrative requirements and distributional impacts for a tax and for tradable permits are very different.[52]

In terms of the future, those who adopt the neoclassical perspective on the economic system are likely to hope that a future economy has features that would be less in evidence with a different perspective. They will look for a preponderance of markets, with minimal or modest government oversight and intervention, supplemented by market-like policy instruments with direct regulation limited to those situations where the case for it is overwhelming. Inequality in the distribution of incomes and wealth is unlikely to get much attention, on the grounds that the market knows best and rewards those according to their contribution. In terms of overshoot, the market does not contain within itself information about the ideal scale of the economy in material, energy, or financial terms and therefore provides no real protection against overshoot. For that, we need to consider the whole economy as a macro phenomenon that cannot be understood adequately if it is seen as nothing more than the outcome of myriad individual decisions. This takes us to the second of our three conceptions of capitalism, inspired by the work of John Maynard Keynes.

The Keynesian and Post-Keynesian Capitalist Economy

John Maynard Keynes was a remarkable Englishman, regarded by many as the most influential economist of the twentieth century. He was also a distinguished public servant, patron of the arts, book collector, highly successful investor, prolific writer, and was generally considered one of the brightest men of his generation. Keynes was at the height of his powers as an economist when the Great Depression descended on the

UK, the USA, and other western countries in the 1930s. The massive reduction in economic output and employment was deeply disturbing on several counts. International trade fell dramatically, hurting both rich and poor countries. Construction almost came to a halt, and farming suffered greatly from the drop in food prices. Primary industries, such as mining and forestry, were particularly hard hit. There was little relief from government, especially in the first years of the Great Depression, and the widespread despair helped fertilize the ground for fascism to flourish in Europe, culminating in World War II.

Prior to Keynes, the economics of the day, with its heavy emphasis on self-regulating markets, had no satisfactory explanation for the Great Depression. It was not the ups and downs of the economy that troubled economists. It was the down without an up that perplexed them. They thought that an increase in unemployment would correct itself because wages would fall, inducing employers to hire more people. Likewise, if there was too little investment to absorb the intended savings, it was reasoned that interest rates would fall, reducing borrowing costs for businesses. This would make investment in new buildings and equipment more profitable and would increase until savings and investment balanced.

Economists did realize that there might be impediments to the adjustment in markets that slowed the pace of recovery. Trade unions that resisted declining wages were a popular target, but the general view of economists in the 1930s was that the economic system would recover by itself and there was little that governments could or should do to speed things up.

Keynes thought differently. He argued that the equilibrium level of output and employment in capitalist economies could be well below their maximum, full-employment levels. He saw no self-adjusting mechanism within capitalism that could be relied upon to bring the economy back to full employment, "where everyone who wants a job and is willing to work at the market wage is in work,"[53] and keep it there.

Before Keynes, economists generally believed that savings and investment in the economy were brought into balance by changes in the

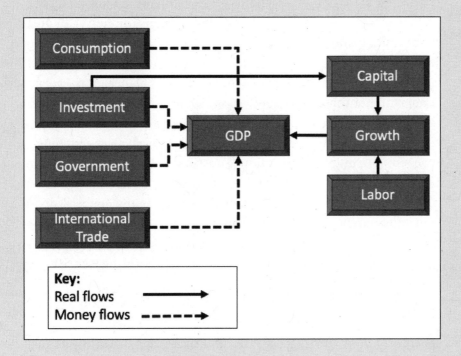

FIGURE 4.4.
Keynesian and
post-Keynesian
economics.

rate of interest, much like in any market, with the rate of interest being
the price borrowers had to pay lenders. Keynes's perspective was different. Looking at an entire economy, and keeping it simple by leaving
aside government and the foreign sector, he realized that incomes can
be spent on consumption or saved. At the same time, the output of the
economy could be devoted to consumption or investment in buildings
and equipment for the longer term. It follows that savings must equal
investment. But decisions to save and decisions to invest are typically
made by different people, so how does this equality of savings and investment come about in practice?

Keynes answered this question not in terms of changes in the interest rate but in terms of changes in the level of total income and output
in the economy. He recognized that people's savings plans could be
quite different from companies' investment plans. He reasoned that

if planned savings by households exceeded planned investment by businesses, households would spend less on consumption than businesses anticipated. Inventories would increase (considered a form of investment), and businesses would reduce their planned investment until actual savings and investment came into balance. In the meantime, with households and businesses spending less, unemployment would rise, and incomes would decline. This, said Keynes, would continue until equilibrium in the economy at large, the macroeconomy, is reached, with output settling down, possibly well below its maximum, with considerable unemployment. If planned investment exceeded planned saving then the adjustments would be in the opposite direction and total income, employment, and output would increase. Most importantly, concluded Keynes, there is nothing inherent in the economic system as he saw it that would automatically bring it back to full employment.

In sum, according to Keynes, changes in national income (essentially the same as GDP) are the main adjustment mechanism in the macroeconomy, not interest rates and other prices. Left to its own devices, a capitalist economy could stabilize at a level far below full employment unless something came along, such as a major war or new invention, which invited renewed investment, jolting the economy out of a very unsatisfactory equilibrium.

Keynes not only provided a new diagnosis of the problems of capitalism, he also had a solution. Achieving full employment was a matter of maintaining the level of total demand in the economy. If total expenditures by the private sector were insufficient, then the government should make up the difference, borrowing to do so if necessary. This is the essence of the New Deal that President Franklin Roosevelt implemented in the USA even before Keynes published his *General Theory of Employment, Interest and Money*[54] in 1936, setting out his macroeconomic theory. What Keynes provided was the theoretical justification for active participation of the government sector in capitalist economies. Younger economists were quick to adopt Keynesian analysis. Older economists, including Keynes's teacher, Arthur C. Pigou, were slower to do so. But with the experience of World War II, where governments in the USA, the UK, and elsewhere spent whatever was necessary for victory, when unemployment evaporated it became clear that Keynes was right. Even before the war was over, meetings were held to work out how international trade could be financed, and total expenditure maintained to avoid another Great Depression in the post-war years. New institutions were established for this very purpose, the most well-known being the International Monetary Fund (IMF) and the World Bank.

For three decades following World War II Keynesian economics reigned supreme. Capitalism flourished, but it was a different capitalism from before the war. After 1945, governments were expected to play a major role in stabilizing the economy. Existing social safety nets were strengthened, and new ones created. Income tax rates were set so that those with higher incomes paid proportionately more than those with lower incomes, and so the distribution of spending power became less unequal. Meanwhile, a new element was added to the Keynesian conception of capitalism. Keynes had made it clear that his theory was for the short term because, as he famously said, "in the long run we are all dead." More prosaically, Keynes did not pay much attention to the fact that the investment expenditures which he considered so important for employment also added to the economy's stock of capital—its buildings, machines, and infrastructure. But as the classical economists had realized more than a century earlier, the accumulation of capital is a fundamental driver of economic growth because it makes labor more productive. From a Keynesian perspective, it also meant that total expenditure in the economy would have to keep increasing if full employment was to be maintained, especially if the labor force was growing as well. Into the 1950s, full employment remained the goal, and economic growth the means. With the Cold War between the USA and the USSR, each with their respective allies, these priorities were switched. Economic growth—the race to have the biggest economy—became the primary goal of government economic policy and, with few exceptions, it has remained that way ever since.

One thing should be clear: Keynesian economics did not replace neoclassical economics. Instead, it became part of a larger set of ideas about capitalism referred to as the "neoclassical synthesis" or "new Keynesian" economics. In this understanding of capitalism, markets continue to play a major role in allocating resources, but the overall level of economic activity is determined by deliberate government actions to stimulate or suppress total demand as need be. In the 1970s, price inflation became a serious problem, and there were proposals, sometimes acted on, to adopt a different, "monetarist" approach to macroeconomics, one based more specifically on the control of the money supply by central banks. Controlling the money supply turned out to be much more difficult than the monetarists expected, not least because of disagreements about what constitutes money and how it should be measured. Also, the speed with which money circulates through the economy, its velocity of circulation, proved to be far less stable than the monetarists had assumed, weakening the link between the quantity of money, inflation, and the macroeconomy.

A parallel development to monetarism was a set of ideas that has come to be known as post-Keynesian economics. In the flurry of enthusiasm for Keynesian economics and the remedy it offered for unemployment, it was often overlooked that Keynes had a lot to say about money. Indeed, he had written a whole book on the subject prior to writing the *General Theory*. Post-Keynesians recognized this and set out to reinterpret Keynes more in keeping with what they believed were his original intentions. One notable insight of the post-Keynesians is that most of the money in a modern capitalist economy is not what central banks print but is created when commercial banks make loans. Through a few keystrokes on a computer keyboard, banks now create the money deposited digitally in the borrower's bank account. As post-Keynesians say, it is not deposits that create loans, but loans that create deposits.

Another insight from the post-Keynesians, and from Hyman Minsky in particular, is the inherent instability of capitalist economies caused by changing sentiments towards risk. Minsky described a repeated progression from conservative lending by banks keen to recover both principal and interest, to riskier loans where recovering interest is sufficient for the time being, and finally to much riskier loans based on the expected increase in the value of the assets that the loans are used to finance. When expectations change and borrowers no longer think that asset values will continue to rise, they sell their assets, which reduces their value. To protect themselves from bad debts banks call in their loans—with mixed success—and the house of cards collapses in on itself. When the financial dust settles, expectations change again, banks start lending conservatively again, and the cycle is repeated.

The picture of a capitalist economy that emerges from the Keynesian and post-Keynesian conceptions is one where markets remain important; unemployment, instability and economic growth are systemic features; and government intervention through taxation, borrowing, and spending is essential to keep the economy on a reasonably even keel. In terms of what this view of capitalism portends for the future, we should remember that Keynes himself was no radical, and was

FIGURE 4.5. The Minsky model of instability.

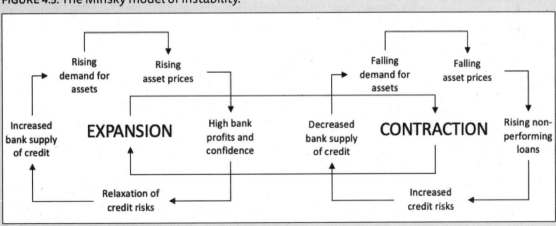

Credit: Author based on G. Riley, Minsky's Financial Instability Hypothesis, www.youtube.com/watch?v=HrXngX2J1Ko.

definitely no socialist. His interest was in managing capitalism, not in replacing it.

Although Keynes did not offer or subscribe to a theory of how economies evolve, the views he expressed in 1930 on the economic possibilities of his grandchildren's generation a hundred years hence were of a society that had solved the economic problem of scarcity. People would be working 15 hours a week, and the biggest problem would be how to use the increased leisure time well. Yet Keynes looked at the prospect of this age of leisure and abundance with dread. He feared there would be too little time for the necessary readjustment in habits and ways of thinking that would be required for the transition to succeed. This may explain why, 90 years after Keynes mused about the future, the immense increase in economic productivity that he correctly anticipated has been used primarily to increase output, not leisure time, with all the attendant environmental consequences leading to overshoot that we now confront. Whether capitalism can be managed to achieve what Keynes thought might soon be possible while at the same time resolving global overshoot, is unclear. Perhaps it will require a transformation away from capitalism equivalent to the transformation from feudalism into capitalism three centuries earlier. To investigate this possibility, we need an analysis of the dynamics of capitalism that has built within it an evolutionary/revolutionary mechanism of change that is absent from the neoclassical and Keynesian perspectives. For that we turn to Marx.

The Marxian and Post-Marxian Capitalist Economy

Karl Marx was a German émigré who spent much of his adult life in London, living in meager circumstances with his wife and children. He supported them through his writing and with funds from his friend and collaborator Friedrich Engels, a prosperous businessman from a German family with a manufacturing plant in Manchester. Marx and his ideas about capitalism are not very popular these days. He still has his followers, of course, but unless today's students of economics, especially in Western countries, choose to take a course on the history of economic thought, should one be offered, they learn little or nothing of Marx. This is unfortunate, since at a time when overshoot is forcing us to rethink our economy and its relation to the biosphere, we have turned our backs on one of the few political economists whose interest was in how economic systems change over time, rather than how to get the one we have to work better.

Marx explained that all societies, other than those at the most basic level of subsistence, generate a surplus beyond the immediate survival needs of its members. How this surplus is generated, by whom and for whom, what it consists of, and how it is used, differentiates various kinds of society. In the ancient civilizations of Egypt, Persia, Greece, Rome, the Incan and Mayan empires, and the dynastic kingdoms of India and China, much of the surplus generated by slave labor accrued to powerful rulers who used it to build monuments, some of which still survive. In all these examples, ownership and control of the surplus was vested in the same person or ruling elite that also held political and military power, so there was no economy distinct from the rest of the society. In European feudal societies, surpluses produced by serfs accrued to their lord. Gradually, in emerging towns and cities, some of the surplus came under the ownership and control of merchants through the profits of trade. Some of these profits were invested in factories, where surplus was produced by wage labor, an arrangement that eventually came to dominate the economy in many countries, after beginning in Western Europe in the latter half of the last millennium. This was the birth of capitalism, which can be defined as a configuration of society in which the main source of surplus is produced by wage labor. What distinguishes capitalism from those other forms of society is the separation of the political, military, and social from the economic. This is not to say that they are entirely independent of each other, but only that the generation and disposal of the society's surplus within capitalism is the primary responsibility of identifiable economic actors—its producers and consumers—who do not themselves hold political or military power, though powerful producers are not without considerable influence on those that do.

Capitalism's distinctive change in surplus creation and disposal, and its separation of economic from political and military power, has had many consequences. One was the emergence of "political economy" developed by the classical economists, such as Smith, Malthus, and Ricardo, who identified and began to study a separate economic realm within society consisting of employers and employees, capitalists and workers, producers and consumers, or whatever categories they found most compelling. These differentiations, and the theories developed to explain their behavior, led to a new form of social analysis that we now call economics. For Marx, the basic structure of capitalism was the division between capitalists, who owned as private property the financial capital and produced capital (buildings and equipment), and workers, who owned only their labor power and depended on paid work for their income. These were the two main classes in Marx's analysis of capitalism, and they had competing and conflicting interests in how the surplus was distributed.

Marx studied the work of the classical economists. He adopted and adapted some of their principles to bring a new understanding to nineteenth-century capitalism. For example, Marx used the classical labor theory of value, which sought to explain the relative prices of commodities in terms of the labor required for their production, to account for the exploitation of labor. He maintained the classical distinction between "use value," which is derived directly from a commodity, and "exchange value," which is the rate at which commodities are traded for each other. Workers, Marx said, are paid only what it costs for the worker and his family to reproduce themselves, (that is, necessary use value, as in food and shelter). Meanwhile the capitalists who employed the workers receive the full exchange value for what the workers produce. The difference is profit. Marx considered this relationship between capitalist and workers exploitative.

Drawing on his extensive knowledge of history, Marx observed that in most precapitalist societies, people could be forced to work and were disciplined, even killed, if they refused. This was true of feudalism which still existed in parts of Europe when Marx was writing. It was also true of many states in the USA under slavery until it was abolished in 1865. In capitalism people can be denied work, but they cannot be made to work by employers—the owners of capital—or by the government.[55] Destitution is an option. The state (i.e., government, judiciary, police, and the military) holds a monopoly of physical force, but under capitalism it lost direct access to the surplus and must rely heavily on taxation to obtain some of it. The power of capitalist employers resides in their ability to withhold work, not to enforce it with punitive sanctions for those who refuse.

Another distinction between capitalism and previous societies analyzed by Marx was the changed nature of trade. Trade is commonplace in history. People have exchanged goods in markets or in personal trade since ancient times. They would make more than they themselves required and trade the surplus with others who had done the same. When money was involved, the sequence would be commodity–money–commodity. Traders would start with excess commodities, sell them for money, which would then be used to buy other commodities for their own use. Under capitalism, said Marx, this sequence or circuit was transformed. Capitalists trade not to transform commodities into other commodities, but to transform money into more money. Starting with an amount of financial capital, capitalists advance funds to buy commodities that they use in production with the intention to sell what they produce for more money than they initially advanced. Today we might say that the purpose of business—of all private sector corporations—is to make money for their owners and they do this by providing goods and services for sale…at a profit.

A related feature of capitalism, already noted, that Marx emphasized, is that capitalists make a profit by paying wages that are less than the market value of the output of what is produced. Were this not so, they would lose money. There are other interpretations of this arrangement, such as profit being capitalists' reward for taking risk, or that as owners of capital, which is just another "factor of production," they are entitled to a return determined by the impersonal forces of demand and supply. But whatever the interpretation, they all share one common feature. They are all predicated on the fact that out of a combination of labor, materials, energy, land, and capital comes an output which belongs entirely to the owners of capital. This is what makes it possible for profit to accrue to those who own capital and not to those who own only their capacity to work. And it is this feature of capitalism that allows owners of capital to accumulate more capital, both financial and produced.

For Marx, the impulse of capitalists to accumulate capital was central to his analysis of capitalism. More than an impulse, the Marxist

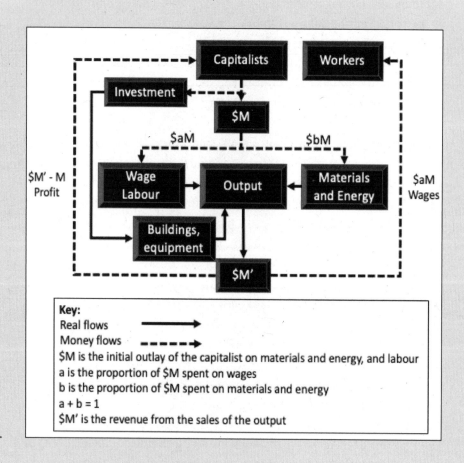

FIGURE 4.6.
Marxian and post-Marxian economics.

view is that capital accumulation is an imperative of capitalism. Failure to accumulate capital as fast as possible puts a capitalist at the mercy of other capitalists who will come to dominate and absorb them. Furthermore, said Marx and classical economists before him, the accumulation of capital accounts for the expansion of economic output for economic growth. But where the classical economists Malthus and Ricardo saw population expansion as inevitably overwhelming the productive capacity of the economy, Marx saw the demise of capitalism as coming from within its own dynamic—a declining ability to generate profit from wage labor because its role in production, said Marx, inevitably declines with the accumulation of capital.

Marx explained that feudalism and slavery gave way to capitalism because the social arrangements were increasingly out of step with factory-based arrangements for production. Looking to the future, he argued that capitalism would inevitably give way to a different form of organization when capitalism was no longer profitable and the workers, by virtue of their impoverished circumstances and increased unionization, demanded change. There is still debate today about whether the rate of profit has declined as Marx predicted, or whether it would have declined but for imperialism and war or both, or whether he was just plain wrong. Marx made other predictions that failed to transpire, though alternative interpretations of events permit different assessments of his record. What is most relevant here is the more general proposition that an expanding economy can generate conditions that undermine the possibilities for further growth, or worse still, can force an uncomfortable and unwanted degree of contraction.

Marx was aware that the concentration of large populations in urban centers and the agricultural practices of his day were depleting the soil of its nutrients. He even related the degradation of soil to international trade, anticipating in some ways the basis for the ecological footprint developed over a century later. However, the pressures of the human economy on the biosphere are now orders of magnitude greater than those that concerned him a century and a half ago. Much of this is attributable to the world's capitalist economies made up largely of the member countries of the Organization for Economic Cooperation and Development (OECD), though the economies of communist USSR (before dissolution, now Russia) and China have also played a major role. Now capitalism faces new threats from the global degradation of the environment. Will it be able to adapt to these new circumstances and still retain the key features that distinguish it from other societal arrangements, or will it lead to the reintegration of political, military, and economic power more characteristic of China—or to something else altogether?

Just as there are post-Keynesians who follow in the footsteps of Keynes, there are post-Marxians who find their inspiration in Marx but have adapted his conceptualization of capitalism to better fit today's cir-

FIGURE 4.7. The countries with the largest cumulative territorial emissions of CO_2 1850–2021 (billions of tonnes of CO_2 from fossil fuels, cement, land use, and forestry).

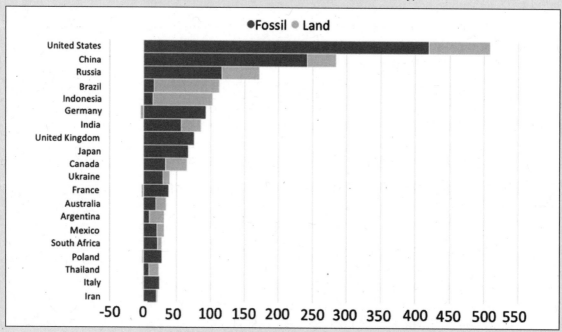

Credit: Source: Carbon Brief analysis of figures from the Global Carbon Project, CDIAC, Our World in Data, Carbon Monitor, Houghton and Nassikas (2017) and Hansis et al. (2015). Chart by Carbon Brief using Highcharts. www.carbonbrief.org/analysis-which-countries-are-historically-responsible-for-climate-change/

cumstances. One such re-conceptualization of capitalism for the twenty-first century is based on the observation that capitalism, especially in the USA, has evolved from the industrial capitalism that Marx analyzed to financial capitalism. Reduced to its simplest form, the M-C-M' circuit of industrial capitalism, where money (M) finances the production of commodities (C) which are sold for a profit (M'), becomes in financial capitalism M-M'. Money makes money simply by charging rent and interest, and making capital gains, without any intermediate production and consumption of commodities. (Hudson, credit in Fig. 4.9.)

When Marx was writing in the nineteenth century, the leading rentiers (people who live on income from property or securities) were landowners. They had been dominant under feudalism but, with

FIGURE 4.8. Financial capitalism.

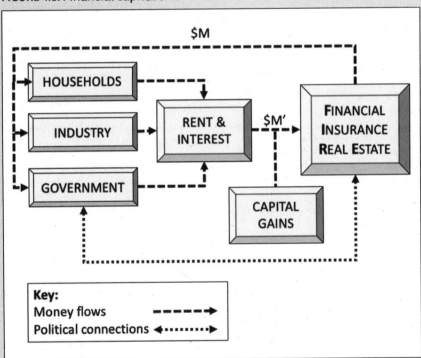

Industrial Capitalism	Financial Capitalism

• Make profits by producing products • Favor industry and labor • Provide public infrastructure at low cost • Reform parliaments to block rent seeking. • Avoid military spending that requires foreign debt • Concentrate economic & social planning in the political capital • Bring prices in line with costs • Banks lend to finance tangible capital investment • Corporate earnings recycled into real capital investment to increase output • Long-term time frame to develop products and marketing plans • Inherently nationalistic, requiring government protection and subsidy of industry	• Extract economic rent and interest • Special tax favoritism to FIRE sectors • Privatize infrastructure to extract monopoly rent • Use international organizations (such as IMF & Nato) to force neoliberal policies • Shift planning and resource allocation to financial centers • Shift monetary policy to central banks representing commercial banking interests • Maximize rent-seeking via land ownership, credit, and monopoly privileges • Banks lend against collateral and bid up rent yielding asset prices • Corporate earnings paid as dividends or used for stock buybacks to increase stock price gains • Short time frame, hit-and-run by financial speculation • Seek prevention of capital controls, imposes free trade libertarian government policies

FIGURE 4.9.
Industrial capitalism versus financial capitalism.

Credit: Text adapted from M. Hudson (2021), "Finance Capitalism versus Industrial Capitalism: The *Rentier* Resurgence and Takeover," *Review of Radical Political Economics*, 1–17. Photos from Pavel Neznanov and Jorge Salvador on Upsplash.

the rise of capitalism, were displaced economically and, to a large extent, politically by industrial capitalists. But rather than disappear as Keynes and others had anticipated, the rentier is alive and thriving in the FIRE (finance, insurance, and real estate) sector of the economy. This sector benefits from favorable taxation of its income through mutually supportive political connections between the FIRE sector and government. Meanwhile, central banks facilitate the financialization of the economy by ensuring, through various means, that sufficient funds are available. This process is further supported by international organizations—the IMF, NATO, the World Trade Organization, and the World Bank—to expand the international scope of financialization, leading to increasing conflict between industrializing countries such as India and China, who are seeking to protect and promote their national economic interests, and countries, such as the USA and Canada, where financial capitalism is ascendant or already well established.

The financialization of capitalism reminds us that capitalism is an evolving system, with many variations reflecting the different circumstances, histories, and ideologies that exist among countries and regions. A recent evolutionary development that began in the twenty-first century, is the emergence of "surveillance capitalism," so well described by social psychologist, philosopher, and scholar Shoshana Zuboff.[56] Zuboff explains how firms such as Google, Facebook, and Verizon went from analyzing data obtained from their users to improve the service they received to "extracting" data from users, often without their knowledge or permission, and claiming it as their own. This data, from multitudes of users, is used by these companies or their clients, to predict behavior. They sell the predictions to advertisers and others to make enormous profits. Zuboff describes the many nefarious methods the companies employ and warns that their success threatens to undermine individual agency and ultimately democracy itself. And that is not all. By stimulating expenditures, which is the main purpose of advertising, the surveillance economy increases overshoot, and by undermining individual agency and democracy, surveillance capitalism reduces our chances of escape.

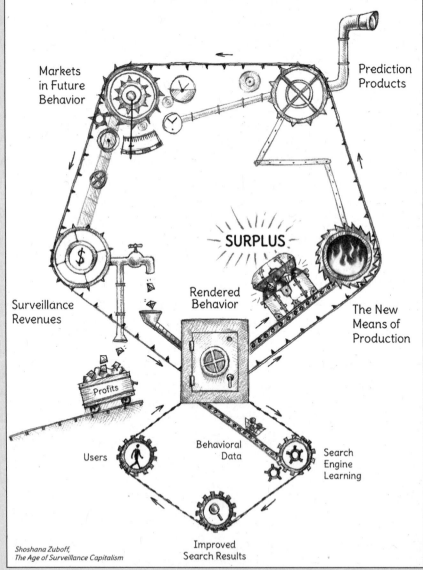

The Discovery of Behavioral Surplus

Surveillance capitalism begins with the discovery of behavioral surplus. More behavioral data are rendered than required for service improvements. This surplus feeds a new means of production that fabricates predictions of user behavior. These products are sold to business customers in new behavioral futures markets. The Behavioral Value Reinvestment Cycle is subordinated to this new logic.

Markets in Future Behavior

Prediction Products

SURPLUS

Surveillance Revenues

Rendered Behavior

The New Means of Production

Profits

Users

Behavioral Data

Search Engine Learning

Improved Search Results

Shoshana Zuboff, The Age of Surveillance Capitalism

FIGURE 4.10. Surveillance Capitalism

Conclusion

The three principal ways of analyzing capitalism that we have briefly described—neo-classical, Keynesian, and Marxian—and the two variants—financial and surveillance capitalism—differ in what they find most compelling about capitalism. The neoclassical (NC) conceptualization of capitalism emphasizes the role of markets. The Keynesian/post-Keynesian (K/PK) conceptualization emphasizes the role of government and central banks for achieving goals relating to employment, economic growth, and price and financial stability. The Marxian/post-Marxian (M/PM) conceptualization highlights the conflicting interests of different classes and the internal pressures this conflict generates, forcing capitalism to change. None of these conceptualizations of capitalism have a monopoly on the truth. There is something to be learned from them all. It is useful, therefore, to consider what the future of capitalism might look like from the perspective of each of them.

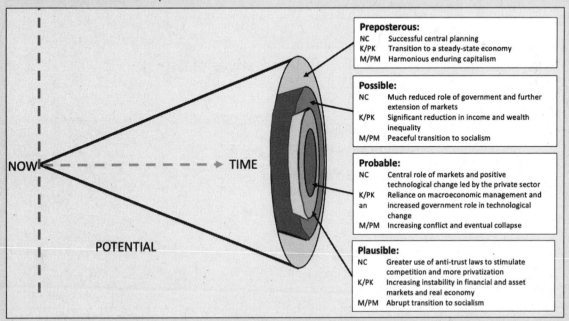

FIGURE 4.11. The future of capitalism.

All the conceptualizations of capitalism considered in this chapter have one important thing in common. They are all concerned, in one way or another, with economic growth. Neoclassical economists are confident that markets can allocate resources over time, as well as among competing uses in the present or short-term. They understand that investment today comes at the expense of consumption today, but it is investment that promises even more consumption in the future by increasing the capacity of the economy to produce. This is economic growth.

It is much the same with Keynesian and post-Keynesian economists, except that they see a larger role for government in influencing the level and direction of investment through a combination of direct public investment and fiscal and monetary policies to spread the benefits of growth more evenly. Keynesians and post-Keynesians also seek to increase the rate of economic growth. Generally, Marxian and post-Marxian economists are also enthusiastic about economic growth. Marx himself lauded capitalism for its productivity and dynamism and

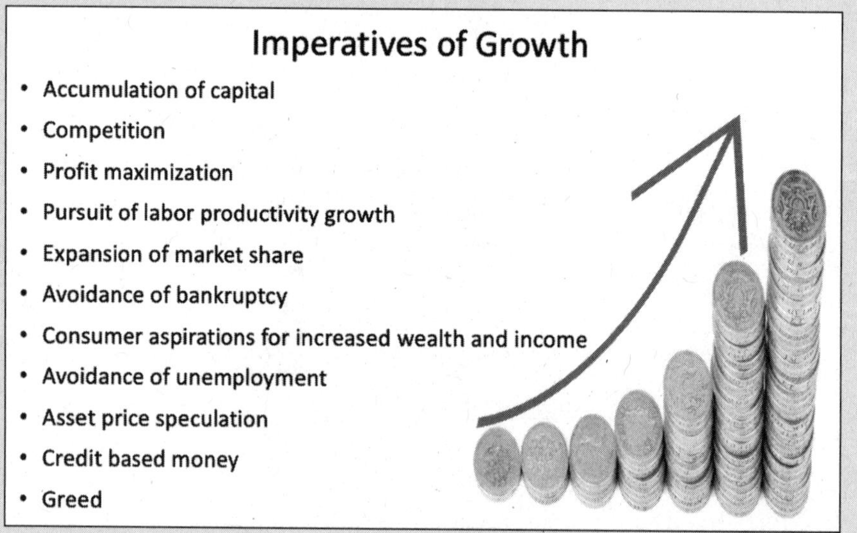

FIGURE 4.12.
Growth
imperatives in
capitalism.

Imperatives of Growth

- Accumulation of capital
- Competition
- Profit maximization
- Pursuit of labor productivity growth
- Expansion of market share
- Avoidance of bankruptcy
- Consumer aspirations for increased wealth and income
- Avoidance of unemployment
- Asset price speculation
- Credit based money
- Greed

Credit: Author, graphic from pxhere.com

the economic growth that resulted. His concern was that wage-earning workers were exploited by their capitalist employers in the process. He was also convinced that economic growth would inevitably cease in capitalist economies when the rate of profit declined to zero, exacerbating conflict between the classes. But this was not intended as a criticism of growth, only of growth under capitalism.

When economic growth is placed within the context of overshoot, it leads naturally to the question of whether growth is essential in capitalist economies. This question is sometimes expressed by asking whether there are growth imperatives in capitalism. Different questions about capitalism arise once overshoot is brought into the picture, such as whether economic growth, as measured by increases in GDP, is possible while pressures on the biosphere are reduced. This is the essence of "green" growth which we consider in Chapter Six. There can be no doubt that the combination of economic growth and population growth as actually experienced has led to overshoot and that the situation will only worsen unless things change. Although the future is essentially uncertain, it must start from the present. In the next chapter we will take stock of the present by looking at trends that suggest where we may be heading in the future, with some trends leading further into overshoot and some leading away from it. Then we will be able to assess various proposals for the best way forward in a world already in overshoot and from which we must strive to escape.

5

CURRENT TRENDS
TO AN UNCERTAIN FUTURE

To think creatively about alternative futures, it is essential to have an appreciation of where we are starting from and how we got here. Such an understanding is not only about the past and present, but also about the trends that connect the present to the future and the forces underlying them. We have already seen how different conceptions of capitalism generate different expectations about the economic future. Now we will look in more detail at trends in some key features of economies that have brought us to overshoot and that will, if they continue, take us further in that direction. We will look at trends especially germane to overshoot: in economic growth, demography, income and wealth inequality, investment, consumption, technology, work, and energy.

It would be a serious mistake to think that any of the many factors that will define the future can be forecast by a simple extrapolation of past trends. A good example of how misleading this can be is to consider data for the minimum height of the river Nile. Many centuries ago, Egyptian tax authorities collected data on the height of the Nile to gauge agricultural prosperity for tax purposes. From the year 811 CE to 842 CE, there was a clear downward trend in the minimum height of the Nile. An extrapolation of this trend would have led the tax authorities and everyone else to expect increasing droughts in the years ahead.

What happened was quite different.

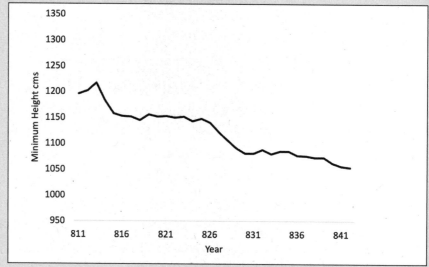

FIGURE 5.1.
Minimum height of the Nile 811 to 842 (5-year moving average in centimeters)

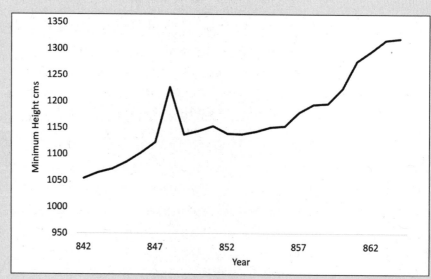

FIGURE 5.2.
Minimum height of the Nile 842 to 864 (5-year moving average in centimeters)

After 864 CE, the minimum height of the Nile declined again, and continued fluctuating with no obvious long-term trend for hundreds of years.

As well as the danger of drawing incorrect conclusions about the future by extrapolating data, there is another important lesson to learn from these two figures. In both, the vertical axis starts at 950 centimeters. Had the axes started at 0 the decline in the minimum height of the Nile and subsequent increase would have appeared much less dramatic. Consider this. From the data, we can tell that the minimum height of the Nile between 811 and 842 declined by 12 percent followed by a 25 percent increase between 841 and 864. Visually, these changes are shown as a 65 percent decline and a 400 percent increase if you measure them with a ruler from the origin. Exaggeration of change over time is avoided if the data are plotted with the vertical axis starting from zero. Then the proportional changes shown visually correspond precisely to the proportional changes in the data. The story is less dramatic, but it is accurate and worth remembering as we consider past trends relevant to overshoot.

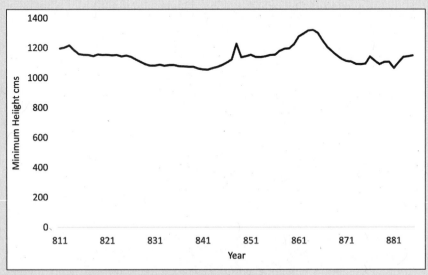

FIGURE 5.3. Minimum height of the Nile 811 to 885 (5-year moving average in centimeters)

Credit: Author. Data from W. J. Baumol, W. E. and Oates, (1979), *Economics, Environmental Policy, and the Quality of Life*, p. 38, Prentice-Hall.

Economic Trends

While it can be a serious error to simply extrapolate from past trends into the future, we can gain a sense of where the world is heading by looking at trends that have brought us to where we are today—to overshoot. Let us begin with trends in world economic output, measured as inflation-adjusted GDP, which increased about eight times between 1961 and 2020 and tripled on a per capita basis.[57] What is not generally appreciated is that the rate of world economic growth trended downwards during this period, with a slight upturn towards the end. (A linear trend line would be downward sloping throughout and if projected forward would result in a zero rate of economic growth in 2031!)

Of course, there was great variation in the world economic growth rate from year to year and among the countries of the world. Without going into too much detail, we can see differences in trends in economic growth at the sub-global level by grouping countries according to their income levels. This is exactly what the World Bank does

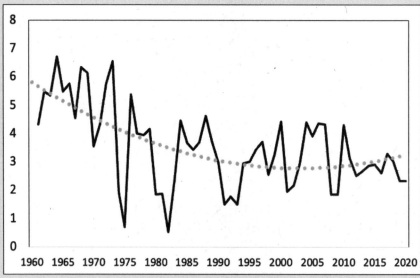

FIGURE 5.4.
World annual rate of economic growth (%) and trend 1961–2020.

Credit: Author. Data from World Development Indicators, World Bank.

when it classifies countries by their gross national incomes (GNI) per capita.[58] In 2022, high-income countries had a per capita GNI of at least US$12,696. Low-income countries had a per capita GNI of US$1,045 or less. Middle-income countries (which the World Bank divides into lower and upper middle-income), had a per capita GNI of between US$1,046 and US$12,695.

Looking at the trends in rates of economic growth in high, middle, and low-income countries (Fig. 5.6), we see that the trend is downwards for high-income countries. (Note, this is the trend. There were considerable ups and downs in the annual rate of economic growth). The declining trend in the rate of economic growth in high-income countries would still have been true in the absence of the COVID-19 pandemic in 2020 and without the financial crisis of 2007/08. Despite the priority given to economic growth in these countries and the policies designed to stimulate growth, economic growth in high-income countries has been slowing over the past six decades.

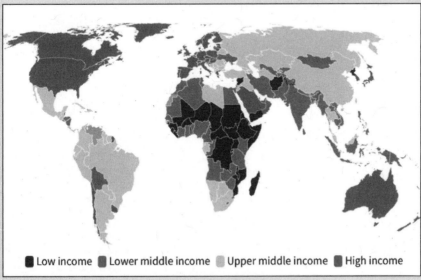

■ Low income ■ Lower middle income ■ Upper middle income ■ High income

FIGURE 5.5.
World annual rate of economic growth (%) 1961–2020.

Credit: World Bank, World Development Indicators, https://datatopics.worldbank.org/world-development-indicators/the-world-by-income-and-region.html

Middle-income countries, which include the BRIC countries (Brazil, Russia, India, and China), tell a different story. The long-term trend in the rate of economic growth in this group of countries shows a modest decline in the first half of the 60-year period, followed by an upturn beginning in the mid-1990s. World Bank data on economic growth in low-income countries only goes back to 1982. The trend in economic growth in these low-income countries shows a substantial rise to 2007, followed by a sharp decline.

Focusing for the moment on high-income countries, we can learn about the causes of the decline in growth rates from Robert Gordon, who studied the history of economic growth in the USA since the 1860s. He points to the slowdown in the growth rate after 1970, which he attributes largely to marked differences between the impact of technologies introduced before then (e.g., electricity, automobiles, jet aircraft, assembly lines, refrigeration, mainframe computers), and

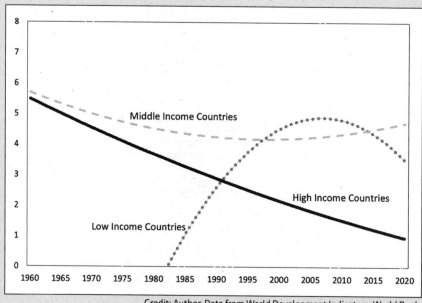

FIGURE 5.6.
Trends in annual rates of economic growth (%) in high-, middle- and low-income countries 1961–2020. (No data for low-income countries before 1982)

Credit: Author. Data from World Development Indicators, World Bank.

those which came after (e.g., the internet, smart phones, e-commerce, personal computers). Looking to the future, Gordon identified six main "headwinds," which he anticipates will continue to slow the rate of economic growth in the USA to below one percent annually between 2015–2040. A similar conclusion concerning growth was expressed by Robert Ayres and Benjamin Warr, who focused on the declining availability of useful energy and the implications for long-term economic growth. Energy is always conserved, but its capacity to do work—*exergy*—decreases when energy is used. This is why new sources of energy are required just to maintain the same level of work, as Soddy, Georgescu-Roegen, Boulding, and Daly emphasized. (See Chapter Three.)

It is highly likely that if the factors that Gordon and Ayres and Warr believe will slow the rate of economic growth in the USA continue to prevail, they will have a similar effect in other high-income countries.

FIGURE 5.7. Economists Robert Gordon and Robert Ayres foresee the end of economic growth in the USA.

Credit: Book covers from R. J. Gordon, (2016), *The Rise and Fall of American Growth*, Princeton University Press, and R. Ayres, and R. Warr, (2009), *The Economic Growth Engine*, Edward Elgar.

Whether this would be helpful in escaping from overshoot would greatly depend on how high-income countries react. Would they make a relatively smooth transition to the new circumstances (see Chapter Eight), or would they adopt a more aggressive stance towards each other and to poorer nations in competition for increasingly scarce resources?

When it comes to forecasting the future rate of economic growth, countries may decide that, faced with overshoot, the best option to reduce pressures on the biosphere and improve well-being is to give priority to other objectives instead of promoting economic growth. Alternatively, it could turn out that measures taken to ameliorate the impacts of overshoot reduce the rate of economic growth (see Chapter Six "Green Investment"). Another possibility is that catastrophic climate change, or some other deterioration of the biosphere from overshoot, will reduce the rate of economic growth. And, in the other direction, contrary to Gordon and Ayres and Warr, some believe that a combination of biotech, artificial intelligence, and breakthroughs in energy and materials technologies will boost economic growth and reduce humanity's pressure on the planet as well.[59] There are many possible futures, some more probable than others. In later chapters we will explore two in particular: a base case where historical trends and relationships continue, and an *Escape* scenario where economic growth ends in high-income countries, and their material and energy throughputs and ecological footprint fall dramatically.

Demographic Trends

Turning to trends in the rate of population growth, we see distinct differences among low-, middle-, and high-income countries. World population growth peaked at 2.1 percent in 1971 and has since declined steadily to just above one percent in 2020. There has been a steady decline in the rate of growth of the population in high-income countries, falling to less than 0.5 percent in 2020. In middle-income countries the rate of population growth fell from over two percent in 1961 to about one percent in 2020, which is where high-income countries were in the early 1970s. Low-income countries show a very different history, with the annual population growth rate peaking above three percent in the early 1990s and declining slightly to about 2.7 percent in 2020. These differences in population growth rates by income category account for the fact that global population growth has been disproportionately high in low-income countries. However, even there fertility rates have declined due to the combined effects of rising living standards, urbanization, and the empowerment of women giving them increased access to family planning and to education for girls.

From the perspective of overshoot, the trends in economic and population growth are encouraging, but they are still insufficient to escape it. Indeed, current population forecasts by the United Nations put the number of humans alive in 2100 at around ten billion, though this number, which could be lower or higher, is very sensitive to changes in the projected fertility rate (the average number or children born per woman of child-bearing age).

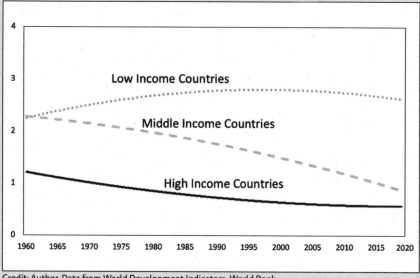

Credit: Author. Data from World Development Indicators, World Bank.

FIGURE 5.8.
Trends in annual rates of population growth (%) in high-, middle- and low-income countries 1961–2020.

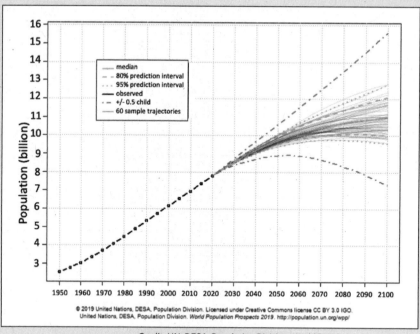

FIGURE 5.9.
World population.

As already noted, the differences in fertility rates among countries with different income levels change the proportion of people living in rich and poor countries. If this continues as expected, then it will also change the distribution of people living in different regions.

One of the consequences of the slowing rate of growth in population, which is expected to continue, is that with proportionately fewer children being born, the average age of the population will rise, especially if life expectancy rises as well, as it has done throughout most of the world since 1900. This will mean a decline in the proportion of people between 15 and 65 who make up the bulk of the labor force, and an increase in the ratio of children and the elderly not in the work force who must depend on those who are. This is true even for retired people who expect to live off their savings and pensions. These funds give them access to whatever is produced in the economy, but the funds

FIGURE 5.10. Total population by region: estimates and projections 1950 to 2100.

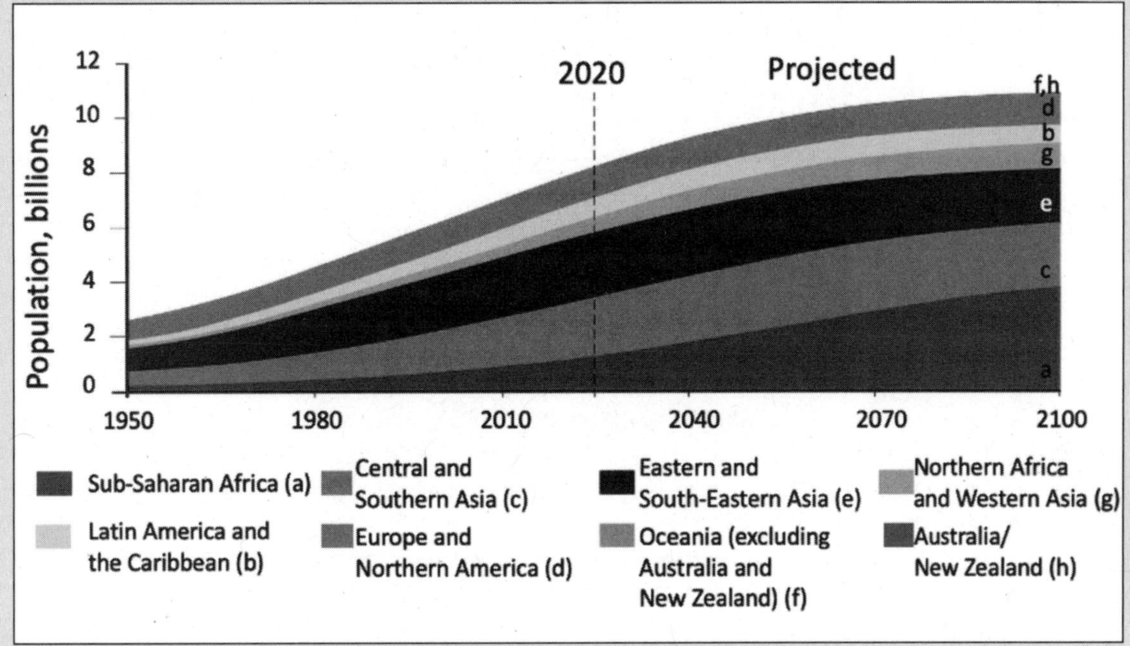

Credit: P. Dasgupta, (2021), *The Economics of Biodiversity: The Dasgupta Review.* Abridged Version. (London: H.M. Treasury.)

themselves do not produce anything. Only the people working do that and they must produce enough for everyone including all those not working for whatever reason.

One last demographic trend that has a significant bearing on overshoot is the increasing concentration of people living and working in urban areas. Urbanization has a long history. It began to accelerate in the early nineteenth century, both as an effect and a cause of industrialization. Factories required people and workers required employment, especially those displaced from the land with no other livelihood. More efficient agriculture, defined narrowly as output per farm worker, allowed these factory workers and their families to be fed, though they themselves played no role in food production. The mutually dependent relationship between factory production and more productive agriculture was based primarily on access to cheap energy

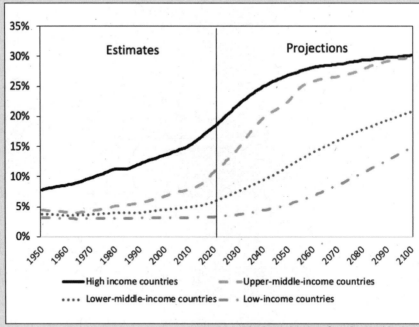

FIGURE 5.11.
Share of total population over 64 years of age by country income group.

from fossil fuels. This will change as the world shifts out of fossil fuels to avoid a climate catastrophe. It is yet to be seen whether the high level of urbanization that now exists will be sustained or whether it will reverse itself in response to changing sources and quantities of energy.

Income Inequality Trends

Looking back over the past century there was a very distinctive U-shaped pattern of change in income inequality within countries. This is shown most clearly in the share of national income going to the top one percent of income recipients in many countries. The share of the one percent typically fell from a peak in 1914, when the earliest estimates of income inequality are generally available, to a low in the mid 1970s because of progressively high tax rates and income redistribution. Income inequality climbed again as these measures

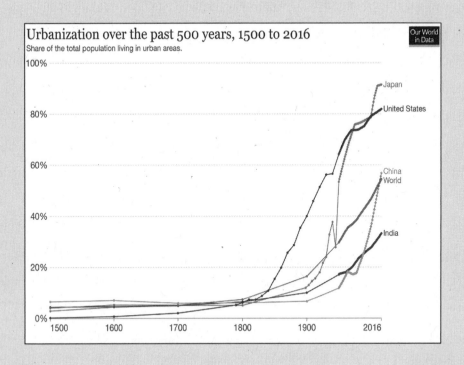

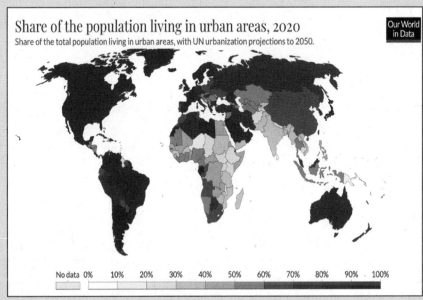

FIGURE 5.12.
Urbanization past and present.

Credit: Hannah Ritchie and Max Roser (2018)—"Urbanization." Published online at OurWorldInData.org. Retrieved from: https://ourworldindata.org/urbanization

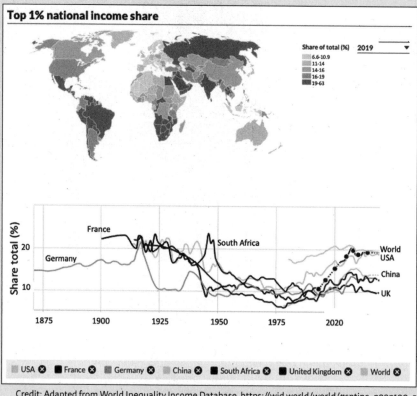

FIGURE 5.13.
Global income
inequality—
top 1% income
share.

Credit: Adapted from World Inequality Income Database, https://wid.world/world/#sptinc_p99p100_z
/US;FR;DE;CN;ZA;GB;WO/2019/eu/k/p/yearly/s/false/5.1754999999999995/30/curve/false/country

were reversed, so that it is now approaching the levels prevailing at the
outbreak of the first World War, prompting some observers to draw
parallels between that era and the growing social disintegration and
disillusion with government seen today.

At first sight, the historical trends in the inequality of distribution
of personal wealth look similar to incomes. This is to be expected
because a significant part of personal wealth comes from the accumulation of savings out of income. Those with higher incomes can
save more and accumulate wealth. However, the other components of
personal wealth, such as capital gains from the appreciation of assets
and inheritance, increase the inequality of the distribution of wealth

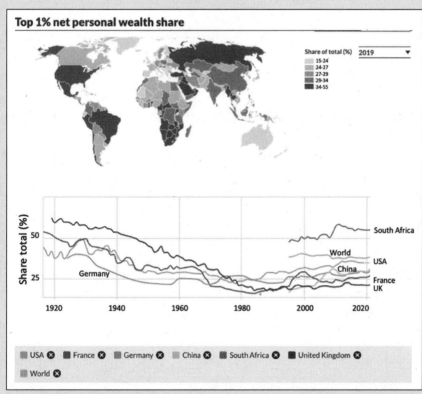

FIGURE 5.14.
Global wealth inequality—top 1% income share.

Credit: Adapted from World Inequality Income Database, https://wid.world/world/#sptinc_p99p100_z /US;FR;DE;CN;ZA;GB;WO/2019/eu/k/p/yearly/s/false/5.1754999999999995/30/curve/false/country

so that it is substantially more concentrated than income. Whereas the top one percent of income earners received about 20 percent of all incomes in 1920 in the USA, France, Germany, South Africa, the UK; the top one percent of wealth owners held 37 percent of personal wealth in the USA in 1920 and as much as 60 percent in the UK. As with income inequality, wealth inequality declined from 1920 until the 1980s when neoliberalism, with its lower taxes, became widely influential, and wealth inequality began to rise, leveling off somewhat in the early twenty-first century. It is estimated globally, that if the trends in wealth inequality continue, by 2050 the top 0.1 percent will own more wealth than the global middle class.[60]

Income and wealth inequality have implications for overshoot, not just because those with high incomes and wealth have disproportionate impacts on the planet through their expenditures, but also because it tends to concentrate political power and influence. Inequality in the political realm presents obstacles to change, especially when the interests of the rich and powerful are threatened, as they may well be in an escape from overshoot requiring a substantial reduction in the physical size of the economy.

Graphs and statistics are useful for displaying and analyzing data, but they are not very good for conveying the human dimension of inequality. An image of the contrast in living conditions within the same

FIGURE 5.15.
Inequality

Credit: Donatas Dabravolskas/shutterstock.com, https://pxhere.com /en/photo/1141148, https://pxhere.com/en/photo/764632

country (Brazil) and the very different opportunities for children in high- and low-income families gives some idea of what the tremendous disparities between wealth and poverty can mean.

So far, we have only considered inequality among people living at the same time. The rise of the youth movement has drawn attention to intergenerational equity, especially in relation to climate change and the lack of good job opportunities and high housing costs. The youth movement was given unexpected impetus by Greta Thunberg's protest about climate change outside the Swedish parliament in 2018. Until recently it was widely assumed, especially in high-income countries, that each generation would have a higher material standard of living than the one preceding it because of economic growth. Overshoot undermines this assumption. Even rich people living in wealthy countries are starting to realize that even they cannot protect themselves and their family against the worst effects of climate change and the degradation of environmental systems. Those most alert to this situation are young

Credit: Li-An Lim, https://unsplash.com/photos/ycW4YxhrWHM

FIGURE 5.16.
Youth concerned about their future.

people still in school, college, or university who face an unprecedented combination of environmental and employment uncertainty and are calling for and working for change.

Investment Trends

All the approaches to understanding the economy described in the previous chapter gave much significance to the accumulation of capital and its contribution to economic growth. One way of understanding economic output is in terms of the numbers of people employed in paid work and their average productivity, i.e., output per hour or year. (Note: this excludes unpaid work which is important in any society but is excluded from GDP, the conventional measurement of economic output and growth.) GDP grows when employed labor and/or average labor productivity increases. Several factors influence labor productivity: education and training, organization and management, number of hours worked, working conditions, and so on, but the most important is the amount of produced capital available to labor: the capital-labor ratio. Compare what a person with a spade can accomplish in a day with what the same person operating a mechanical digger and the energy to run it can do. The same is true of an accountant working with a pencil and paper compared to one working with a computer linked to the internet. This realization is why economists from Adam Smith onwards have seen the accumulation of physical (as distinct from financial) capital as key to economic growth.

Physical capital accumulates with investment. It also depreciates through use, lack of maintenance, or being left idle. This means that some investment is required if capital is to be maintained in good working order. An economy's stock of capital increases when investment exceeds depreciation. All this is straightforward. What may be less obvious is that investment today determines the capital stock of tomorrow, just as investment in past years determined the capital stock available today. If you live in a community well served by roads and rail it is because decisions were made years, even decades ago, to build the

Credit: https://www.publicdomainpictures.net/en/free
-download.php?image=confederation-bridge&id=243280

FIGURE 5.17.
Investment: the
bridge to the future.

rail and road infrastructure from which you now benefit. The schools, colleges, and universities that students attend are the result of previous investments in buildings, equipment, and training staff. The same is true of all the infrastructure in villages, towns, and cities that provide clean drinking water, sewage treatment and disposal, hospitals, theatres, transportation, energy, houses, offices, factories, and all the equipment and buildings that goes with them, plus that used by the military, police and firefighters, farms, fisheries, and mines. There is more but you get the picture. Investment is the bridge to the future.

There are two questions to be decided in any economy when it comes to investment. How much of today's output should be devoted to investment rather than consumption, and how should investment be divided among all the available alternative types? The answers to these questions have considerable influence on what the future will be. In the short-term, more investment means less consumption today (assuming no significant slack in the economy). It also means the possibility of more consumption tomorrow, made possible by the larger capital stock that investment today helped create. The range of products and services that will be produced and available for consumption or trade in the future depends on the composition of the capital stock at that time, which will be determined by investment today and in the years to come.

Economies differ greatly in how these critical choices are made and by whom. In some economies, the public sector plays a major role in determining the level and composition of investment. In others there is much greater reliance on the private sector to make these decisions, keeping government involvement to a minimum. The motivation, risk, and rewards relating to these investment decisions can be quite different depending on which sector is making the investment and why.

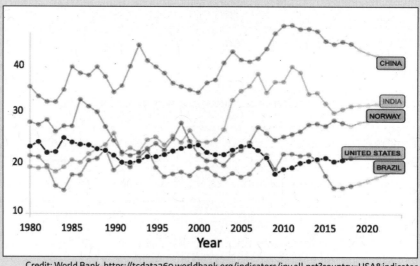

FIGURE 5.18.
Investment share of GDP (%) in five countries.

Credit: World Bank. https://tcdata360.worldbank.org/indicators/inv.all.pct?country=USA&indicator=345&countries=BRA,CHN,IND,NOR&viz=line_chart&years=1980,2024&compareBy=reg

The Chinese and US economies provide a sharp contrast in this respect, with the public sector having considerable control in China over decisions made more commonly by the private sector in the USA.

The wide difference in the proportion of GDP devoted to investment in different countries is striking. Compared with other countries, since 1980 and even before, China has consistently given greater emphasis to investment rather than current consumption, building up the productive capacity of its economy to supply export markets and obtain foreign exchange. Since 2000, India has also invested proportionately more of its GDP than high-income countries such as the USA and Norway. In Brazil, investment has lagged all four of these countries.

Countries also differ in the allocation of investment to different purposes. The OECD divides investment into six groups: dwellings (excluding land); other buildings and structures (e.g., roads, bridges, airfields, dams); transport equipment (e.g., ships, trains, aircraft); cultivated biological resources (e.g., managed forests, livestock raised for milk production); information and communication technology equipment (e.g., computer software and databases, telecommunications equipment and computer hardware); and intellectual property products (e.g., research and development, mineral exploration, software, databases, and literary and artistic originals). From 1972 to 2019, the USA saw an increasing percentage of investment going to information and communication technology and intellectual property and a declining percentage going to biological resources. As countries try to navigate their way through and out of overshoot, we can expect changes in the allocation of investment away from resource- and energy-intensive activities to those which will reduce the demand for materials and energy, such as improved home insulation and more efficient modes of transport. The rapid shift from fossil fuels towards renewable sources will require a massive realignment of investment in the energy sector, which in turn will increase the use of materials in solar arrays, wind turbines, and other technologies for capturing renewable energy.

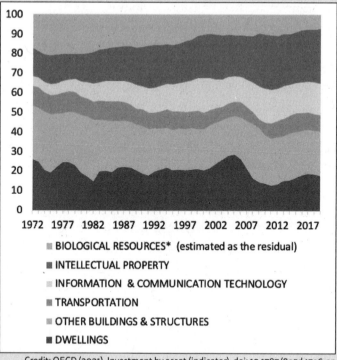

■ BIOLOGICAL RESOURCES* (estimated as the residual)
■ INTELLECTUAL PROPERTY
▪ INFORMATION & COMMUNICATION TECHNOLOGY
■ TRANSPORTATION
■ OTHER BUILDINGS & STRUCTURES
■ DWELLINGS

FIGURE 5.19.
Percent of investment by category (%), USA 1972–2019.

Credit: OECD (2021), Investment by asset (indicator). doi: 10.1787/8e5d47e6-en

Consumption Trends

Household expenditure on consumption is more stable and more predictable than private investment. It is also the largest component of GDP. According to neoclassical economics, consumption generates utility, which is immaterial. One consequence of this view of consumption is that its physical dimensions are overlooked. Utility does not require disposal, but the materials and energy embodied in the goods and services that provide utility certainly do. The term "consumption" is really a misnomer since goods are not consumed, they are used. The same is true for energy. Neither are consumed in the sense that they disappear. The same is true for "production" which requires inputs of materials and energy obtained from the environment, only a portion of which ends up in marketable products. The rest is waste to be recycled or disposed of.

The distinction between goods and services can also be misleading. All goods provide services. Cars provide the service of mobility and, depending on the make and model, status as well. Fossil fuels provide energy for a variety of services such as space heating and transportation. Food provides nutrition and a temporary feeling of being well fed. The goods that provide these services are degraded with use. The materials they are made of can be reused, repurposed, or recycled—some more easily than others—but eventually they become so degraded that disposal is all that is left. Energy can be used more efficiently to provide services, such as by replacing incandescent with LED lighting, but it cannot be recycled to perform the same work over again. The second law of thermodynamics will not allow it. Inevitably, economies require new supplies of materials and energy just to keep going—and increasing amounts if they keep growing to satisfy rising levels of consumption—unless efficiency improvements keep pace.

Services can be obtained from goods, or they can be purchased directly. In high-income economies, services account for about 70–80 percent of all consumer expenditures by the private and public sectors.[61] The provision of these services also requires the use of materials and energy, the difference being that the consumer does not normally own the equipment used to provide the service, say by a hairdresser, car mechanic, landscaper, taxi or Uber driver, decorator, cinema, or gym. Nonetheless, it is fair to say that the purchase of these services also generates waste materials and energy though the quantities, especially of materials, may well be less than if each consumer bought their own equipment. Possibilities for shared ownership and greater use of renting and leasing that reduce material requirements can contribute to the escape from overshoot, though to what degree is unclear.

When Thorstein Veblen wrote about conspicuous consumption at the end of the nineteenth century, advertising was still in its infancy. At that time, most people in the USA and the richer European countries had little discretionary income, and so advertisements were generally

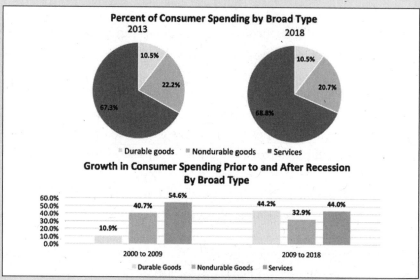

FIGURE 5.20. Percent of consumer expenditure by broad type USA 2013 and 2018.

FIGURE 5.21. The Changing face of Coca–Cola— 1906 and 2012.

directed towards the small proportion of the population that did have money to spend on nonessential items. The ads themselves were also very different from today. They were wordy and provided more information about the advertised product than is now usual.

Advertisers love to tell us that whatever your problem—loneliness, hair loss, obesity, lack of status, poverty, unhappiness—there is a product that promises to solve it. We are shown images of beautiful people using some product, implying that, if we were to use it too, we would be just as beautiful; or images of groups of attractive people enjoying a drink together, suggesting that if we would just buy that drink, we too could be among friends like that. Perhaps the most egregious ads of all are those showing an ecstatic lottery winner, but not the hoards of losers, some getting deeper and deeper in debt to feed their gambling habit.

Another aspect of advertising that has changed are the types of media that carries it. First it was print, then came radio, cinema, TV, and now the internet, which has opened many new possibilities for

Credit: https://www.flickr.com/photos/izziebutton/27704498586

FIGURE 5.22. Body & Face Beach Sand. Another product you didn't know you needed.

FIGURE 5.23. Ad Evolution 1980–2020.

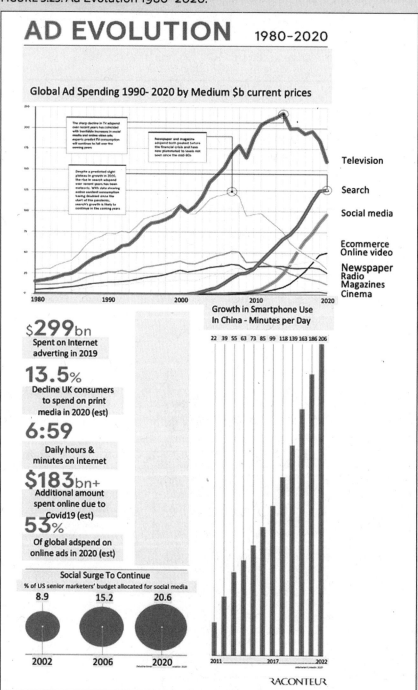

Credit: Adapted from R. Wood (2020), "Visualizing the Evolution of Global Advertising Spend (1980–2020)" *Visual Capitalist*, www.visualcapitalist.com /evolution-global-advertising -spend-1980-2020/

advertising that interrupts our lives whether we like it or not. In the USA it is estimated that, on average, people see between 6,000 and 10,000 ads each day, which is nearly double what it was in 2007.[62] Before the pandemic, global expenditure on advertising was US$600 billion. It took a sharp dip in 2020 but is expected to exceed the 2019 level by 2022 and then grow considerably faster than GDP.

It has been understood for some time that advertising is less about the product and more about lifestyle. The Merriam-Webster dictionary definition of lifestyle tells us that it is "the typical way of life of an individual, group, or culture." In other words, advertisers attempt to associate a product with a lifestyle, not as it is really lived, but as some sort of ideal that is available simply by buying the advertised product. In this way advertising ends up promoting a high-consumption lifestyle, starting at a very early age and then through all the stages of life to old age where coffins and funeral homes are grist for the advertisers' mill. Consumption as the way to the good life has inevitable consequences for materials and energy use, land transformation, and ultimately for overshoot.

The increasing expenditure on consumption, aided and abetted by advertising, has had some curious results. Between 1973 and 2015 the

FIGURE 5.24.
The false promises of advertising.

Credit: Photos by Campbell on Unsplash. https://unsplash.com/photos/3ZUsNJhi_Ik, https://unsplash.com/photos/oWU2woJuHnE and Iwona Castiello d'Antonio on Unsplash https://unsplash.com/photos/oWU2woJuHnE

average size of a new single-family dwelling in the USA increased by 62 percent while the average number of people per household fell from 3 to 2.5. This means the average space per person in a new house in the USA nearly doubled in 42 years. You might have thought that all this extra living space gave people ample storage space at home for all their worldly goods, yet one of the fastest growing service sectors in the USA is self-storage, where almost ten percent of US residents pay to store the material overflow of the American dream. What began as a nation's dream has become a planetary nightmare. We need a new American dream.[63]

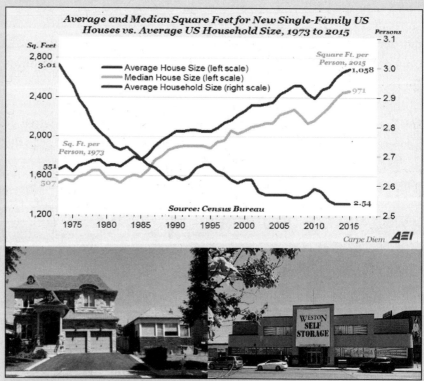

FIGURE 5.25. Increased house size in USA 1973–2015 and increased self-storage

Credit: Chart: M.J. Perry (2016), "New US Homes Today Are 1,000 Square Feet Larger Than in 1973 and Living Space per Person Has Nearly Doubled," AEI June 5. www.aei .org/carpe-diem/new-us-homes-today-are-1000-square-feet-larger-than-in-1973 -and-living-space-per-person-has-nearly-doubled/; housing. Photos: Author.

A new American Dream, one more in keeping with overshoot, may be an easier sell than it might first appear, simply because many who dreamed of a single-family dwelling with a two-car garage, in a quiet, safe suburb with good schools and public services, achieved through hard, well-paid work in a secure job, have failed to achieve it. Stagnant wages, increasing debt, expensive housing, and poor job prospects stood in their way. But an even bigger obstacle of a different kind is the Easterlin Paradox, named after Richard Easterlin, who first wrote about it in the 1970s. Easterlin observed what seems to be a contradiction. On the one hand, at a point in time both within and among many countries, richer people are on average happier than poorer people. On the other hand, when incomes rise over time the population does not on average become any happier. Easterlin explained this paradox by noting that at any moment people's happiness depends on how they compare themselves with others. It is their relative income and how their consumption compares with others that counts. Consequently, if everyone's income rises with economic growth and relative incomes remain the same, people do not feel any happier.

Easterlin also noticed that people are not very good at anticipating how their aspirations will change as their income increases. If a person's happiness depends on the relationship between their aspirations and attainments, happiness will not rise with an increase in consumption if aspirations rise as well. In the boating world this is referred to as Two-Footitis—a boat owner's need to acquire a boat two feet longer than the one they already have. No matter how big your boat is, it is never big enough, especially if others are getting bigger boats.

If Easterlin is correct that, after a certain material level of income and consumption, relative rather than absolute levels are what makes people happier, then further economic growth will not make a population happier unless it also comes with redistribution towards those at the lower end of the income scale. Likewise, income redistribution can make many happier, even without economic growth, by narrowing the gap between rich and poor, so income (and wealth) redistribution could be an important component of an escape from overshoot.

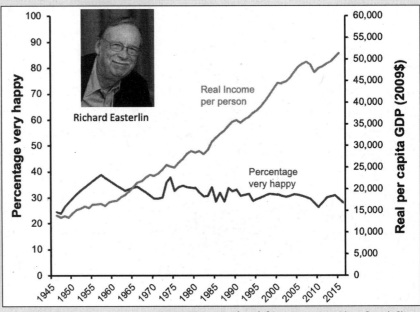

Credits: P. A. Victor, (2019), fig 9.1, *Managing without Growth: Slower by Design, not Disaster*, Edward Elgar Publishing.

FIGURE 5.26.
Income and happiness in the USA 1945–2014.

It will be no surprise to most people to learn of research that shows there is much more to happiness than money. In the past couple of decades there has been an explosion of research into the sources of happiness, well-being, life satisfaction—terms which mean much the same thing. Much of this research informs the annual *World Happiness Report* published by the Sustainable Development Solutions Network. These reports use results from the Gallup World Poll for assessing life satisfaction according to a device known as the Cantril ladder. Respondents to a survey in about 150 countries are asked to think of a ladder. The top rung of the ladder represents the best possible life for them and is given a 10. The bottom rung of the ladder represents the worst possible life and is given a 0. They are then asked to rate their own current life on the 11-point, 0 to 10 scale of the ladder.

Looking at changes in the Cantril ladder scores by region between 2006 and 2019, when GDP per capita increased in every region, several trends stand out. The North America and Australasia region show a declining trend though the score remains the highest among the regions. In Western Europe the trend is U-shaped, and in the Latin America-Caribbean region it is an inverted U-shape declining in the last third. South Asia, dominated by India, shows a downward trend throughout.

Statistical analysis of responses to the Gallup World Poll reveals that GDP per capita is only one of a number of factors that account for differences in life satisfaction among countries. The others are social support, healthy life expectancy, freedom to make life choices,

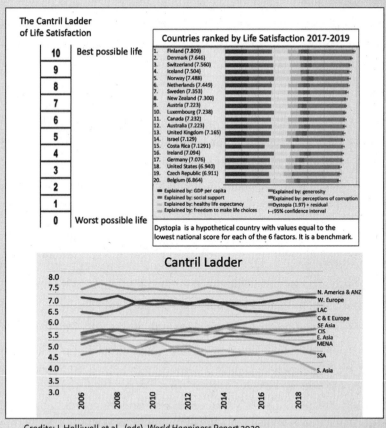

Credits: J. Helliwell et al., (eds), *World Happiness Report 2020*, Sustainable Development Solutions Network.

FIGURE 5.27.
Life satisfaction by country and region.

generosity, and freedom from corruption, leaving about a quarter of the differences unexplained. Taken together, these five factors make a greater contribution to differences in life satisfaction than GDP per capita.[64] Since these five factors need lower material and energy inputs than the production of GDP, this finding suggests ways of improving human well-being with considerably less environmental impact than increases in GDP, especially among high-income countries. It also presents opportunities for closing the gap in life satisfaction between low-, middle-, and high-income countries in ways that might reduce overshoot without relying on economic growth.

Technology Trends

We are often told that we live in the age of technology, yet technology is as old as humanity itself. In the Stone Age, early humans made tools from stone and did so for some 3.4 million years before the invention of metalworking around 3,000 BCE, first in bronze then in iron. Throughout this long era, technological advance was slow and was based largely on transforming materials for use as tools, weapons, and structures. What energy was required came from renewable sources such as solar, wind, and wood; humans; and domesticated animals. The next era of technological change in the second half of the second millennium was mainly about the transformation of energy. It began with water power, then steam power, followed by electric power and the combustion of petroleum in transportation and industrial processes. These transformations of materials and energy are ongoing. What defines the technological age of today is the transformation of information and advances in the life sciences.

Technology does not exist in isolation; it is embodied in human artifacts. Even the oddly named "cloud" refers to software and services that run on the internet, stored digitally in physical equipment powered by electricity. It requires a network of servers to find the information, entertainment, business, and social connections we increasingly rely on. What makes this age different when it comes to technology has a lot to do with the pace of change. Technologies tend to become invisible when they are familiar. For example, when teachers write on

FIGURE 5.28. Transformations in economic history.

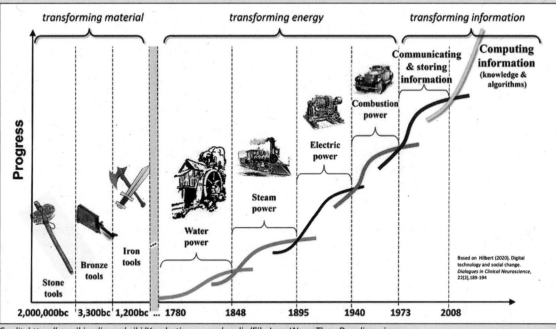

Credit: https://en.wikipedia.org/wiki/Kondratiev_wave#/media/File:LongWavesThreeParadigms.jpg

blackboards, they are using technology. Students sitting on chairs and writing on paper with pen and ink are using technology. No one who went through their whole education exposed to only these technologies gave them a second thought. They were invisible, in the sense that both teachers and students were oblivious to the tools they were using because they had always been there, or so it seemed. Only when computers were first introduced into the classroom was it obvious to teachers and students alike that they were using technology.

For a brief time starting in the mid-1970s, independently operated desktop computers, laptops, boom boxes, the Sony Walkman music player, and early mobile phones were emblematic of the age of technology. Then came the internet which massively expanded what was possible with electronic technology in industry and the delivery of music, videos, games, news, online banking, crypto currencies, and other novel commercial activities. It opened a whole new world of information to anyone with a suitable device and a Wi-Fi connection. Perhaps most profound of all in terms of societal impacts was the invention and proliferation of multifunction, integrated, smartphones—a technology that is literally in your face and hard to ignore—and the explosion of social media that came with them. The first iPhone was released in 2007. In 2022 people in the USA were spending an average of 5.4 hours each day on their smartphones with almost all households owning at least one. The rate of ownership is even higher in the UK and Mexico. When time spent on tablets, video games, personal computers, multimedia devices, TVs, radios, DVRs, and DVDs is included, the average US resident spends about 10 hours and 40 minutes each day on screen.[65]

Computers play a major role in processing and transforming information. The earliest electronic computers were huge machines. They contained an enormous number of fragile vacuum tubes that switched electronic signals in the computer to do calculations. ENIAC had 18,000 vacuum tubes and weighed 33 tons. These machines were marvels in their time but had an annoying tendency to overheat and break down. In 1947 John Bardeen, Walter Brittain, and William Shockley built the first transistor, which is a solid state, semi-conductor device

FIGURE 5.29. ENIAC—the first general purpose electronic computer, 1946. Four vacuum tubes typical of those used in ENIAC.

Credit: Penn Engineering, "Celebrating Penn Engineering. History: ENIAC." https://www.seas.upenn.edu/about/history-heritage/eniac/, https://pxhere.com/en/photo/1071095

that could perform the same function as a vacuum tube but was much smaller, more robust, and used far less electricity, generating much less heat. Transistors rapidly replaced vacuum tubes in computers and other electronic devices.

The speed with which a computer, smartphone, or almost any electronic device can process information depends to a large extent on the number of transistors that can be built on a single silicon chip. In 1965 Gordon Moore, co-founder of Intel, predicted that this number would double each year for another ten years, reaching the seemingly astonishing number of 65,000. This forecast was simply an extrapolation of the trend before 1965. Moore's predicted rate of increase turned out to be on the high side. Building 65,000 transistors on a single chip was not reached until 1979. Moore subsequently over-adjusted by predicting a doubling every two years whereas from 1961 for about 50 years the doubling period was approximately eighteen months, reaching 2.6 billion transistors on a single chip in 2011 and, though rising more slowly, almost 57 billion in 2021. Still, as predictions go, Moore did very

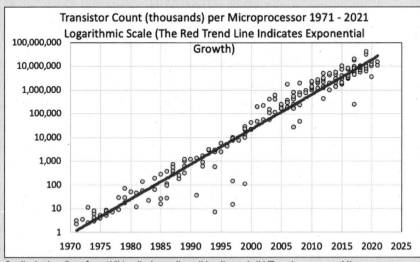

Credit: Author. Data from Wikipedia: https://en.wikipedia.org/wiki/Transistor_count#Microprocessors

FIGURE 5.30. Exponential increase in transistors on a microprocessor.

well, so much so that a doubling rate of 18 months has become known as Moore's law.[66]

The number of transistors on a single chip is an important determinant of processing time but it is not the only one. When processing time is measured directly, it turns out that it has been increasing even faster than Moore's law would suggest, making possible new functions such as face recognition, natural language processing, augmented reality, and virtual reality. These are all examples of artificial intelligence—the simulation of human intelligence by machines—that is increasingly becoming part of the contemporary human experience, whether we are aware of it, like it, want it, or not. No doubt there is much more to come, so much so that some observers warn of the technological "singularity," a point when intelligent machines become self-improving and surpass human intelligence, signaling the end of the human era. If they are right, then what seems preposterous now to most people will become possible—with unforeseeable consequences.

All new technologies have unintended consequences which may be beneficial or damaging. As an example, in the 1940s DDT was hailed as a wonderful new insecticide when first used to protect soldiers and civilians from malaria and typhus. It was so successful that Paul Müller, who discovered DDT's insecticidal properties, was awarded the Nobel Prize for Medicine in 1948. DDT quickly became popular among farmers for controlling pests but side effects were waiting in the wings. In 1962 Rachel Carson wrote about the carcinogenic effects of DDT and its effects on wildlife in *Silent Spring*.[67] This caused considerable public concern and, after much struggle and vilification of Carson by some chemical companies, DDT was banned for use in agriculture in the USA in 1972. Other countries followed the US and ultimately DDT was banned globally in 2004, leading to the recovery of the once-threatened bald eagle and peregrine falcon whose eggshells had become thin and fragile because of ingesting DDT.[68]

A more contemporary example of a technology with both positive and negative effects is social media. It has brought friends and families together from around the world in ways that were undreamed of

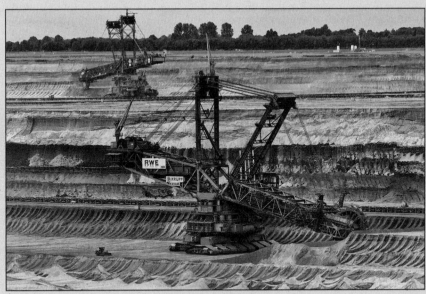

FIGURE 5.31. Bagger 288 (foreground) German open pit mining machine. Taller than the Statue of Liberty, heavier than the Eiffel Tower. A crew of three to four can mine 265,000 tons of fuel per day.[69] Note the bulldozer to the left for comparison.

Credit: Raymond Spekking. https://en.wikipedia.org/wiki/File:Garzweiler
_Tagebau-1230.jpg#/media/File:Garzweiler_Tagebau-1230.jpg

before the internet. But social media has also led to public shaming and bullying on a scale never seen before, causing depression and suicide, especially in teenagers, and it has led to the spread of a lot of misinformation and propaganda. Who can tell where this will lead?

The miniaturization that Moore predicted, and which made much of the current phase of technological innovation possible, has had an impact at the other end of the size scale that is not always appreciated. It is a version of the rebound effect first observed by Jevons in relation to more efficient steam engines and coal consumption (see Chapter Three). Miniaturization of information and control technologies and the vast increase in the speed of data processing has made it possible to design, build, and operate enormous machines that have become commonplace in cities, on farms, in the resources sector, and in the military. All of this has contributed to overshoot.

It would be foolish to deny the many achievements of modern technology, but it would be equally foolish to assume that technology,

FIGURE 5.32.
COSCO Container Ship "Universe Class," 400 meters long, capacity 21,337 20-foot containers, operated by a crew of 26.[70]

Credit: Alf van Beem https://commons.wikimedia.org/wiki/File:Cosco_Shipping _Universe_(ship,_2018)_IMO_9795610,_Port_of_Rotterdam_pic4.jpg

having got us into overshoot, will also get us out of it. Consider the following:

- Some problems do not lend themselves to technological solutions.
- New technologies often solve one problem and create others.
- Technologies developed in the lab do not necessarily operate at scale.
- The pace of technology diffusion is often much slower than assumed or expected.
- The rebound effect reduces and sometimes eliminates gains from improved efficiency.
- Technology and the science behind it are often developed and supported to serve commercial and political interests which may not be in the public interest.
- The social processes out of which technology and science arise are difficult to understand, regulate, and control and may be completely invisible.

The role that technology can and ought to play in dealing with over-shoot is hotly debated. We will consider its potential for reconciling continued economic growth with reduced environmental impacts in the next chapter.

Work Trends

Just as economic systems and technology have evolved, so has the nature of work, both paid and unpaid. The proportion of men of work-ing age (15+) in low- and middle-income countries in paid work is very similar, having declined about seven percent between 1991 and 2019. The comparable statistic for men in high-income countries is much lower, possibly due to the longer number of years spent in formal education and earlier retirement in high-income countries, though it began trending up in 2009. When it comes to the employment of women the story is rather different. There is a much higher propor-tion of women employed in low-income countries than in middle- or high-income countries. Also, the employment proportion of women in

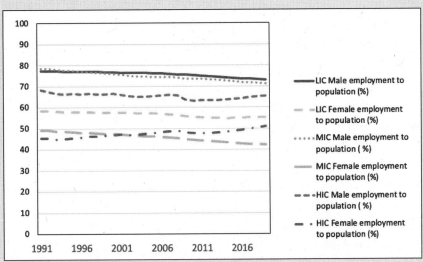

Credit: Author. Data from World Development Indicators, World Bank.

FIGURE 5.33. Employment to population ratio of men and women in low-, middle- and high-income countries, 1991 to 2019.

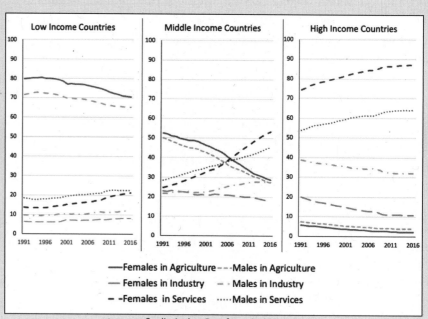

FIGURE 5.34.
Employment of
males and females
in agriculture,
industry, and
services in low-,
medium-, and high-
income countries
1991–2016 as % of
total employment
of males and
females.

Credit: Author. Data from World Development Indicators, World Bank.

middle-income countries declined steadily from 1991 to 2019 but went in the other direction for women in high-income countries.

When we look at employment in the three sectors—agriculture, industry, and services—we can see marked differences in levels and trends within and among high-, medium-, and low-income countries. The general trends in middle-income countries are similar to low-income countries though they started from very different levels in 1970. By 2016 the proportions of men and women employed in the services sector in middle-income countries had far surpassed the proportions of men and women employed in agriculture. By comparing low-income and middle-income countries we see that the employment proportions in the low-income countries in 2016 were approaching those of the middle-income countries in 1970.

A comparison of the middle- and high-income countries shows something similar. The employment pattern in the middle-income

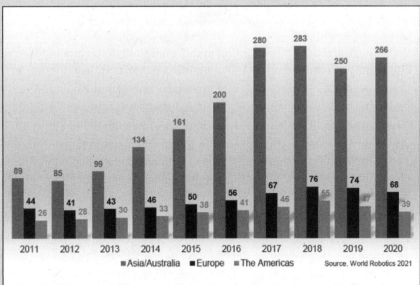

FIGURE 5.35.
Annual installation
of industrial robots
('000 of units).

Credit: Executive Summary, World Robotics 2021 Industrial Robots, https://ifr.org
/img/worldrobotics/Executive_Summary_WR_Industrial_Robots_2021.pdf

countries in 2016 was beginning to approximate the employment
pattern in the high-income countries in 1991. Taking the three income
groups of countries together, we see employment in agriculture giving
way to employment in industry which, in turn, gives way to employment in services.

The declining proportion of people employed in industry does not
mean that industrial output has declined. Far from it. In this sector, as
in agriculture and to a lesser extent in services, production has been
increasingly automated. One indication of this is the rapid increase in
the number of industrial robots installed annually, which more than
tripled between 2011 and 2017.

Robots, and other applications of artificial intelligence more
generally, have spread primarily through the economies of high and
middle-income countries, making an increasing range of occupations vulnerable to human labor being displaced by machines. This
trend raises serious questions about the ownership and control of the

Most exposed occupations	Least exposed occupations
Clinical laboratory technicians	Animal caretakers, except farm
Chemical engineers	Food preparation workers
Optometrists	Mail carriers for postal service
Power plant operators	Subject instructors, college
Dispatchers	Art/entertainment performers

Notes: Table displays census occupation title for the five occupations with the highest exposure scores and with the lowest exposure scores above employment threshold of 150.

FIGURE 5.36. Occupations with highest and lowest exposure to artificial intelligence.

Credit: M. Webb, (2019), "The Impact of Artificial Intelligence on the Labor Market," November 6. https://ssrn.com/abstract=3482150 or http://dx.doi.org/10.2139/ssrn.3482150

machines, including the algorithms and data that are generated, as well as whether overshoot will be exacerbated or mitigated.

The changing distribution of employment by sector has been accompanied by a gradual reduction in paid working hours. Because the data coverage for working hours is incomplete, we can only describe the trend in working hours for OECD member countries, rather than for the whole world. There has been a continuous downward trend in the annual average hours of paid work (full and part-time work combined) from 1970 to 2020 in OECD countries as a group. The substantial drop in 2020 was due to the COVID-19 pandemic, which also changed the location of work, with more people working from home. It remains to be seen whether this will be a lasting change.

When we look at selected countries, we see that the substantial differences in average work time in 1970 have narrowed, especially since 1995. Working hours changed little in the USA; they decreased the most in Japan; and in Sweden they declined then increased from a low point in 1980. In 2019 the average annual hours in paid work were 1,777 in the USA and 1,440 in the Netherlands. Norway and Denmark had the lowest hours worked in OECD countries in that year with 1,381, while Germany had 1,383. At the other end of the scale was Colombia at 2,172.

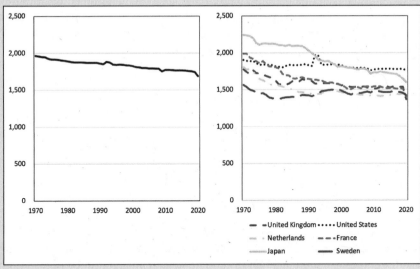

FIGURE 5.37.
Average annual hours in paid work per worker 1970–2020.

Credit: Author. Data from OECD "Hours worked", https://data.oecd.org/emp/hours-worked.htm

These trends in paid work, in terms of gender, sector, automation, and hours worked, reflect a combination of the changing structure of economies and the changing age structure of populations. Both have implications for overshoot that are difficult to predict, especially since they can be influenced by deliberate policies, making plenty of room for differences of opinion about what is plausible, probable, and preferable.

Energy Trends

Beginning in the eighteenth century, the availability of cheap energy first from coal and then from oil and natural gas, fundamentally changed humanity's relationship with the rest of nature. If there is a single, explanatory cause of overshoot this is it. Fossil fuels have provided the energy that has driven economic growth for two centuries. At the same time, through increased food production, they relaxed constraints on human population growth. Cheap, convenient, transportable energy made it possible to obtain prodigious amounts of materials

FIGURE 5.38. Global primary energy and GDP.

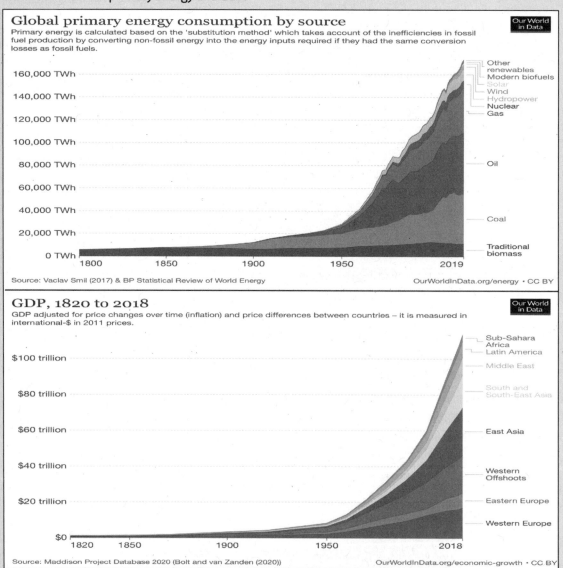

Credit: Hannah Ritchie, Max Roser and Pablo Rosado (2020), "Energy." https://ourworldindata.org/energy; Max Roser (2013), "Economic Growth". https://ourworldindata.org/economic-growth

and convert landscapes on an unprecedented scale, overwhelming the regenerative capacity of the biosphere. A climate catastrophe looms, land is being transformed, soils degraded, oceans are warming, ice caps are melting, and habitats of countless species are being damaged and destroyed. This is overshoot.

In 2020, fossil fuels provided over 84.3 percent of global primary energy consumption, down from 87.7 percent in 1990 and 93.8 percent in 1970. Nevertheless, the total consumption of fossil fuels increased over this period because of the substantial increase in total energy use. Renewable sources of energy provided 11.4 percent of primary energy consumption in 2020, with solar and wind contributing just 4.1 percent, hydro 6.9 percent, and other renewables 0.5 percent. Nuclear energy, providing 4.4 percent, made up the rest.[71]

With so much concern about climate change, the push for another energy transition is underway. This time it will be a reversal of past trends, away from fossil fuels. Solar, wind, and other renewable sources of energy are favored by many. Others look to a much greater deployment of nuclear energy, and still others are counting on carbon capture and storage to mop up greenhouse gases from fossil fuels at least and until the transition away from them is complete. There is considerable disagreement about whether this energy transition can be accomplished while economic growth continues apace, or whether the energy transition will absorb so much of the investment required for other purposes that it will slow economic growth. There is also disagreement about whether the transition can be accomplished fast enough to avoid a climate catastrophe. On top of this is a concern about making the transition in a way that is equitable.

The distinguished scientist Vaclav Smil has examined in considerable depth the transition from traditional sources of energy, such as wood and other biomass, to coal, oil, and natural gas.[72] He cautions against undue optimism about how rapidly a transition from fossil fuels to renewable sources of energy can be achieved.

One consideration that is often overlooked in considering a transition to renewable energy is that while the energy is renewable, the

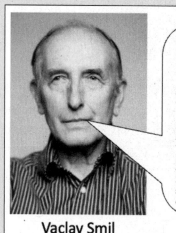

Energy transitions are not sudden revolutionary advances that follow periods of prolonged stagnation, but rather continuously unfolding processes that gradually change the composition of sources used to generate heat, motion, and light ... The most important historical lesson is that new resources require extended periods of development. The verdict is clear: only small economies endowed with suitable resources can undergo very rapid resource transitions ... The scale of large economies makes everything more inertial, and global resource transitions unfold across generations. Even though the country is endowed with abundant hydrocarbon resources, it took the United States 25 years to raise the share of oil consumption from 5% to 25%, and for natural gas it took 33 years. After crude oil reached 5% of global primary energy supply, it took another 40 years to rise to 25%, and the comparable period was even longer, 55 years, for natural gas.

Vaclav Smil

FIGURE 5.39.
Vaclav Smil on
energy transitions.

Credit: V. Smil (no date), "Energy Transitions," World Economic Forum,
http://vaclavsmil.com/wp-content/uploads/WEF_EN_IndustryVision-12.pdf

materials required to capture it and distribute the output to users are not. The total material requirements[73] can be very considerable, much greater than for the fossil fuels they are expected to replace. Their manufacture and distribution uses energy which, in the early years of the transition at least, will require fossil fuels, and additional equipment and infrastructure, such as wind turbines and solar arrays, require energy and materials which should be included in an overall assessment of an energy transition.

The types and amounts of materials involved will depend on the technologies employed and the rate of expansion of their use. With good design and suitable institutional arrangements in place, materials can be recovered, reused, and recycled. However, the result will always be less than complete. The transition away from fossil fuels towards renewable sources of energy to avoid catastrophic climate change may be confounded by a lack of readily accessible materials. It will also entail difficult decisions about land use as biomass, solar arrays, and wind turbines compete with other uses of land.

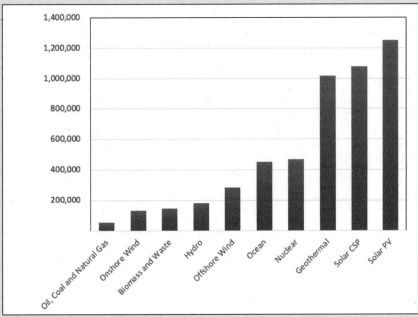

FIGURE 5.40.
Total material
requirements of
energy technologies
(tonnes per
gigawatt).

Credit: Author, from data in T. Watari et al., Supplementary material for "Total
material requirement for the global energy transition to 2050: A focus on transport
and electricity," *Resources, Conservation & Recycling*, 148, 91–103.

A critical aspect of making a rapid transition away from fossil fuels
is what it will mean for the energy available to the rest of the economy. It takes energy to get energy. The difference between the energy
derived from any source and the energy used in its production and
distribution is known as net energy. This is the energy that all other
activities in the economy use and rely on. Net energy is energy output
minus energy input. It can be calculated for a single solar panel, wind
turbine, or barrel of oil, and for a city or entire economy, which raises
the question of what is likely to happen to total net energy in a transition away from fossil fuels?

A useful energy metric for tackling this question is the ratio of net
energy to energy input. This ratio is the energy return on energy invested (EROI or EROEI). If a technology has an EROI less than one, then

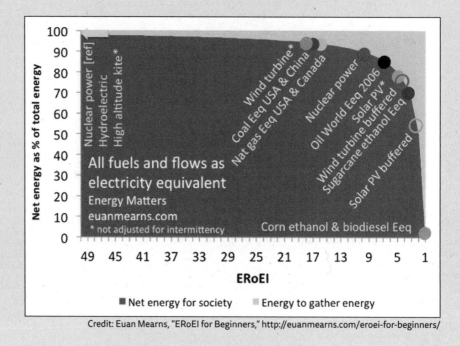

FIGURE 5.41.
The Net Energy
Cliff—Summary
of the EROI for a
range of fuels and
renewable energies.
(Eeq = electricity
equivalent.)

Credit: Euan Mearns, "ERoEI for Beginners," http://euanmearns.com/eroei-for-beginners/

it is an energy sink rather than a source. The calculation of EROI for energy technologies or energy systems is complicated by the question of boundaries. For example, does the energy input of ethanol from corn include the energy used to produce the tractors and harvesters and the energy to run them? Does it include the energy used to transport the ethanol to the point of use? Different boundary definitions generate different values for EROI.

Estimates of EROI have been made for many energy technologies, ranging from 1000:1 for oil produced in the USA in 1919[74] to 0.7 for bioethanol derived from wood in Ecuador in 2018.[75] Euan Mearns created a powerful image relating the EROI values of various energy technologies to their net energy. He called it the Net Energy Cliff. For energy sources with an EROI of 50, 98 percent of the energy input is available for consumption (i.e., use by others). This percentage declines as EROI declines but even when EROI is only 10, 90 percent of the energy input is still available for consumption. When EROI falls below 10, the percentage of the energy input available for consumption begins to decline rapidly so that at an EROI of 5, only 80 percent is available for others to use because 20 percent of energy output is required for energy production.

If EROI in an economy declines over time, an increasing proportion of the energy output is absorbed by the energy sector leaving less and less for other sectors. The EROI of fossil fuels has been declining as the richest and easiest to access deposits have been exploited, a trend which is expected to continue. It may already be as low as 6 for fossil fuels when calculated at the final energy stage, ready for use; a value that is comparable to values for renewables. This similarity would appear to make the transition from fossil fuels to renewables more feasible than previously believed.[76] However, to put this in context, it is estimated that an EROI of at least 7 is required to support the economies of OECD countries and 11 for the USA economy specifically.[77] High-income economies may already be in energy jeopardy.

Conclusion

At the start of this chapter, I cautioned against a naive extrapolation from the past into the future. The prevailing growth paradigm, and the stories we tell ourselves about the future, tend to reinforce the idea that the future will look a lot like the present, with a linear progression to ever-greater prosperity and technological complexity—until, because of overshoot and its effects, it doesn't. Another danger is that projecting trends by one variable at a time can lead to conclusions about what is possible and probable different from when several, interdependent trends are considered together. In the next chapter, we will examine a particular combination of trends that bear on a possible escape route from overshoot: whether economic growth can continue while the GHG intensity of GDP (tonnes of emissions per dollar of GDP) declines fast enough to avoid a climate catastrophe. This is the appealing, but contentious, promise of green growth.

6

GREEN GROWTH: A DANGEROUS DISTRACTION?

In recent years several revealing adjectives have been placed ahead of the word growth, words such as inclusive, smart, clean, shared, sustainable, climate-friendly, and green. These adjectives tell us that something has been lacking in economic growth, not as idealized by many economists, politicians, and the media, but in our lived experiences. Growth has seldom been inclusive, smart, clean, shared, sustainable, climate friendly, or green. The shortcomings of economic growth, signaled by adjectives such as these, are all interesting and important. They seem many, but they boil down to just three: growth has not benefited everyone—it has not been inclusive or shared; it has been environmentally damaging—hence the call for clean, climate-friendly, green growth; and because of the first two, it is not sustainable.

A common assumption underlying these different types of economic growth is that growth per se is not the problem, only some feature of growth that, it is assumed, can be remedied with the right policies. Growth can and should continue, or so we are told, providing it is the right kind of growth. More than that, we are led to believe that the right kind of growth will be even faster than the wrong, unsustainable kind. For example, the promise of green growth, which is at the heart of proposals for a Green New Deal and Ecomodernism, is that it will be an economic stimulus, a foundation for stronger and even faster economic growth.

FIGURE 6.1. Towards a green economy

Credit: UNEP https://sustainabledevelopment.un.org
/content/documents/126GER_synthesis_en.pdf,

But is that a probable, plausible, or even a possible outcome? Does green growth provide an escape from overshoot, or is it a dangerous distraction that is diverting attention away from what really needs to be done to save a planet in peril? Of course green growth, should it be possible, will not be sufficient. To be sustainable it will also have to be inclusive, so that everyone gets a fair shake, where inclusive is not to be defined by national borders but should encompass everyone. Let's take a deeper look.

Defining Green Growth

There are many definitions of green growth, each expressing in some way the idea that economic growth can continue indefinitely while at the same time resource requirements and environmental impacts decline. If economic growth was measured in purely physical terms, such as tons of material inputs and wastes and joules of energy, then most would agree that eternal growth would be impossible on a planet with finite resources and waste sinks. Some might think that the physical size of the economy could continue to increase by expanding its reach into outer space—mining asteroids and other planets, colonizing the solar system—but even they would have to agree that this possibility will provide no relief to overshoot for decades, even centuries, to come, if at all, making it preposterous in terms of the futures cone.

Economic growth, however, is not measured in physical terms. Prospects for green growth rest on the observation that GDP, the most common measure of economic output, is a measure of the market, that is the money, *value* of economic output. This opens the possibility that the value of output can increase, while the *physical* size of the economy, measured in appropriate physical units, declines. This is what is meant by decoupling economic growth from an economy's resource requirements and environmental impacts. Other possibilities include decoupling well-being from economic activity and decoupling environmental pressures and impacts from resource use. Illustrating these different possibilities is easy. Achieving them is another matter. Here we will concentrate on decoupling resources and environmental impacts from economic activity, i.e., physical decoupling.

There are at least three types of physical decoupling: (1) *relative* decoupling, which means a decline in resource use and/or environmental pressures and impacts per dollar of GDP; (2) *absolute* decoupling, which means a decline in resource use and/or environmental pressures and impacts as GDP increases, and (3) *strong or sufficient absolute* decoupling, which means a fast enough decline in the accumulated stock of a pollutant such as atmospheric greenhouse gases, or a fast enough increase in the stock of a resource such as forests, to avoid serious environmental pressures and impacts, as GDP increases.

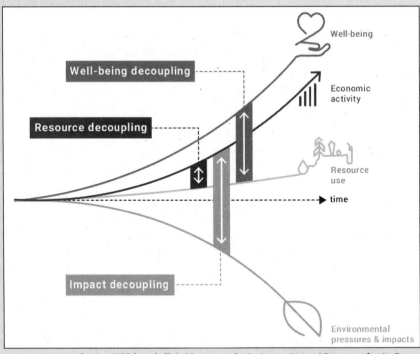

FIGURE 6.2.
The decoupling
concept.

It is essential to be clear which type of decoupling is contemplated
when discussing green growth, because it can make a big difference
as to whether green growth will add to overshoot or help reduce it. For
example, if impact per dollar of GDP declines more slowly than GDP increases, total impact will increase; or if net GHG emissions decline but
remain positive, the atmospheric concentration of GHGs will continue
to rise even though annual emissions decline absolutely.

These distinctions among different types of decoupling should not
be dismissed lightly. In 2002, President George W. Bush set a national
target for the USA of reducing greenhouse gas intensity by 18 percent
by 2012. By "greenhouse gas intensity" the president meant greenhouse gas emissions per dollar of GDP. Bush was committing the USA
to a version of green growth based on relative decoupling. As it turned
out, the USA exceeded the target. The GHG intensity of the USA econ-

Credit: Whitehouse archives. https://georgewbush-whitehouse.archives
.gov/news/releases/2002/02/images/20020214-5.html

FIGURE 6.3.
President Bush's commitment to green growth, 2002.

omy declined by 32 percent between 2002 and 2012, a clear example of relative decoupling. It is also an example of absolute decoupling because even with the 17 percent increase in GDP during the same period total GHG emissions declined by ten percent. No doubt President Bush would be very pleased at this turn of events, even though GHG emissions in the USA remained second only to China's, adding to the already excessive accumulated stock of GHGs in the atmosphere, which increased the risk of catastrophic climate change.

This example of reduced GHG emissions in the USA, while economic growth continued, is often cited as an example of green growth, even though, as of 2018, emissions were still greater than in 1992,[78] the year the USA, together with 153 other countries, signed the United Nations Framework on Climate Change. Still, US emissions of GHGs peaked in 2007 and began a slow decline over the next 12 years. Several factors contributed to this promising example of green growth, at least defined in terms of relative and absolute decoupling, though not the sufficient or strong decoupling needed to reduce the worst risks of climate change. The first is that the energy intensity (i.e., energy/GDP) of the US economy has been in a steady decline since at least as far back as 1965 due to improvements in technology and energy efficiency, and to the gradual shift of the US economy away from natural resource sectors to manufacturing and services. At the same time, the GHG emissions intensity of energy in the US declined as the share of energy used in the USA from fossil fuels fell, and there was also a transition away from coal and oil to natural gas. The combination of a decline in both the energy intensity of GDP and the GHG intensity of energy continued to reduce the emissions intensity of GDP. Further reductions are expected, though not guaranteed.

The third factor behind the absolute decoupling of GHG emissions from economic growth in the USA is a different matter. It concerns the effect of changes in US trade patterns with the rest of the world. To understand this, we must make a further distinction. On one hand, we have GHG emissions released in the USA known as its "territorial" or "production-based" emissions. On the other hand, we have GHG emissions released anywhere in world from the production, distribution, and use of goods and services purchased by the USA. This includes emissions from production in other countries that export products to the USA. These emissions are called "consumption-based." Each country's consumption-based emissions are equal to its territorial emissions plus emissions associated with its imports minus the emissions associated with its exports. At the global level, consumption-based and territorial emissions are identical.

In the closing years of the twentieth century, US territorial and consumption-based emissions of carbon dioxide, the predominant greenhouse gas, were virtually equal. (We have estimates of consumption-based emissions of carbon dioxide over time but not for all GHG emissions so the comparison here is restricted to carbon dioxide.) This relationship began to change in 1997. In 2002, when President Bush made the commitment about GHG intensity reduction, US consumption-based emissions of carbon dioxide were already six percent greater than its territorial emissions. The percentage difference reached a peak of nine percent in 2006 and remained close to seven percent through to 2020. The main reason for this divergence between territorial and consumption-based emissions in the USA is the increasing reliance of the USA on imports of manufactured goods from China and other developing countries. These countries typically have lower production costs than the US but higher energy and GHG emissions intensities, so while the US may show reductions in territorial-based GHG emissions, global GHG emissions can increase when the location of production changes. It is unclear how this will play out in the future, but from the perspective of overshoot, nothing is gained in terms of global GHG emissions when one country reduces its territorial emissions through increased imports, shifting the GHG emissions abroad, especially if the exporting country's emissions intensity of production is greater than that of the importing country. And this is not even accounting for the GHG emissions from international shipping that are usually not attributed to either country.

As you might expect, the excess of consumption-based emissions over territorial (production-based) emissions in the USA is matched by an excess of territorial emissions over consumption-based emissions in other countries, especially China with its large trade surplus. Between 1990 and 2019 CO_2 emissions in China increased, while emissions per yuan of GDP declined, satisfying only the first of the three definitions of green growth given earlier—relative decoupling.

Growth of Many Colors

The USA is not alone in reducing its territorial emissions of GHGs while its economy grew. It did this by reducing emissions intensity faster than the rate of economic growth. Several other European countries have done the same. We can use this comparison of rates of change in economic output and in emissions intensity to define different colors of growth.

Using GHG emissions as an example, when the rate of reduction in the emissions intensity of GDP exceeds the rate of economic growth there is an absolute reduction in emissions. This is the second of

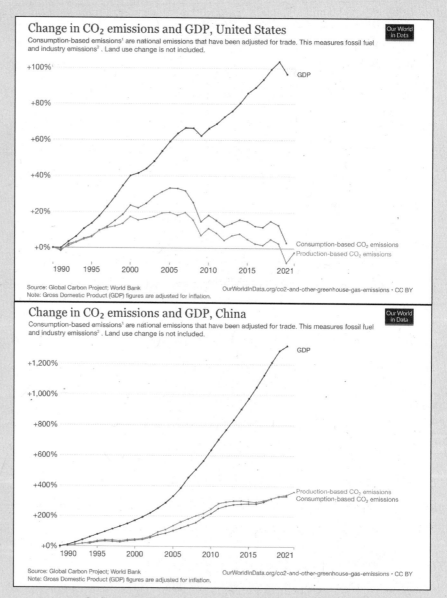

FIGURE 6.4.
Changes in
CO₂ emissions
and GDP in
USA and China
1990–2021.

Credit: Hannah Ritchie, Max Roser, and Pablo Rosado (2020), "CO₂ and Greenhouse Gas
Emissions." https://ourworldindata.org/co2-and-other-greenhouse-gas-emissions
Note the different scales in the graphs for China and the USA, making simple
quantitative comparisons between the two countries difficult.

the three definitions of green growth given earlier, i.e., absolute de-coupling.[79] The greater the difference between the rate of emissions intensity reduction and the rate of economic growth, the greater is the rate of reduction in emissions. Were the difference in intensity reduction and economic growth to be large enough, then emissions would decline sufficiently rapidly to keep cumulative emissions below a target threshold. This would be a case of *strong or sufficient absolute decoupling*, necessary for *deep green growth*. Otherwise, we have *light green growth*, which is good, but not good enough as a response to overshoot.

Growth is a different color when the rate of reduction in emissions intensity is positive but less than the rate of economic growth. This is *amber growth*, which is characterized by relative decoupling: economic growth with increasing emissions. When a traffic light turns amber, we should be cautious and be prepared to stop. The same is true for amber growth. Increasing GHG emissions or any increase in environmental impact causing overshoot and threatening catastrophe must be reversed. Amber growth is not the answer.

If the rate of reduction in emissions intensity is zero or negative, meaning that emissions per dollar of GDP is constant or increasing, then emissions increase with any positive rate of economic growth. This is *red growth* and as the traffic signal tells us, immediate action is necessary to avoid disaster.

A key point, when considering the relationship between emissions intensity and economic growth, is that the rate of economic growth and the rate of reduction in emissions intensity pull emissions in opposite directions. If the rate of economic growth is large enough, it will overwhelm the rate of reduction in emissions intensity, causing emissions to increase even if the rate of reduction in intensity is positive.

In short, if the rate of emissions intensity minus the rate of economic growth is positive then emissions decline, and if it is negative emissions increase. A simple plot of the trends in the difference between the rate of reduction in territorial CO_2 emissions intensity and the rate of economic growth from 1991 to 2018 for low-, middle-,

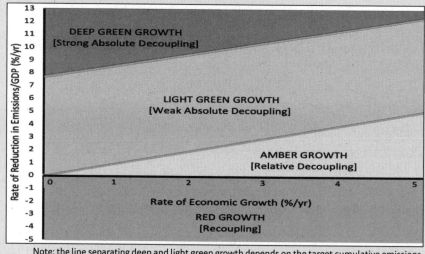

FIGURE 6.5.
The colors of
growth.

Note: the line separating deep and light green growth depends on the target cumulative emissions,
time frame, and projected negative emissions. In this example, the target cumulative emissions is
ten times the starting annual emissions, the time frame is 2022 to 2050, and negative emissions
in 2050, which rise linearly over time, are assumed to be ten percent of the starting emissions.

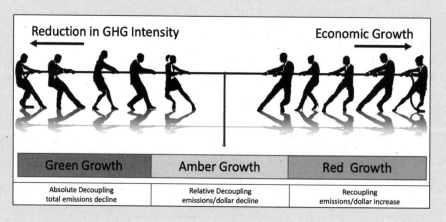

FIGURE 6.6.
Reduction in GHG
intensity and increase
in rate of economic
growth pull emissions
in opposite directions
[GHG emissions =
emissions/GDP x
GDP].

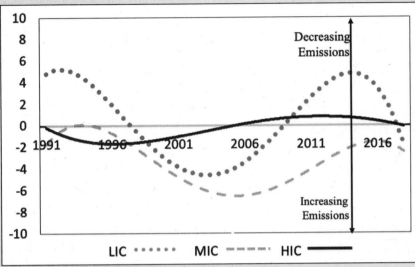

FIGURE 6.7.
Absolute decoupling in low-, medium-, and high-income countries: CO_2/GDP reduction (%/yr)—rate of economic growth (%/yr) 1991–2018—smoothed.

Credit: Author. Data from World Development Indicators, World Bank.

and high-income countries reveals that CO_2 emissions from middle-income countries increased throughout the entire period. Low-income countries show three periods of about the same duration: in the first from 1991 to 1998 CO_2 emissions declined. Then to 2009 they increased, declining again to 2017. The trend in high-income countries was an increase in CO_2 emissions until 2005 and then a decrease to 2018.

Does Increased Efficiency Lead to Decoupling?

One more important point is that green, amber, and red growth are distinguished by the relative sizes of the rate of reduction in emissions intensity and the rate of economic growth, but these rates are not necessarily unrelated. As Jevons pointed out long ago, increases in the efficiency of coal combustion to produce energy led to an increase in coal consumption. This is an example of relative decoupling, when improved efficiency reduces production costs, bringing lower prices and increased sales. The rebound effect, as this sequence of events is commonly known, can overwhelm the effect of increased efficiency on the reduced demand for resources, or at least result in the reduced demand being much less than anticipated. One obvious example of the rebound effect is how lighting standards have changed with improvements in technology, from incandescent to halogen to mini-fluorescent to LED lights. As lighting costs have decreased, the understanding of what is meant by a brightly lit area has changed, and many people think nothing of leaving the lights on in empty rooms because the cost of doing so is so low. This exemplifies the vitally important sociocultural aspect of demand—i.e., the ever-shifting expectations of needs versus wants. Like a ratchet, upward cultural shifts in expectations around material comfort are extremely hard to undo.

The link between efficiency and economic growth is highly germane to green growth. It means that reductions in the emissions intensity of GDP anticipated from advances in technology may not only have an immediate rebound effect but may also stimulate economic growth. Indeed, this outcome is sometimes used by proponents of

FIGURE 6.8. Living room lighting, 19th and 21st century, an example of the Jevons effect.

| A 19ᵗʰ Century Victorian Drawing Room Lit by Electric Light | A 21st Century Example of Living Room Lighting |

Credit: https://commons.wikimedia.org/wiki/File:The_Drawing_Room_(5509581411).jpg, Pavel L. Photo and Video/Shutterstock.com

green growth to support their case, without realizing that faster growth requires faster reductions in emissions intensity if total emissions are to decline sufficiently.

Future Prospects for Green Growth

Data can tell us what has happened in the past and prompt us to develop explanations for the changes we observe. But data alone cannot tell us what is likely to happen in the future, so there is plenty of room for disagreement about the potential for green growth to help us escape from overshoot. However, what is beyond dispute is that for green growth to result in absolute reductions in resource use or in emissions of GHGs and other contaminants, the rate of reduction in these flows must exceed the rate of economic growth. From this it follows that, to achieve any absolute reduction target, the faster the rate of economic growth, the faster must be the rate of reduction in resource intensity or emissions intensity. To continue with the example of GHG emissions, suppose we have an emissions reduction target of net zero in 2050 starting in 2022, and suppose this is to be achieved by a 90 percent reduction in emissions and a ten percent contribution from negative emissions from nature-based solutions (e.g., tree planting) and technology-based solutions (e.g., engineered carbon capture

Rate of Economic Growth	Rate of Reduction in Emissions Intensity	Rate of Reduction in Emissions Intensity after 1 year Delay	Rate of Reduction in Emissions Intensity after 2 year Delay
0.0%	7.9%	8.2%	9.7%
1.0%	8.8%	9.1%	10.6%
2.0%	9.7%	10.0%	11.5%
3.0%	10.6%	10.8%	12.4%
4.0%	11.4%	11.7%	13.2%
5.0%	12.3%	12.5%	14.0%

FIGURE 6.9. The rate of reduction in emissions intensity to meet a net zero emissions target in 2050 from 2022 depends on the rate of economic growth and any delay in starting.

and storage). Further suppose that the contribution from these negative emissions increases steadily from zero to ten percent over the period. Then we can calculate the rate of reduction in GHG emissions needed to reduce them by 90 percent over 28 years for any given rate of economic growth, allowing for any delay in starting.

Unsurprisingly, but crucially, the required rate of reduction in GHG intensity must increase with faster rates of economic growth to reach net zero emissions in 2050. At an annual rate of economic growth of three percent, the annual rate of reduction in GHG intensity must be 10.6 percent to meet the net zero target, allowing for a ten percent contribution of negative emissions. *Even with zero percent growth in GDP, GHG emissions intensity must decline by 7.9 percent annually for 28 consecutive years to achieve net zero in 2050.* What might appear to be modest differences between rates of reduction in GHG emissions intensity—from 10.6 percent to 7.9 percent—can be deceptive. They translate into considerable differences in the required reduction in GHG intensity of GDP in 2050 for net zero emissions.

For example, at an annual rate of reduction in GHG intensity of 7.9 percent, by 2050 GHG emissions per dollar of GDP will be just 9.2 percent of its value in 2022. This would be a remarkable achievement across the entire economy. But if the annual rate of GHG intensity decline is 10.6 percent, as is required to meet a net zero emissions target with an economic growth of three percent per year allowing for negative emissions, GHG emissions per dollar of GDP will be only 3.9 percent of its value in 2022. *The faster rate of economic growth requires close to a complete elimination of GHG emissions from each dollar of GDP by mid-century simply because the size of the economy will have more than doubled in size.*

Delay in reducing the GHG intensity of GDP only makes matters worse. For delays of a few years, each year of delay, roughly speaking, increases the required rate of reduction in emissions intensity by almost one percent for any rate of economic growth. The shorter the time left to reach net zero, the faster must be the rate of reduction in emissions intensity, to such a degree that what was once possible may

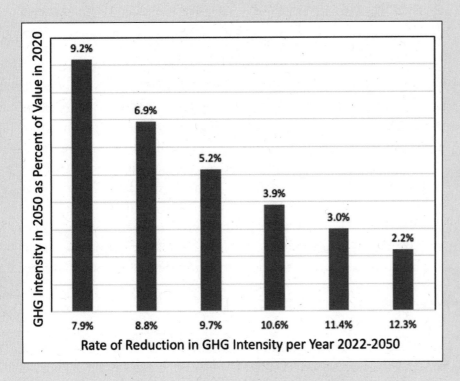

FIGURE 6.10.
Reduction in GHG
Emissions Intensity
2022–2050 for Net
Zero.

now be preposterous, the more so in the presence of substantial economic growth.

Stocks not Flows: The Achilles Heel of Green Growth

We have seen that economic growth and reductions in emissions intensity pull total emissions in opposite directions. The same applies to the tension between economic growth and reductions in resource intensity. Delay further exacerbates the problem. Consequently, relative decoupling of resource and environmental impacts from growth in GDP is easier to achieve than absolute decoupling, but absolute decoupling is essential for green growth to be part of a plan to escape from overshoot. That alone is a problem for green growth, but there is another more daunting one: how to avoid excessive accumulation of unwanted stocks and excessive depletion of valuable ones while the economy continues to grow.

Most resource and environmental problems are problems of stocks, not flows. A stock, in the sense used here, is an accumulation of a flow. For example, the water in a bathtub is a stock made from the inflow of water into the bathtub. When the plug is removed, the outflow of water empties the bathtub. If water is flowing into the bathtub at the same time as water flows out the stock of water will increase, decrease, or stay the same depending on the relative sizes of the inflow and outflow. It is the stocks of urban air pollutants that put human health at risk; it is the stock of GHGs in the atmosphere that causes climate change; and it is the stock of GHGs in the oceans that is making them more acidic, compromising their capacity to support life. Other examples include the build-up of toxic wastes in landfills and the storage of radioactive wastes from nuclear power plants. These are all undesirable stocks. There are also stocks that we want to increase, such as forest cover and wildlife habitat.

These stocks are all determined by inflows and outflows, but it is the stocks themselves—whether too large or too small—that put human and ecological well-being at risk. So it is the stocks, not just the flows that give rise to them, that must be decoupled from economic growth. This is much more challenging than the absolute decoupling of flows. To prevent stocks from increasing, net flows must be zero. For stocks to decline, net flows must be negative, and for desired stocks to increase, net flows must be positive. This means removing GHGs from the atmosphere and oceans, ensuring that birth rates of wildlife species exceed their death rates, neutralizing stored toxic wastes at a faster rate than they are generated, allowing degraded lands to regenerate, and achieving rates of afforestation greater that deforestation without creating monocultures. The list goes on.

Unlike biological resources which can regenerate, mineral deposits that provide materials for the economy cannot be used without being depleted. Recovery and recycling can alleviate the need for new supplies, but not to the point where all requirements are met from non-virgin sources, especially if economic output continues to grow.

Credit: https://pxhere.com/en/photo/949615?utm_content=shareClip&utm
_medium=referral&utm_source=pxhere

FIGURE 6.11.
An example of
clear-cutting.

We can see the significance of these stock-flow considerations by turning once again to climate change. In the ongoing discussions of climate change a great deal of emphasis is placed on reaching net zero emissions by a target date. At the COP 21 meeting in Paris in 2015 countries made commitments to reduce their territorial emissions. At COP 26 in Glasgow in 2021 these commitments were revisited, with many countries committing to net zero GHG emissions by 2050, some earlier, some later. But what does this mean for the accumulation of GHGs in the atmosphere?

There are many paths to net zero, each with different implications for the accumulation of GHGs in the atmosphere and hence for climate change. Let's consider three paths, each a version of green growth.

Initial emissions in 2022 start at 100. You can interpret this as an index of net GHG emissions with a starting value of 100, or 100 million tonnes of GHG. It makes no difference to the examples. The red (dashed) path to net zero is a simple linear reduction in net emissions until zero is reached in 2050. The black (solid) path to net zero represents a rapid deployment of a technological breakthrough starting

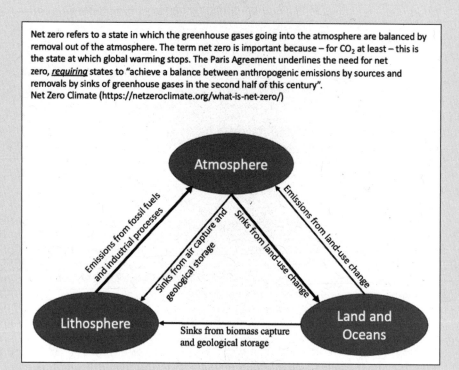

FIGURE 6.12.
Net zero explained.

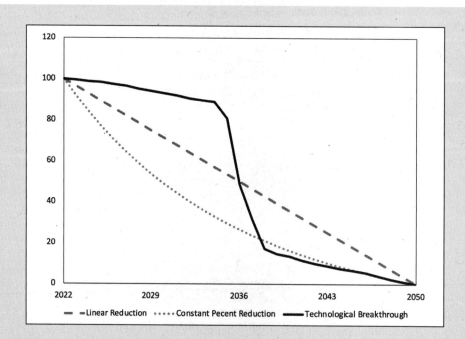

FIGURE 6.13.
Three paths to net zero—annual GHG emissions.

in 2035 that, after a slow initial decline, brings net emissions down to ten in only eight years and continues to decline to zero in 2050. The green (dotted) path goes from 100 to zero at a constant rate of decline in emissions.

These three paths start and end with the same level of net emissions. However, they differ considerably in terms of their cumulative emissions. In 2018 the Intergovernmental Panel on Climate Change (IPCC) issued a report in which it was estimated that to have a 66 percent chance of keeping global warming to 1.5 degrees C, the remaining global carbon budget—i.e., additional allowable cumulative emissions of CO_2 in the atmosphere—was ten times global annual emission in 2018.[80] In 2021 the IPCC published a table with estimates of the remaining global carbon budgets starting from 1 January 2021, and

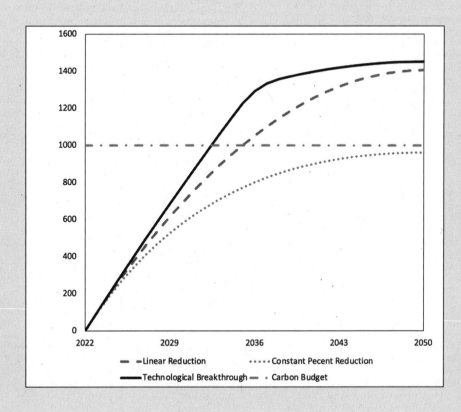

FIGURE 6.14.
Three paths to net zero—cumulative GHG Emissions.

their uncertainties. It gives a slightly lower estimate of the remaining carbon budget (400 $GtCO_2$).[81] For this example, we will use the 10 to 1 ratio for setting the budget at 1,000. The problem it illustrates can only become more troublesome as time passes and major cuts in emissions are delayed.

As can be seen, the linear decline scenario and the technological breakthrough scenario both exhaust the remaining carbon budget of 1,000 in the first half of the next decade. Only the scenario with a constant rate of reduction in net emissions remains within the carbon budget. The main reason for this is the much greater reduction in net emissions in the early years compared with the other scenarios. The historical record, characterized by postponement rather than by early, very large reductions in emissions, provides little reason for optimism in this regard. Time marches on and it is difficult to be optimistic about achieving net zero GHG emissions fast enough to remain within an ever-diminishing remaining budget, especially when so much reliance is placed on unproven technologies and delay, rather than determination and commitment being the order of the day.

Although the past is not necessarily a reliable guide to the future, it can be a source of comfort, even inspiration, if examples can be found of what is now required. But it can also be a cause for concern and despair if past achievements fall well short of what is now so urgently needed. The World Bank maintains a large database of World Development Indicators (WDI) which includes the CO_2 emissions intensity of GDP for countries. From these indicators we can see how often this emissions intensity declined by any specified amount, from one year to the next. We have already seen that to meet a net zero GHG emissions target in 2050 from 2022, when the rate of economic growth is two percent, will require emissions intensity of GDP to decline by 9.7 per year for 28 consecutive years, even allowing for a ten percent contribution from negative emissions from nature-based and technology-based solutions.

It is sobering to discover that of the more than 15,000 year-to-year reductions in CO_2 intensity available from the WDI data base covering

Countries with 3 or More Consecutive Years in which the Rate of Reduction in the CO_2 Intensity of GDP exceeded 9.7 percent since 1990			
Country	**Number of Consecutive Years**	**Country**	**Number of Consecutive Years**
Qatar	6	Kenya	3
Democratic Republic of Congo	5	Liberia	3
Lebanon	4	Libya	3
Afghanistan	3	Mongolia	3
Albania	3	Romania	3
Angola	3	Sudan	3
Azerbaijan	3	Togo	3
Bahrain	3	Turkmenistan	3
Cote d'Ivoire	3	United Arab Emirates	3
Equatorial Africa	3	Uzbekistan	3
Iraq	3		

Credit: Author. Data from World Development Indicators, World Bank.

FIGURE 6.15. Countries with three or more consecutive years in which the rate of reduction in the CO_2 intensity of GDP exceeded 9.7 percent 1990–2018.

most of the countries in the world, only 12 percent were at least 9.7 percent, and that was for a single year. We need to sustain this rate of emissions intensity reduction for the next 28 years with only a two percent annual average rate of economic growth. When we look for instances of consecutive years in which the rate of reduction met this 9.7 percent criterion in the years since 1990 when the world began to wake up to the seriousness of climate change, what we find is not encouraging. Not a single country exhibited more than six consecutive years in which the rate of reduction in CO_2 intensity declined by more than 9.7 percent. In only 20 countries was there a string of at least three such years, not one of them members of the OECD apart from Romania. All the rest were from Africa and Asia and collectively their emissions of CO_2 were a very small proportion of the global total. None of the countries with the highest current or cumulative emissions of CO_2 were included, most notably the USA and China, and global emissions continued to rise.

Looking forward, the prospects for long-term green growth are discouraging and they become more so the faster an economy grows.

Despite this, there are lessons to be learned from thinking about green growth and what it will take to escape from overshoot. One of the most important of these is the kind and level of investment required to transform economies from dependence on the increasing exploitation of nature to economies that allow natural systems to flourish.

Green Investment

Tomorrow's economy depends very much on the investments undertaken today: the types of transportation systems we build, the buildings and other infrastructure that we construct, the sources of energy we rely on, the provisions we make for recovering and reusing materials, for designing better, more durable products and sharing them, and the measures we take to preserve and protect nature and to avoid the worst effects of climate change. Transitioning to an economy that has a reduced requirement for resources, generates less wastes of all kinds, and reverses the land transformation that has destroyed habitat for so many species, requires a different scale and pattern of investment. It requires investment whose primary purpose is to reduce the environmental impacts of economic activity through mitigation and adaptation and not just to expand economic output. This is a very important distinction from conventional investment in pursuit of profit. As we shall see, the two can have very different macroeconomic consequences. Reductions in greenhouse gas emissions through investment in carbon capture and storage, or in large-scale battery storage to handle the intermittency of solar and wind, are green investments for mitigation. The construction of sea walls to prevent flooding from rising water levels, or increasing home insulation to cope with greater temperature extremes, are examples of green investment for adaptation. Green investment can also stimulate and reinforce behavior change to reduce environmental impacts when, for example, investment in shared public transit induces people to switch from individually operated cars.

This green investment can be contrasted with non-green investment intended to add to the productive capital stock of the economy and increase economic output, regardless of whether the investment

Credit: https://pxhere.com/en/photo/170379

FIGURE 6.16.
Urban green space.

is by the private or public sector. Some green investments, such as improved lighting that increases productivity, can also be productive, and some non-green investments, such as the replacement of an inefficient machine with a more efficient one, can reduce environmental impacts, but their main purposes are quite different.

A further useful distinction that bears on the transformation of economies to escape from overshoot is between "additional" and "non-additional" green investment. Green investment is additional if it adds to total investment, and non-additional if it displaces non-green investment, leaving total investment expenditures unchanged. For example, if a company is obliged by regulation to install pollution abatement equipment and reduces its non-green investment by the same amount, total investment expenditures are unaffected. The green investment is non-additional. Additional green investment adds to aggregate demand (GDP), but non-additional green investment does not.

The distinction between productive and unproductive green investments, and between green investments that are additional or non-additional, gives rise to four categories of green investment. Each category has different implications for the macro economy. Short-term effects depend on the extent to which green investment is additional and long-term effects depend on the extent to which it is productive. They also differ in the extent to which they can contribute to an escape from overshoot.

Aggregate demand consists of consumption expenditures, investment expenditures, government expenditures, and exports minus imports. In the 1930s John Maynard Keynes explained how persistent high levels of unemployment were largely due to a deficiency in aggregate demand (see Chapter Three). He saw no inherent reason why, left to itself, the private sector would spend enough to keep the workforce fully employed. Keynes thought that investment—expenditures on new equipment and buildings—by the private sector were especially volatile, being highly dependent on the "animal spirits" of entrepreneurs. His solution was for government to step in with additional expenditures to make up for deficiencies in aggregate demand. These days government expenditures account for a substantial proportion

	Productive Green Investment	Non-productive Green Investment
Additional Green Investment	Increases productive capital stock Adds to aggregate demand [Worst for escape from overshoot: stimulates economic growth]	No effect on productive capital stock Adds to aggregate demand [Next worse for escape from overshoot: stimulates economic growth]
Non-additional Green Investment	No effect on productive capital stock No effect on aggregate demand [Reduces overshoot: no effect on economic growth]	Reduces productive capital stock No effect on aggregate demand [Reduces overshoot more and economic growth. Best for escape from overshoot]

FIGURE 6.17.
Four categories of green investment.

of GDP in most countries. They help build the capital stock of transportation networks, schools, universities, hospitals, water treatment and sewage disposal facilities, and so on. Some governments go further and own and operate large facilities, such as electricity generating stations and pipelines. All this requires direct investment by the public sector, and public ownership makes it that much easier for governments to directly influence aggregate demand to maintain high levels of employment. Governments also use monetary and tax policy to stimulate or damp down private sector investment expenditures as macroeconomic conditions require, and they induce the private sector through regulation to spend funds on various measures to reduce environmental impacts.

If we want to transition the economy so that we can escape from overshoot, the pattern of investment will have to shift rapidly and in large degree to green investment. Green investment that is productive will be attractive to the private sector if it is sufficiently profitable. Investment in resource recovery that saves on the purchase of virgin materials falls into this category. Non-productive green investments, almost by definition, will not be funded by the private sector unless they are required by law or incentivized by a tax or subsidy. It will be up to government to make these green investments on a significant scale and to pay for them through a combination of taxation and borrowing, supplemented sometimes from revenues.

The question of the additionality of green investments has implications for further growth of the economy. If green investment is additional and productive, it expands the productive capital stock of the economy and hence its ability to produce goods and services, demanding more resources and generating more wastes. If green investment is non-additional and productive, it will not affect the productive capital stock or the rate of economic growth, but if it is not productive and displaces non-green investment then the economy's capital stock will be less than otherwise, and so will the rate of growth. This is not something that is favored in countries that judge their success by their growth rate, but if they do not choose to follow a truly green path, one

FIGURE 6.18. Seven barriers to green growth.

7 barriers to green growth

7. Cost shifting

What has been observed and termed as decoupling in some local cases was generally only apparent decoupling resulting mostly from an externalisation of environmental impact from high-consumption to low-consumption countries enabled by international trade. Accounting on a footprint basis reveals a much less optimistic picture and casts further doubt on the possibility of a consistent decoupling in the future.

6. Insufficient and inappropriate technological change

Technological progress is not targeting the factors of production that matter for ecological sustainability and not leading to the type of innovations that reduce environmental pressures; it is not disruptive enough as it fails to displace other undesirable technologies; and it is not in itself fast enough to enable a sufficient decoupling.

5. Limited potential of recycling

Recycling rates are currently low and only slowly increasing, and recycling processes generally still require a significant amount of energy and virgin raw materials. Most importantly, recycling is strictly limited in its ability to provide resources for an expanding material economy.

4. The underestimated impact of services

The service economy can only exist on top of the material economy, not instead of it. Services have a significant footprint that often adds to, rather than substitute, that of goods.

3. Problem shifting

Technological solutions to one environmental problem can create new ones and/or exacerbate others. For example, the production of private electric vehicles puts pressure on lithium, copper, and cobalt resources; the production of biofuel raises concerns about land use; while nuclear power generation produces nuclear risks and logistical concerns regarding nuclear waste disposal.

2. Rebound effects

Efficiency improvements are often partly or totally compensated by a reallocation of saved resources and money to either more of the same consumption (e.g. using a fuel-efficient car more often), or other impactful consumptions (e.g. buying plane tickets for remote holidays with the money saved from fuel economies). It can also generate structural changes in the economy that induce higher consumption (e.g. more fuel-efficient cars reinforce a car-based transport system at the expense of greener alternatives, such as public transport and cycling).

1. Rising energy expenditures

When extracting a resource, cheaper options are generally used first, the extraction of remaining stocks then becoming a more resource- and energy-intensive process resulting in a rising total environmental degradation per unit of resource extracted.

defined by increases in the stocks we want and reductions in the stocks we do not, then in all likelihood it will be forced upon them by the increasingly adverse consequences of overshoot.

Barriers to Green Growth

In a careful assessment of the evidence for green growth based on decoupling, published by the European Environmental Bureau (EEB), Tim Parrique and his co-authors concluded: "Of all the studies reviewed, we have found no trace that would warrant the hopes currently invested into the decoupling strategy. Overall, the idea that green growth can effectively address the ongoing environmental crises is insufficiently supported by empirical foundations."[82] They identified seven barriers to green growth.

Conclusion

We can now answer the question about green growth posed at the start of this chapter: Does it provide an escape from overshoot, or is it a dangerous distraction that is diverting attention away from what really needs to be done to save a planet in peril? Based on the information and analysis of this chapter, at best green growth, even with absolute decoupling, will only contribute to escape from overshoot in the short term. More and more goods and services cannot be produced out of less and less forever. Green growth, which depends on the endless dematerialization of GDP, does not offer a plausible, even possible, long-term solution. Decoupling material and energy throughput from economic activity will remain essential, but on its own it cannot save us. We need an alternative route of escape. Increasingly, ideas are being discussed about a new era of *post growth* to be led by the rich countries, with poorer countries that can still benefit from growth to follow. But what will a post growth economy look like? Fortunately, much has already been written about this and it is time to look at some of the most promising ideas.

7

POST GROWTH POSSIBILITIES

As shown in the previous chapter, the idea that green growth offers a comparatively painless escape from overshoot does not stand up to scrutiny. But if green growth is not the answer to overshoot, what is? It is not the color of growth that matters, green or otherwise, but growth itself that must be tackled. It is time to challenge the fixation on economic growth as anything more than a passing phase in the human experience, and to think about and plan for life in the coming era of post growth. Fortunately, we are not starting from scratch. Much has already been said on the issue to help us.

The first thing to get straight about post growth is what it is that will cease to grow. We certainly want to see growth in human and ecological well-being, in happiness, fulfillment, justice, trust, equity, peace, love, security, longevity, human rights… The list is extensive and while the elements may not change much from one community to another, the priorities can and do. They change over time as well. Post growth is not stagnation. Quite the opposite in fact. There is plenty of evidence showing that once a reasonable material level of living standards has been achieved, well-being is more likely to be increased through means with very low or no material content. A post growth era in which wellbeing increases while throughput stabilizes then declines is what makes post growth both plausible, preferable, and a potential escape from overshoot.

What must not grow in all countries sooner or later, and must decrease right now, starting in rich countries, is the material inflows to and outflows (waste) from their economies and the entire global economy. This is essential to reduce overshoot caused by excessive use of minerals and biomass and the transformation of land. It is also essential to reduce the demands on the limited capacity of the planet to absorb the wastes from economic activities. These material inflows and outflows are the material throughput of an economy. Some material inputs, such as those used in buildings, infrastructure, and equipment, remain in the economy for many years so in any one year the material inflows exceed the material outflows by the quantity of materials accumulated, allowing for demolition and discards that are not reused, repurposed, or recycled. This is simply an application of the law of conservation of mass. A similar conservation law applies to energy and is known as the first law of thermodynamics: in any process the quantity of energy remains unchanged.

The combustion of fossil fuels and biomass which converts chemi-

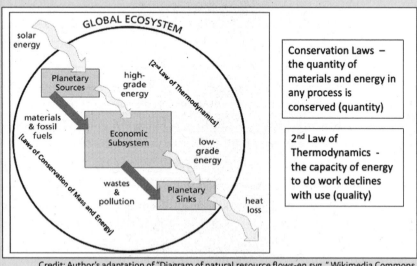

FIGURE 7.1.
The economy as a subsystem of the global ecosystem.

Credit: Author's adaptation of "Diagram of natural resource flows-en.svg," Wikimedia Commons.

cal energy into heat brings into play the second law of thermodynamics which is concerned with the quality of energy, in particular its capacity to do work (i.e., as a force causing the movement of an object) rather than its quantity. While the quantity of energy remains unchanged in the economic activities of production, distribution, and consumption, the capacity of energy to do work declines with use. The second law rules out the possibility of perpetual motion machines, machines that can run forever without requiring any new supplies of high-quality energy to keep them going. As an example, cars fuelled by gasoline cannot run on the low temperature heat of their exhaust. New fuel is required to keep them running.

Nobel prize-winning chemist Frederick Soddy was the first person to appreciate the significance of these laws of thermodynamics for

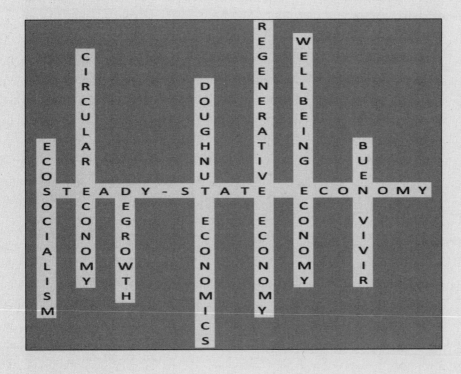

FIGURE 7.2.
Post growth economics.

economics. He was followed 40 years later by Kenneth Boulding and Nicolas Georgescu-Roegen (see Chapter Three) but very few econo-mists paid attention. One who did was Herman Daly, who proposed a post growth economy which, following the lead of demographers, he termed a steady-state economy.

Daly's proposal for a steady-state economy was in direct response to his concern with overshoot, so it is sensible to start there as we con-sider several approaches to post growth economics, most, if not all of which were influenced by Daly's work. We can learn something useful from all of them.

Steady-State Economy

Daly defines a steady-state economy in two different but complemen-tary ways. The first one is based on maintaining a constant human population and stock of built capital over time. These stocks of people and artifacts are to be maintained with a throughput of energy and materials that is within the capacity of the biosphere to regenerate the resource inputs and assimilate the waste outputs.[83] Daly's second definition of a steady-state economy is one where throughput is held constant at a sustainable level, based on the capacity of the biosphere to regenerate the resource inputs and assimilate the waste outputs. The size of the human population and the stock of capital is then free to adjust to whatever size the constant throughput can maintain.[84]

The first definition holds population and capital stock constant and allows throughput to vary. The second definition holds throughput constant and allows population and capital stock to vary. An advantage of the second definition is that it avoids the practical problem of de-termining when the total stock of capital in an economy is constant in physical terms and the associated problem of what is to be included as capital for this purpose. Is it just the artifacts produced by humans, as Daly presumably intended, or does it also include natural capital, social capital, and any of the other types of capital that some have sug-gested? It also has the advantage of focusing attention on material and energy throughput which, through extraction and disposal, are the main connections between the economy and the biosphere. Overshoot is largely attributable to throughput causing excessive accumulation of unwanted stocks (e.g., atmospheric greenhouse gases, plastics in the ocean) or decumulation of valuable stocks (e.g., forests, fish, minerals) so a definition of a steady-state economy that puts throughput front and center and allows flexibility in relation to population and the capital stock is preferable.

One of Daly's many contributions to post growth economics was to situate economics within a much broader framework of human knowledge. In the middle of the ends-means spectrum we see "intermediate means"—the stocks of artifacts, labor power, and energy—being used to meet "intermediate ends"—health, education, comfort, etc.—which is the purpose of economic activity. How the production and distribution of intermediate ends from intermediate means is done, or how it

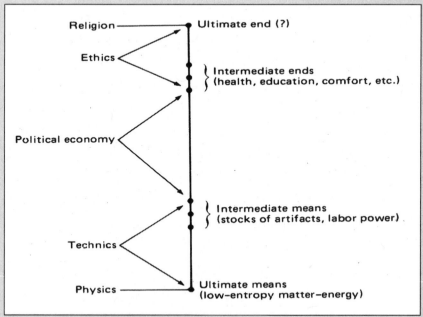

Credit: H. E. Daly, (1977), *Steady-State Economics: The Economics of Biophysical Equilibrium and Moral Growth*, W. H. Freeman.

FIGURE 7.3.
Daly's ends-means spectrum.

could be done differently, is the domain of political economy. Political economy is both an older name for economics, or, as it is practiced today, an outlook broader in scope, encompassing the history and evolution of economic systems and considerations of power.

Limiting the scope of economics to intermediate means and intermediate ends risks losing sight of what intermediate means are made from, and what higher goals the intermediate ends are intended to serve. Daly's ends-means spectrum shows that intermediate means are made from "ultimate means"—the stuff from which the planet is made plus sunlight—and intermediate ends are to serve the "ultimate end"—the highest or ultimate good. Consideration of ultimate means and ultimate end(s) provides the intellectual and ethical framework for the steady-state economy, an economy that is ecologically sustainable, distributionally just, and economically efficient, in that order.

Overshoot from the perspective of a steady-state economy can be seen as the result of the transition from an "empty world" to a "full world," with empty and full referring to the physical increase in humans and their artifacts within the context of a fixed ecosystem or ecosphere.

FIGURE 7.4.
From empty world to full world.

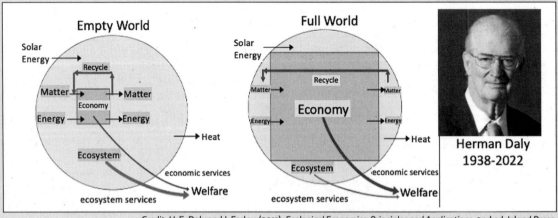

Credit: H. E. Daly and J. Farley, (2011), *Ecological Economics: Principles and Applications*, 2nd ed. Island Press.

Overshoot has many dimensions but at its core is the excessive impact on planetary systems by humanity to such an extent that the planet's capacity to support humans and countless other species is undermined with the very real risk that there is no escaping catastrophe. If we are to fashion an escape from overshoot, then one place to start is Daly's proposal for a steady-state economy; its emphasis on the physical scale of the economy is what overshoot is all about. We must find ways to keep the throughput of energy and materials in the economy within the capacity of the biosphere to sustain their sources and assimilate their wastes. This is a fundamental feature of a steady-state economy. It is also explicit in some of the other approaches to a post growth economy and, if not stated as such, is consistent with them. Moving beyond definition, Daly provides three operational principles to limit the human scale to a level within carrying capacity and sustainability.

Adoption and implementation of these principles are the minimum requirement for escaping from overshoot. Advocates of a steady-state economy, such as the Center for the Advancement of the Steady State

1.Renewable resources: **harvest not to exceed regeneration rate**

2.Non-renewable resources: **rate of depletion not to exceed rate of creation of renewable substitutes**

3.Waste emissions: **not to exceed assimilative capacity**

Credit: Author. Adapted from H. E. Daly, (1990), "Toward Some Operational Principles of Sustainable Development," *Ecological Economics*, 2, 1–6.

FIGURE 7.5.
Daly's operational principles.

Economy, and advocates of other approaches to post growth economies even more so, draw attention to social, cultural, political, financial, and ethical dimensions which must also be factored in for a successful and desirable future. But given the centrality of the physical dimension of the economy for escaping from overshoot, we must look deeper into what this means and its broader implications for an escape from overshot, which we will do in Chapter Eight when we consider the principle of contraction and convergence.

Thinking about the physical dimensions of an economy is essential for dealing with overshoot but it is not common practice within economics and governments where the size of economies is described in terms of GDP—the total money value of market transactions for final goods and services. Market prices reflect information about production costs and personal values best known to producers and consumers. But this does not include information about the physical scale of the economy. Even a market system working according to all the precepts laid down by generations of economic theorists cannot be relied upon to limit the physical size of an economy to avoid overshoot or escape from it. Such a scale must be determined through a political process, as is commonly the case for dealing with issues like urban air and water pollution, land and water use, and the protection of local biodiversity where there are clear jurisdictional responsibilities. Political processes work less well for transboundary and global issues where jurisdiction is unclear or nonexistent, as in the case of overshoot from the excessive release of greenhouse gases and overfishing on the high seas.

The distribution of incomes and wealth, which is a matter of justice as well as reward for effort, is also beyond the competence of markets to determine in an entirely defensible way. Increasing inequality, especially when it lacks social approval, can be socially disruptive, sometimes leading to violence. In a steady-state economy as envisaged by Daly, there would be one or more institutions concerned with determining the distribution of incomes and wealth. Again, this is not without precedent in the modern world. Progressive income taxes where a person's tax rate increases with the size of their income, inheritance

FIGURE 7.6. Income and wealth inequality increasing in the USA.

taxes of one sort or another, and systems of social support, are examples of politically determined attempts to moderate the degree of inequality determined by markets. Nonetheless, the marked increase in income and wealth inequality since the 1970s in the USA and the UK, with their comparatively high acceptance of market-determined distributions of income and wealth, is generating increasingly loud calls for something more effective.

In a world dominated by various versions of capitalism where markets play a major role, any transition to a post growth economy must wrestle with the question of what role markets should continue to play. The answer to this question distinguishes the different approaches to post growth. Daly sees markets having a significant role in a steady-state economy by allocating resources to alternative ends, providing the economy's physical scale avoids overshoot and the distribution of incomes and wealth is kept within widely accepted bounds. But even then he recognizes that markets have their limitations. As explained in Chapter Four, markets can allocate rival goods and services reasonably well, providing exclusion is possible and given the caveats about scale and distribution. But for goods and services that are non-rival, meaning that one person's consumption does not reduce another's, even if market allocation is possible, it is hardly desirable.

Overshoot can be caused by excessive use of "common pool" resources which are rival but where exclusion is low (e.g., fishing in protected waters with weak enforcement) or non-existent (e.g., fishing on the high seas not bound by limits). Whereas economists typically propose the creation of markets to fix this problem by creating some form of property right through tradable permits, or imposing payments such as a price on emissions, other institutional arrangements are possible and may well be superior.

Forty years ago, Elinor Ostrom began publishing her findings on the different ways that common pool resources have, in fact, been successfully managed in and around the world for a very long time, without recourse to markets and prices. From her work and that of numerous colleagues, Ostrom distilled a set of principles for stable local manage-

1. Define clear group boundaries.
2. Match rules governing use of common goods to local needs and conditions.
3. Ensure that those affected by the rules can participate in modifying the rules.
4. Make sure the rule-making rights of community members are respected by outside authorities.
5. Develop a system, carried out by community members, for monitoring members' behavior.
6. Use graduated sanctions for rule violators.
7. Provide accessible, low-cost means for dispute resolution.
8. Build responsibility for governing the common resource in nested tiers from the lowest level up to the entire interconnected system.

Elinor Ostrom
1933-2012

Credit: Author. Adapted from J. Walljasper, (2011), "Elinor Ostrom's 8 Principles for Managing a Commons." http://www.onthecommons.org/magazine/elinor-ostroms-8-principles-managing-commmons

FIGURE 7.7.
Ostrom's eight principles for managing common pool resources.

ment of common pool resources that have been successful in avoiding excessive use, especially at the local level with strong community involvement. These non-market approaches to the management of common pool resources expand the possibilities for escaping from overshoot well beyond creating property rights and markets where none exist, or imposing prices directly through fees of various kinds, as well as the more conventional approaches of subsidies and direct regulation.

There is much more to be said about a steady-state economy beyond the defining characteristics of limiting throughput to address scale and the need for complementary institutional arrangements for determining distribution and allocation. But we have covered the basics, enough to explore and compare other approaches to a post growth world.

Circular Economy

In 2005 Ellen MacArthur sailed alone around the world faster than anyone else before her. On her retirement from competitive sailing, she established the Ellen MacArthur Foundation to promote the concept of a circular economy. Working with business, policymakers, NGOs, and academics, the Foundation has been very successful in getting circular economy ideas and principles on the agendas of governments and corporations in many countries such as Japan, China, Canada, and the member countries of the European Union.

There is no one definition of a circular economy. Here's one from the Ellen MacArthur Foundation:

> The circular economy is based on three principles, driven by design: eliminate waste and pollution; circulate products and materials (at their highest value); and regenerate nature.

FIGURE 7.8. Circular economy.

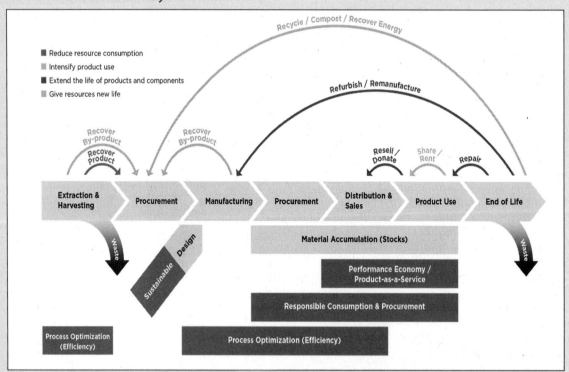

Credit: The expert panel on the circular economy in Canada (2021), *Turning Point*, Canadian Council of Academies, Ottawa, https://cca-reports.ca/reports/the-circular-economy-in-canada/

It is underpinned by a transition to renewable energy and materials. A circular economy decouples economic activity from the consumption of finite resources. It is a resilient system that is good for business, people, and the environment.[85]

The report of the Council of Canadian Academies' expert panel on the circular economy defined the circular economy as:

A systemic approach to production and consumption for living within planetary boundaries that conserves material resources, reduces energy and water use, and generates less waste and pollution.[86]

We should be clear that a completely circular economy is ruled out by the unavoidable degradation of materials and energy that comes with their use in economic activity. Even in a steady-state economy, new sources of materials and energy will always be required. In the kind of economy envisaged by the MacArthur Foundation, even if it were possible to recover and/or reuse 100 percent of materials by decoupling economic activity from the consumption of finite resources, which of course it is not, it would only be sufficient for maintaining a constant level of output. Expanding output would require additional material and energy inputs from virgin sources unless technology and the composition of output keeps changing fast enough to reduce material requirements per unit of output. This amounts to green growth on a very grand scale over a very long time which, in terms of the futures cone, lies somewhere between possible and preposterous. A completely circular economy is not a realistic goal. The term also evokes the misleading circular flow diagram in the first chapter of conventional economics textbooks. And while recycling materials is often possible and should be done up to an economic and energetic limit, though energy can be used more efficiently, it can never be recycled in the sense of performing the same work over again. The second law of thermodynamics will not allow it. So, a circular economy is an aspirational goal, a direction in which to move rather than a destination that can ever be reached. In 2020 the European Union, which is far ahead of North America in pursuing circularity, had a circular material use rate of 12.8 percent, ranging from a low of 1.3 percent in Romania to a high of 30.9 percent in the Netherlands. Even a 50 percent circularity rate will be very difficult to reach, especially in the time frame that an escape from overshoot requires.[87]

This is not to say that there is nothing to learn from the idea of a circular economy. On the contrary, there are many examples showing that the design and redesign of products, production, and distribution systems can make an enormous difference to the resource requirements of particular goods and services. Providing steps are also taken to avoid the rebound effect, resources can be saved, wastes reduced, and nature regenerated, which is all to the good.

Wellbeing Economy

The steady-state economy with its emphasis on physical throughput and scale provides the macroeconomic framework for escaping from overshoot. Only by reducing throughput to levels compatible with regenerative and assimilative capacities of ecosystems can we hope to return to a safe operating space within planetary boundaries. The circular economy also adopts a physical view of the economy, adding valuable detail about how to reduce throughput by extending the time that materials are kept usefully employed through better design, as well as various measures to increase reuse and recovery. Both the steady-state economy and the circular economy are intended to promote human and ecological wellbeing, implicitly if not explicitly. In the wellbeing economy, wellbeing is fundamental. Wellbeing, which is best understood as a set of experiences, not a collection of physical products, is the ultimate value produced by an economy.

According to the Wellbeing Economy Alliance's *Wellbeing Economy Policy Design Guide*, the wellbeing economy is "an economy that is designed with the purpose of serving the wellbeing of people and the planet first and foremost; in doing so, it delivers social justice on a healthy planet."[88] In a wellbeing economy there is a deliberate move

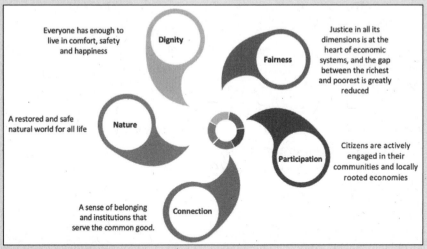

Everyone has enough to live in comfort, safety and happiness — **Dignity**

Fairness — Justice in all its dimensions is at the heart of economic systems, and the gap between the richest and poorest is greatly reduced

A restored and safe natural world for all life — **Nature**

Participation — Citizens are actively engaged in their communities and locally rooted economies

A sense of belonging and institutions that serve the common good. — **Connection**

Credit: Author. Based on Wellbeing Economic Policy Design Guide https://wellbeingeconomy .org/wp-content/uploads/Wellbeing-Economy-Policy-Design-Guide_Mar17_FINAL.pdf

FIGURE 7.9.
Core dimensions of wellbeing economies.

beyond GDP to new metrics of progress. This is not a complete rejection of GDP as an indicator of wellbeing, though it is seen as a measure of means rather than ends. Neither is it a commitment to a steady-state economy at some suitable level of throughput. Rather, it is a call for a change in direction towards wellbeing, based on a comprehensive, culturally sensitive understanding of the meaning of wellbeing derived from and informed by grassroots participation, networking, and sharing of information. *The Wellbeing Economy Policy Design Guide* is full of useful information and ideas to help communities develop a wellbeing vision, design a wellbeing economy strategy, assess, select, and implement wellbeing economy policies, and evaluate policy impacts on wellbeing.

Thinking about economies in terms of wellbeing rather than growth answers the question of what an economy is for. It is an answer that has begun to find political favor. Through the efforts of the Wellbeing Economy Alliance, the governments of Finland, Wales, Scotland, and Iceland have formed the Wellbeing Economy Governments (WEGo) partnership to provide mutual support for building wellbeing economies.[89] Other governments, such as those in Germany and the UK, have also embarked on a range of wellbeing initiatives, as has the OECD through the development of a wellbeing framework and metrics for measuring progress, as in its 2020 report, "Beyond Growth: Towards a New Economic Approach." Governments using public policy to move in the direction of a wellbeing economy have generally used one or more of the following: legislation requiring the consideration of the wellbeing of current and future generations, new institutions to promote wellbeing, and reform of the budget process to align economic policy with the objectives of a wellbeing economy.

Although there is some mention of planetary boundaries in discussions and reports about a wellbeing economy, the relationship between them is unclear. This may be due to.the difficulty of translating planetary boundaries down to the national and subnational, where most of the proposals for wellbeing economies have been directed. More significantly perhaps is that there is no mention of overshoot, throughput, or steady-state in *The Wellbeing Economy Policy Design Guide*. Furthermore, statements from the Scottish and German governments describing their understanding of a wellbeing economy show a close affinity with green growth, though the term itself is not used. This is something that a wellbeing economy as currently envisaged has in common with a circular economy, suggesting that even those governments leading the way are not yet ready to give up on growth in GDP.

Buen Vivir

Buen Vivir (Ecuador) and Vivir Bien (Bolivia) mean essentially the same thing. They are Spanish words used in Latin America meaning the Good Life. Buen Vivir was conceived as an alternative to the Eurocentric ideas of development and economic growth, especially as embodied in neoliberalism. It focuses on the Good Life in a broad sense where wellbeing is understood within community and not just as the agglomeration of individual assessments of utility derived from consumption. Drawing on Indigenous traditions of the region, Buen Vivir includes Nature not as an object to be exploited for human benefit, but

FIGURE 7.10.
Buen Vivir

as a subject with intrinsic value and rights, dissolving the Eurocentric dualism of society and nature. This represents a rejection of the reductionism embodied in economic values and commodification, as entailed, for example, in the concepts of natural and human capital. Buen Vivir is pluralistic and is open to different interpretations depending on cultural, historical, and ecological settings.

Buen Vivir was included in the constitution of Ecuador in 2008 and Vivir Bien in Bolivia's in 2009, though in somewhat different ways. In Ecuador, Buen Vivir is described as a set of rights to such necessities as health, shelter, education, and food within a framework that is intercultural, respectful of diversity, and in harmony with Nature which also has rights. Vivir Bien in the Bolivian constitution draws on Indigenous ideas and is included in the section on ethical and moral principles that define the values, ends, and objectives of the state's efforts to increase quality of life. In this way Vivir Bien is incorporated as an ethical principle rather than as a set of rights.

After the constitutional adoptions of Buen Vivir and Vivir Bien, new governments in Ecuador and Bolivia came to power that were not in sympathy with these initiatives and did not act in accordance with them. However, the constitutions were left intact, providing the basis for later governments to continue setting examples for the world of alternative approaches to development that can help the escape from overshoot.

Even though the steady-state economy and wellbeing economy were not inspired by Indigenous cultures, there is much they have in common with them. The idea of person-in-community, which is central to Buen Vivir, has been adopted by Herman Daly, the modern architect of the steady-state economy, through his collaboration with theologian John Cobb Jr.[90] Even stronger is the link between a wellbeing economy and Buen Vivir. Indeed, Buen Vivir is given as an example of crafting and communicating a wellbeing vision in *The Wellbeing Economy Policy Design Guide*. However, it is not what Buen Vivir has in common with approaches largely developed in the global North that makes it so significant for addressing overshoot. It is the fact that it comes from the global South and is a deliberate effort to find alternative development paths based on an ethical and moral stance that is distinct from modern Western culture, rejecting its individualistic utilitarianism and what has proven to be a disastrous instrumental view of nature. Buen Vivir will be insufficient in and of itself to overcome the pressures of capitalism on the biosphere, but in calling for a redefinition of the good life and how to achieve it, Buen Vivir provides an essential component of an escape from overshoot.

Doughnut Economics

One of the most powerful images of overshoot shows a circular map of the world divided into cake-like slices. (See Chapter One, Figure 1.12). Each slice represents a globally significant environmental feature vulnerable to overshoot such as climate change, biodiversity loss, and

FIGURE 7.11. Doughnut Economics.

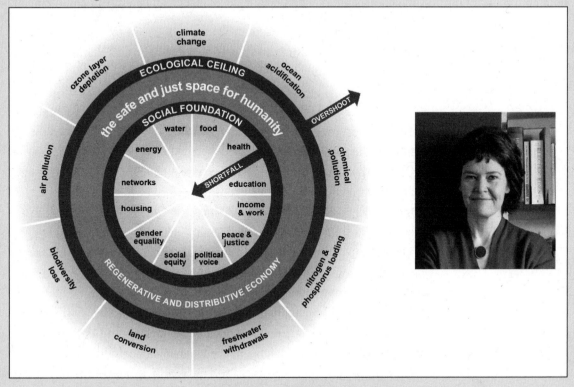

Credit: K. Raworth, (2017), *Doughnut Economics: Seven Ways to Think Like a 21st Century Economist*, Chelsea Green Publishing. Image from https://en.wikipedia.org/wiki/Doughnut_(economic_model)

land conversion. In the centre of the image is a smaller circle labeled "safe operating space" which is defined by a set of boundaries based on science and risk assessment. The idea is that—providing humanity remains within the safe operating space defined by these boundaries— the risk of triggering irreversible changes in critical Earth systems is very low. That several planetary boundaries have already been surpassed and others are getting close, is compelling evidence that we are in global overshoot.

Confronted with this image, economist Kate Raworth went one critical step further. She superimposed on the planetary boundaries image a set of social indicators to be achieved within the safe operating space.

Raworth derived these social indicators from the UN's Sustainable Development Goals (SDGs). She modified the planetary boundaries image by hollowing out the centre to make room for 12 social priorities: health, education, income and work, peace and justice, political voice, social equity, gender equality, housing, networks, energy, water, and food. The effect was to create a North American style doughnut, with the body of the doughnut representing the safe and just space for humanity bounded on the outside by the ecological ceiling and on the inside by the social foundation.

Raworth offers this inspiring image of the Doughnut as the goal for the twenty-first century to replace the twentieth-century goal of compounding economic growth. This is the first of seven ways she proposes for transforming economics to make it more useful for tackling the problems of this century and which comprise Doughnut Economics. In a single image the Doughnut encapsulates the double dilemma of development: achieving a broad set of social goals that define conditions for fulfilling lives for everyone while remaining within those planetary boundaries that have not been transgressed and retreating from those that have. How might this work? Raworth has documented numerous examples from around the world of communities, businesses, governments, and individuals that have adopted the Doughnut perspective and changed their ways to move in the direction of a safe and just space for humanity. They have done this by reducing energy and materials use, changing product designs, using regenerative methods in agriculture, fishing, and forestry, redistributing incomes and wealth among and within nations, restructuring financial systems to serve the real economy, and increasing public participation in governance at all levels.[91]

What remains unclear is whether these types of changes, even if adopted worldwide, would be sufficient to bring all eight+ billion humans within the safe and just operating space of the Doughnut. How large is that space? How thick is the doughnut? Without answers to these questions, we cannot say whether what is on offer is a plausible escape route from overshoot especially when we are told by Raworth to be "agnostic about growth."

7 Ways to to Think Like a 21st Century Economist

1. **Change the goal:**
   - from GDP growth to the Doughnut
2. **See the big picture:**
   - from self-contained market to embedded economy
3. **Nurture human nature:**
   - from rational economic man to social adaptable humans
4. **Get savvy with systems:**
   - from mechanical equilibrium to dynamic complexity
5. **Design to distribute:**
   - from growth will even it up again to distributive by design
6. **Create to regenerate:**
   - from growth will clean it up again to regenerative by design
7. **Be agnostic about growth:**
   - from growth addicted to growth agnostic

Credit: Adapted from Raworth 2017. Image from https://blog.p2pfoundation.net
/doughnut-economics-an-economic-model-for-the-future/2018/01/08

FIGURE 7.12.
Seven ways to think like a twenty-first century economist.

To be fair, however, the growth that Raworth is talking about is growth in GDP, not growth in material and energy throughput and land conversion, though these have historically all generally moved together. And the growth agnosticism that she advocates is to create economies that are no longer structurally dependent—financially, politically, or socially—upon endless GDP growth. As she puts it, "We have inherited economies that need to grow, whether or not it makes us thrive. What we need are economies that make us thrive, whether or not they grow."

Fortunately, others have taken up the challenge of estimating the thickness of the Doughnut. Jason Hickel, using data for 151 countries

FIGURE 7.13. Social and biophysical indicators covered in the dataset provided by O'Neill et al. (2019).

Social indicator	Threshold
Life Satisfaction	6.5 on 0–10 Cantril Scale (Gallup World Poll)
Healthy Life Expectancy	65 healthy life years
Nutrition *	2700 kcal per person per day
Sanitation *	95% with access to improved sanitation facilities
Income *	95% living on more than US$1.90 per day
Access to Energy *	95% with access to electricity
Education *	95% enrolment in secondary school
Social Support	90% say they have relatives or friends they can depend on
Democratic Quality	0.8 on −2.5–2.5 scale, average of Worldwide Governance Indicators on voice, accountability and political stability
Equality	70 on 0–100 scale, based on Gini coefficient of household disposable income
Employment	94% of the labour force employed

Biophysical indicator	Boundary
CO_2 Emissions	1.6 tonnes of CO_2 per person per year
Phosphorous	0.9 kilograms P per person year
Nitrogen	8.9 kilograms N per person per year
Blue Water	574 cubic meters H_2O per person per year
eHANPP	2.6 tonnes C per person per year
Ecological Footprint	1.7 global hectares (gha) per person per year
Material Footprint	7.2 tonnes per person per year

* Social indicators that require significant resource inputs

Credit: J. Hickel, (2018), Table 1 in "Is it possible to achieve a good life for all within planetary boundaries?", *Third World Quarterly*, 40, 1, 18–35.

assembled by O'Neill and colleagues,[92] reached the conclusion that, "achieving a good life for all within planetary boundaries will require overshoot nations to reduce their biophysical footprints by at least 40–50% on average from current levels, assuming poor nations can achieve social thresholds within planetary boundaries." To answer the question of whether this can be achieved while GDP continues to increase, Hickel reviewed several empirical studies and cites Ward et al. who concluded that: "Growth in GDP ultimately cannot plausibly be decoupled from growth in material and energy use, demonstrating categorically that GDP growth cannot be sustained indefinitely."[93]

Like all useful conceptual frameworks, Doughnut Economics answers some questions and raises others. Is there a better way to think about prospects for the twenty-first century than offered by conventional economics which treats the economy as a self-contained system isolated from the biosphere; regards humans as well-informed, far-sighted, self-interested, rational, and socially isolated; emphasizes equilibrium rather than disequilibrium; and assumes that increasing inequality and environmental degradation associated with rising incomes will be resolved by further increases in income? The answer from Raworth's Doughnut economics is a clear Yes. There is a better way. Is it possible to provide a good life for all within planetary boundaries and from available sources of materials energy not included in the boundaries? That is an empirical question that Raworth herself has not addressed but the evidence to date suggests it will require very substantial reductions in material and energy throughput in nations most responsible for overshoot.

Hickel has attempted to answer this question about the feasibility of living within the Doughnut. He distinguishes between social targets or thresholds that require significant inputs of resources such as access to energy and sanitation, and those whose achievement is more through improved social arrangements, such as reduced income inequality and life satisfaction.

A plot of the average per capita biophysical impact of nations with respect to planetary boundaries against their social achievement in meeting resource-intensive social thresholds shows that several middle-income countries come close to achieving both, but none succeeds entirely. It also shows that many countries that fall short on social achievement have the lowest per capita biophysical impact and many that meet the social thresholds have per capita biophysical impacts far greater than planetary boundaries allow. These are the high-income countries responsible for extraordinarily large throughputs of materials and energy. Moving them into the safe and just space for humanity within the Doughnut will require extensive changes to their economies and social systems that may be hard to imagine but which escape from overshoot requires.

Regenerative Economy

The Doughnut Economy draws together in a single compelling image several features that have been presented by others as alternative frameworks for post growth economies. One of these is the Regenerative

FIGURE 7.14. Ecological efficiency of nations.[94]

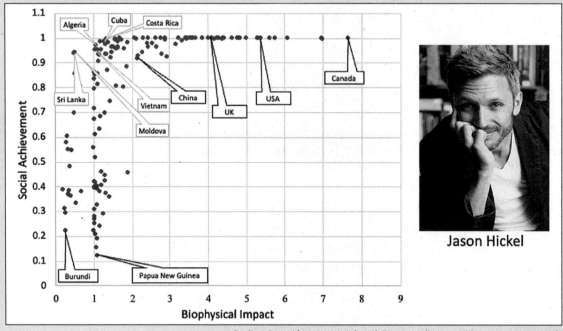

Jason Hickel

Credit: Adapted from J. Hickel, (2019), Figure 3 in "Is it possible to achieve a good life for all within planetary boundaries?", *Third World Quarterly*, 40, 1, 18–35.

Economy promoted by John Fullerton. In 2010 Fullerton left a successful career as a Wall Street banker to establish the Capital Institute with the goal of reimagining our economy. His work experience had convinced him that the relentless pursuit of endless growth both in returns on invested capital and in GDP was a fundamental cause of overshoot. The answer, he believes, lies in a redesign of economic and financial systems based on principles of regeneration derived from the modern understanding of nature and its self-organizing, self-regulating, continuously adapting living systems. This does not amount to a rejection of capitalism, but rather an extensive redesign.

The purpose of a Regenerative Economy is to promote and sustain human prosperity and wellbeing in an economy of permanence.[95] It uses the universal principles and patterns underlying stable, healthy, and sustainable living and nonliving systems throughout the real

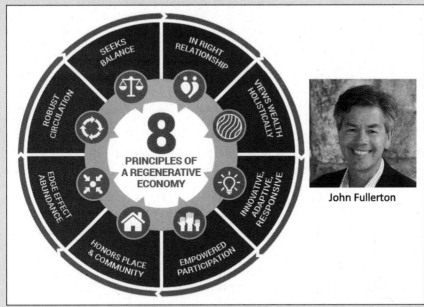

Credit: Capital Institute /8-principles-regenerative-economy/

FIGURE 7.15.
Principles of a regenerative economy.

world as a model for economic system design. This purpose of a Regenerative Economy is to be achieved by redesigning the economy according to eight key principles that have much in common with Doughnut Economics such as the rejection of "exponential undifferentiated growth" but not economic growth in its entirety, and seeking balance among "efficiency and resilience; collaboration and competition; diversity and coherence; and small, medium, and large organizations and needs." The Regenerative Economy also draws on biomimicry—which promotes strategies inspired by nature—and has much in common with the steady-state economy, especially in relation to throughput limits and the regeneration of natural systems as well as human-produced capital assets.

In addition to its insistence on the significance of regeneration as fundamental, the Regenerative Economy really comes into its own in considering finance: how it works, its role in overshoot, and how it has come to dominate the real economy rather than serve it. Working from the eight Principles for a Regenerative Economy, Fullerton has proposed a policy agenda for reforming the financial system in the United States that can be adapted to other countries. He believes that if these reforms were adopted, they would help redirect investment towards regenerative activities and reduce income and wealth inequality. Although his agenda is ambitious, even more changes in the financial system may well be required to create a system fit for reducing overshoot fairly and fast such as in the role of central banks and in the ownership of private financial institutions.

Degrowth

"Degrowth is a planned reduction of energy and resource throughput designed to bring the economy back into balance with the living world in a way that reduces inequality and improves human well-being."[96] Degrowth is a "missile" word, says Giorgos Kallis, by which he means that is it intended to unsettle people by attacking the cherished belief in economic growth. Hickel, another key contributor to the burgeoning degrowth literature, says degrowth is a word that cannot be co-opted in the way that sustainable has as in "sustainable growth." Degrowth, which is a translation of the French word *décroissance*, has a long history with many roots in philosophy, the social sciences, Indigenous thought, and economics, especially ecological economics which understands the economy as a subsystem of the biosphere. But degrowth is more than a critique of economic growth, it is a critique of capitalism and its dependency on growth based on the drive for the accumulation of capital, an idea most forcefully expressed by Karl Marx in the nineteenth century.

Degrowth is also a social movement centered primarily in continental Europe but with an increasing presence in other parts of the world. Young people especially are attracted to it, sharing the view that growth, particularly in rich countries, is the root cause of overshoot, that much of this growth in consumption does not increase well-being and may be detrimental to it, that growth is an excuse for not dealing

FIGURE 7.16. Ten-part framework for financial reform.

1. Curtail Speculation • Curb excessive speculation. • Encourage capital to flow into real investment, and particularly into projects aligned with the transition to regenerative economies.	**6. Test Sovereign Money** • Launch multiple diverse, controlled, regionally-designed, sovereign money experiments • Target renewable energy infrastructure assets, labor-intensive infrastructure repairs and upgrades, green infrastructure projects that restore vital ecosystem function, regenerative agriculture and related regional food system infrastructures. • Experiment with education and healthcare investment and a guaranteed minimum income.
2. Reduce Leverage Financial leverage in its many forms enhances capital efficiency while reducing systemic resiliency. • Reduce or eliminate incentives for excess leverage. • Increase incentives for equity and risk-sharing partnership models.	**7. Realign Fiscal Spending and Investment Priorities** • Cut government waste and outdated priorities that are not adapted to the new context. • Eliminate extractive and degenerative public investments and tax policies such as fossil fuel subsidies, capital investment subsidies over labor, and out of proportion defense expenditures. • Replace with regenerative public investments in education of all types and in: health focused on prevention, the public health system, innovative social enterprises, and the social safety net.
3. Regulate for Fractal Structure A healthy financial metabolism ensures circulation of money into small and mid-sized enterprises at regional and local scale rather than allowing ever more concentration at the top. • Rebalance structure of the finance industry to heavily penalize systemic risk and concentration. • Encourage structural diversity and broad circulation in the flow of capital by following the design of effective circulatory systems, such as our fractal cardiovascular system.	**8. Realign Public Research Investment** In the new world of complexity, public investment must prioritize addressing root causes over responding to the never-ending escalation of symptoms. Bold new commitments to research in energy technologies, advanced material science, green chemistry, soil science and regenerative agriculture, in public health systems and an understanding of how to invest in human immune systems are all essential to catalyze innovation in these vital areas.
4. Prioritize Business Formation • Encourage capital flow into new business clusters, and into small business expansion, with emphasis on "green" business and social enterprises addressing societal well-being. • Curtail emphasis on state-sponsored subsidies to large and concentrated business enterprises, while updating anti-trust laws for the 21st century.	**9. Redesign Philanthropic Incentives and Constraints to Accelerate Impact** • Increase incentives to accelerate shift of dynastic wealth into charitable vehicles with greater accountability to the common good. • Unblock the sclerosis within the philanthropic sector that prolongs perpetuity of individual foundations.
5. Reform Tax System • Reimagine tax structure to tax "bads" like pollution and excess speculation rather than "goods" like ordinary income. • Socialize windfall profits and dynastic wealth into both social and natural capital stocks that have been systematically depleted. • Shift the tax burden toward capital with offsetting incentives to high regenerative impact capital projects. • Enhance systemic resiliency by upgrading and simplifying the social safety net to include a broad-based, guaranteed minimum income.	**10. Establish Capital Investment Review Board (CIRB)** • Establish a Capital Investment Review Board, perhaps at each of the twelve regional Federal Reserve Districts, to review the regenerative quality of all public and private real capital investment programs greater than $250 million.

Credit: Adapted from Capital Institute "An Agenda for Genuine Financial Reform,"
https://capitalinstitute.org/blog/an-agenda-for-genuine-financial-reform/

FIGURE 7.17.
Degrowth—
a movement.

with rampant inequality, and that scarcity is a creation of capitalism rather than fundamental to the human condition.

When it comes to policy proposals, those from proponents of degrowth have much in common with others. For example, there is shared agreement that degrowth and a steady-state economy are about reducing the physical scale of the economy which will most likely reduce GDP, though that is not the objective of degrowth or a steady-state. A comparison of the ten-point policy proposals of Kallis and Daly shows further similarities. These are not complete lists. Hickel for example, also calls for an end to planned obsolescence, a shift from ownership to usership, ending food waste, scaling down ecologically destructive industries, decommodifying public goods, and expanding the commons.

One notable difference between Daly's vision for a steady-state economy and that of the degrowth movement concerns human population. The total consumption of goods and services which drives the throughput of materials and energy is found by multiplying population by average consumption per person. Daly observes that in rich

Degrowth Policy Proposal: Kallis	Steady-State Policy Proposals: Daly
1. Citizen debt audit 2. Work sharing 3. Basic and maximum income 4. Green tax reform 5. Stop subsidies and public investment for polluting activities 6. Support the social and solidarity economy 7. Social use of vacant buildings and houses 8. Reduce and restrict advertising 9. Establish environmental limits 10. Abolish GDP 	1. Cap-auction-trade systems for basic resources 2. Ecological tax reform 3. Set a minimum income and a maximum income 4. Free up the length of the working day, week and year – allow greater options for part time or personal work 5. Re-regulate international commerce – move away from free-trade, free capital mobility and globalization 6. Downgrade the WTO/WB/IMF 7. Move away from fractional reserve banking towards a system of 100% reserve requirements 8. Enclose the remaining open access commons in public trusts, and price them by cap-auction-trade systems, or by taxes 9. Stabilize population 10. Reform national accounts – separate GDP into a cost account and a benefits account

Gorgios Kallis

FIGURE 7.18.
Degrowth and steady-state policy proposals.

Credit: G. Kallis, (2015), "Yes we can prosper without growth," https://degrowth.org/2015/05/15/yes-we-can-prosper-without-growth/, Daly (2015), "Economics for a Full World," The Great Transition Initiative, https://greattransition.org/

countries growth in throughput is largely due to increases in consumption per person not in population and so he says emphasis should be on reducing consumption per capita to reduce throughput in rich countries. In poorer countries, with much lower consumption per capita, growth in throughput comes primarily from increases in population which Daly suggests should be addressed through measures such as the education of women and the availability of birth control. Advocates of degrowth agree with this approach but are cautious about population measures directed at poor people, seeing remnants of colonial ideas—which they vehemently oppose—in play.[97] They also call for a reimagining of society in which "enough" replaces growth as the overarching objective for an economy's output of goods and services, where there is a more balanced blend of provisioning between individual and collective action, and where self-limitation premised on sharing provides an escape from overshoot.

The full range of degrowth policy proposals is nicely illustrated by the "Iceberg of Degrowth" showing the wide range of policies described in the degrowth literature, many of which are shared with others writing about post growth. But even this impressive collection of degrowth policy measures fails to capture what, in the view of some, is the full scope of what degrowth encompasses—a more far-reaching reconceptualization of what society is, and what it ought to be to escape from overshoot.[98]

Ecosocialism

In 2001 Michael Löwy, a French-Brazilian Marxist sociologist and philosopher co-authored with American scholar Joel Kovel An Ecosocialist Manifesto.[99] They were following the example of Marx and Engels' Communist Manifesto of 1848, presenting it "only as a line of reasoning" rather than a concrete plan. Their Ecosocialist Manifesto is grounded in the proposition that ecological crises and societal breakdown are interrelated and result from the same cause: the expansion of capitalism around the world. They describe capitalism as a system inherently unable to solve these crises because to do so requires setting limits on the accumulation of capital which cannot be done under capitalism. Such limits, says the manifesto, require socialism, and if the limits are to be for ecological purposes as well as the more traditional one of reuniting workers with the means of production, then it must be cast in an ecological framework. Hence ecosocialism.

FIGURE 7.19. Iceberg of degrowth policy proposals: core instruments on top (in descending order of citations 2005–2020); themed goals below (in random positions).

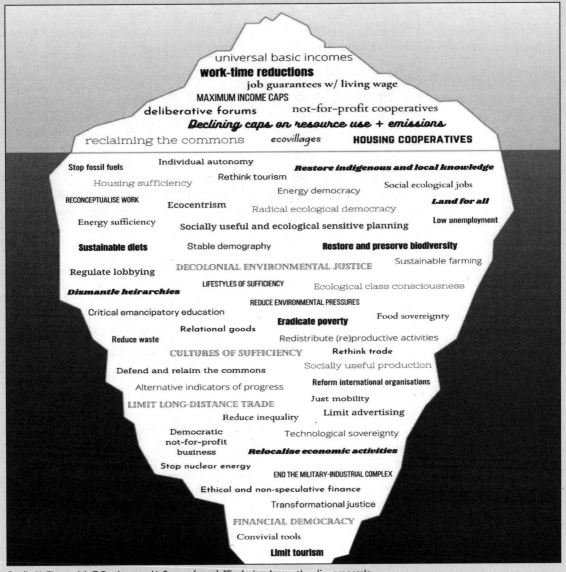

Credit: N. Fitzpatrick, T. Parrique, and I. Cosme, (2022). "Exploring degrowth policy proposals: A systematic mapping with thematic synthesis," *Journal of Cleaner Production*, in press.

FIGURE 7.20.
Ecosocialism.

Credit: https://www.politicalanimalmagazine.com/2019/02/21/ecosocialism-vs-the-green-new-deal/

"A fundamental premise of ecosocialism is that in a society without sharp class divisions and capitalist alienation, 'being' will take precedence over 'having.' Instead of seeking endless goods, people pursue greater free time, and the personal achievements and meaning it can bring through cultural, athletic, recreational, scientific, erotic, artistic, and political activities." The Ecosocialist Manifesto sees the need to develop a path to ecosocialism in accord with the "limits to growth essential for the sustainability of society," but in a way that insists "upon redefining both the path and the goal of socialist production in an ecological framework." Such a path and goal are to be achieved by shifting toward qualitative development and away from quantitative growth without imposing "scarcity, hardship and repression." Such a path, should it prove feasible, would be an escape from overshoot.

The authors of the Communist Manifesto recognized that the political, social, and economic changes they were calling for would not happen immediately so they proposed ten measures, different in different countries, that would lead in their desired direction of change, each one necessitating further changes until the ownership and control of capital and the conditions of employment were totally revolutionized. Some of these measures have been introduced in many countries in one form or another without, it seems, weaning them off capitalism towards socialism. No equivalent list of measures to help bring about ecosocialism is included in the Ecosocialist Manifesto but one can be created from Löwy's other publications that is useful for comparison with those of other approaches.

This list of ecosocialist measures contain several that are found in the lists for the other approaches to post growth such as reduced worktime, restrictions on advertising, redefinition of the standard of living, and replacing energy from fossil fuels with energy from renewable sources. But it also contains measures that differentiate it concerning the transformation from capitalism to ecosocialism, namely the widespread use of democratic planning and a much-reduced role for markets. In this important sense, ecosocialism is the most political of all the approaches to post growth described in this chapter.

Conclusion

These brief accounts of several approaches to post growth approaches for an escape from overshoot in a fair and equitable manner are intended to bring out their main features. There is an extensive printed and online literature for all of them that is richer in content, including important internal disputes, than can be captured in a few pages. There is also a substantial literature on post growth by authors who do not identify with any of these approaches in particular, Tim Jackson being one of the most interesting and influential,[100] as well as organizations committed to post growth such as the Post Growth Institute.[101] All have something useful to offer.

The various post growth approaches described in this chapter share a common interest in economy-society-environment interrelation-

FIGURE 7.21. Ecosocialism measures.

1. Transform the productive system through democratic planning of the economy taking into account the preservation of ecological equilibrium.

2. Discontinue branches of production such as nuclear power plants, industrial fishing, destructive logging of tropical forests.

3. Replace fossil fuels with renewable sources of energy: water, wind, sun.

4. Create conditions for full and equitable employment with equal conditions of work and wages.

5. Redefine the meaning of standard of living to connote a way of life that is actually richer, while consuming less.

6. Base socialist planning on democratic and pluralist debate at all the levels where decisions are to be made. Plan the main economic options, not the administration of local restaurants, groceries and bakeries, small shops, and artisan enterprises or services.

7. Remove decisions on investment and technological change from the banks and capitalist enterprises and replace them with public decisions that serve society's common good.

8. Replace advertising with information on goods and services provided by consumer associations.

9. Set prices of goods according to social, political, and ecological criteria, not by demand and supply. Products and services will result from planning based on use value and more and more products will be distributed free of charge according to the will of the citizens.

10. Reduce labour time so that working people can participate in the democratic discussion and management of the economy and society.

11. Rejection of the definition of progress based on market growth and quantitative expansion. Development should be a qualitative. Orient production toward satisfying authentic needs such as for water, food, clothing, housing, and basic services such as health, education, transportation, and culture.

12. Countries in the global South should build needed railroads, hospitals, sewage systems, and other infrastructures with a productive system that is environmentally friendly and based on renewable energy. Their food production should be through peasant biological agriculture based on family units, cooperatives, or collectivist farms, not the destructive and antisocial methods of industrialized agribusiness.

13. The North should provide technical and economic help to the South but not via the monstrous debt system and imperialist exploitation of the resources of the South, and without the need for Europe and North America to reduce their standard of living in absolute terms.

Credit: Author. Based on M. Löwy, (2015), *Ecosocialism: A Radical Alternative to Capitalist Catastrophe*, Chapter 2: Ecosocialism and Democratic Planning, Haymarket Books, and M. Löwy, (2018), *Ecosocialism and Democratic Planning*.

ships. They all agree that different measures of success should replace increasing growth in GDP, working time should be reduced, finance needs an overhaul, and energy from renewable sources should replace fossil fuels. They differ considerably when it comes to possibilities for a reformed capitalism and more generally about the place of politics in achieving real change. Yet despite their differences, or because of them, we can learn something from them all in mapping an escape from overshoot.

FIGURE 7.22. From degrowth to steady-state.

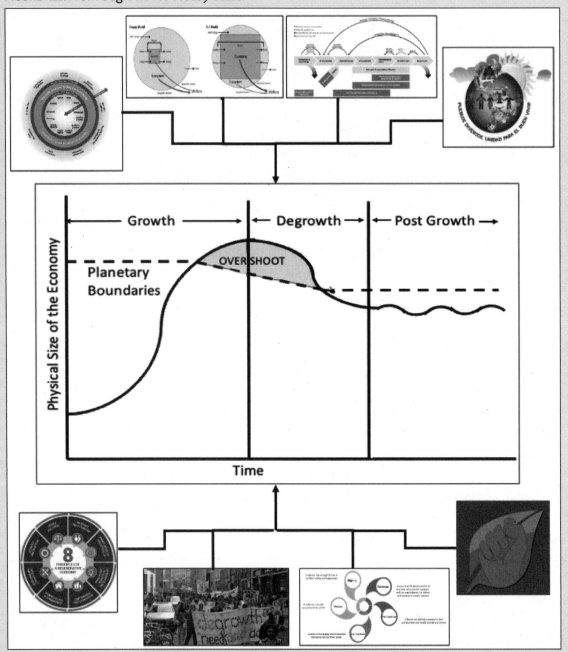

Credit: Based on D. W. O'Neill, (2012), "Measuring progress in the degrowth transition to a steady state economy," *Ecological Economics*, 84, 221–23

8

MODELING AN ESCAPE FROM OVERSHOOT

The Story So Far

We began this book with an investigation into overshoot—the unsustainable demands being placed on the biosphere by eight billion humans, expected to increase to 10± billion by 2100 according to UN forecasts. How will they fare? Despite abundant evidence of overshoot, responses to date have been only piecemeal at best. Even with climate change, and the succession of meetings of world leaders addressing it, there has been much more talk than action. There has been a continuous upward trend in the atmospheric concentration of carbon dioxide and the often overlooked associated increasing acidification of the oceans, damaging marine life.

Or take the biodiversity crisis. From 1900 to 2015 the human population more than quadrupled, and the mass of wild land mammals declined by 70 percent. Now only four percent of mammals on land and sea are wild and a quarter of these are threatened with extinction.[102] This decline in wild mammals and related increase in species extinction has a long history, going back millennia. It predates the rise of agriculture which began roughly 10,000 years ago, though it is now driven by the land conversion and habitat destruction largely associated with agriculture. These changes have accelerated to the point where our current situation is being described as the sixth extinction, and far too little is being done to stop it.

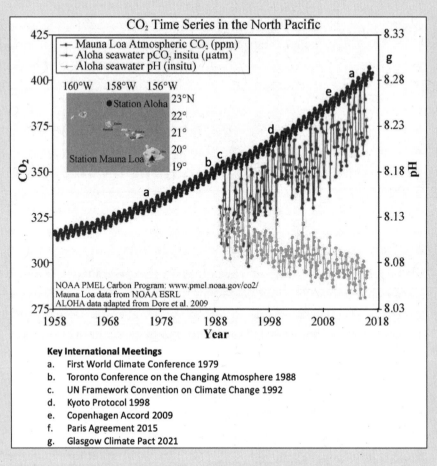

CO₂ Time Series in the North Pacific

- Mauna Loa Atmospheric CO₂ (ppm)
- Aloha seawater pCO₂ insitu (μatm)
- Aloha seawater pH (insitu)

NOAA PMEL Carbon Program: www.pmel.noaa.gov/co2/
Mauna Loa data from NOAA ESRL
ALOHA data adapted from Dore et al. 2009

Key International Meetings
a. First World Climate Conference 1979
b. Toronto Conference on the Changing Atmosphere 1988
c. UN Framework Convention on Climate Change 1992
d. Kyoto Protocol 1998
e. Copenhagen Accord 2009
f. Paris Agreement 2015
g. Glasgow Climate Pact 2021

FIGURE 8.1.
Atmospheric and oceanic concentration of carbon dioxide and the Mauna Loa Observatory.

Credit: Chart NOAA; photo NOAA photo library.

So where can we turn for help? Many explanations have been given for overshoot. Biological explanations emphasize the natural tendency of populations of all species to expand to the limits of their environment's capacity to sustain them. In the case of humans, the biological propensity to breed has been reinforced by religious and political encouragement to propagate. Others see the powers of science and technology and society's unwillingness and/or inability to restrain them as fundamental to overshoot. All these factors play into overshoot, working within and through economic, political, and social systems that bring them together in ways that are hard to understand. Yet understand them we must if we are to find an escape from overshoot by design, not disaster.

In this book, we began by looking for insights from the founders of economics who witnessed the rise of capitalism first in Britain and conceived of the economy as a discrete component of society worthy of study. Their analysis placed considerable emphasis on agriculture, which was the dominant sector in eighteenth-century Europe, where economics as we know it today has its roots, and where the roles of land and labor in production were obvious. Gradually, as factory-based manufacturing spread, cities, towns, and ways of life were transformed, and the role of land in economic production became less obvious. In the nineteenth century, owners of capital displaced landowners as the most economically powerful group in capitalist societies. This shift in economic power went hand in hand with a shift in political power. In the late nineteenth and early twentieth centuries capitalism became entrenched in many countries, and in economics the study of markets based on private property flourished. Enthralled by the capacity of prices to signal emerging scarcities and to incentivize appropriate behavioral and technological responses, most economists paid little attention to the sources of materials and energy needed to run economies, and to what happened to them when they were no longer useful.

The Great Depression of the 1930s witnessed the development of macroeconomics—the study of whole economies—and the realization that full employment was not a normal or even necessary outcome of capitalism. Keynes explained that governments had a key role to play in maintaining total spending in the economy to ensure high levels of employment. In the stagflation of the 1970s, combining low rates of economic growth, high unemployment, and inflation, three decades of successful Keynesian economic policy gave way to monetarism and the view that the single best macroeconomic lever was control of the money supply. This idea proved more difficult in practice than imagined. Control of the money supply was supplanted by control over interest rates by central banks to tame inflation, while governments concentrated on fiscal policy (i.e., taxation and spending) and trade policy—arrangements being tested once again by rates of inflation not seen for 30 years. Rapid technological change and the spread of globalization have transformed economies by breaking down barriers to trade, removing restrictions on the movement of financial capital, and creating whole new markets for cryptocurrencies and for data obtained surreptitiously by companies like Google and Facebook from users of their services. Whether the renewed, active participation of governments in the economy brought about by the financial crisis of 2009 and the COVID-19 pandemic of 2019–2022—as well as the structural changes in work and educational arrangements—will last only time will tell.

In the past century, with few exceptions, such as the interruptions in oil supplies in the 1970s, little attention was given in the public and private sectors to the consequences of growing economies' rapidly rising requirements for inputs of materials and energy, the increase in wastes of all kinds, and the ongoing transformation and degradation of land. This was also true of economists who should have known better since they had a lot to say about production but did so without considering the materials and energy that went into it and the wastes that came out. Of course, there were exceptions. The rise of the conservation movement, and environmentalism more generally, being one. Periodic concern about the availability of raw materials, such as the report of the US President's Materials Policy Commission in 1952 is another. Other exceptions to the neglect of the biophysical dimension of economic activity were the few economists, some of whom we met in Chapters Three and Seven, who worked largely outside and against the mainstream. Both their insights into the economy as a subsystem of the biosphere and a broader appreciation of what successful economies and the societies of which they are a part should mean, give us some of the concepts and ways of thinking that we need to escape from overshoot.

The past and present are not infallible guides to the future, but they are the best available. Some very smart, insightful people have, in their own time, made impressively accurate statements about what lay ahead. Others, not necessarily less smart or less insightful, made predictions that were not borne out by experience. Perhaps this was because of a different assessment of the balance of forces in play, or simply because a combination of the unknown and unexpected derailed even the most reasonable accounts of what was to come. Sometimes it was simply a lack of, or too much, imagination. Our problem is that, at any moment, we can be confronted by very different predictions or expectations about the future. What one person considers probable, others might think possible or even preposterous. How are we to tell the difference, other than by hindsight when it is too late? At the very least, we can look at past trends and consider the likelihood of whether they will continue, and if so for how long, which is what we tried to do in Chapter Five. One lesson from that exercise is that short-term trends can be a poor guide to the long term (the height of the river Nile for example) and a simple extrapolation of trends is no substitute for an analysis of the system or systems from which these trends arise.

This observation holds true when it comes to economic growth—the upward trend in economic output. We live at a time when most nations still place the pursuit of economic growth at or very near the top of their economic policy agendas. It has been there since the end of World War II, when governments of nations with rich economies and equipped with Keynesian economics took responsibility for full employment, which they soon came to believe could best be achieved through economic growth. Enthusiasm for economic growth was spurred by the Cold War and has remained strong, especially in official circles, ever since. We should not be surprised, therefore, that when faced with evidence of overshoot, governments and international organizations such as the World Bank, the IMF, and the OECD, are loathe to sacrifice economic growth. They prefer the idea of green growth—more output from the economy coupled with reduced use of resources and generation of wastes, assuming this can be done fast enough to escape from overshoot and avoid its worst consequences along the way. Then, with an economy of ever-increasing size, so many other problems could be dealt with through a more inclusive approach than we have seen in the past—or so it is believed.

It makes for an attractive prospect but, as we saw in Chapter Six, not a plausible one. The rates at which economies grow and resource inputs and waste outputs per dollar must decline to meet any resource or environmental target, pull in opposite directions. Faster economic growth *necessitates* faster reductions in resource use and waste per dollar of GDP simply to stand still, let alone reverse direction. Examples of where this has happened, such as when a new technology such as more efficient lighting was introduced, should not mislead us into thinking it applies, or can apply, to entire economies.

As for inclusivity, in the USA for example, GDP per person increased by some 230 percent in inflation-adjusted dollars in the 50 years following 1970, the year of the first Earth Day, and yet the need for more inclusivity in all its social, economic, and political dimensions is stronger today than ever. If anything, economic growth became an excuse for not dealing with inclusivity, and especially inequality, in the belief that as it continued, everyone could and would become richer. This view of the future has been confounded by the dramatic increase in the unequal distribution of income and wealth in the USA and many other high-income countries since the 1970s (see Chapter Five). It also overlooks the significance of the Easterlin Paradox, which says that people's sense of wellbeing depends more on their relative position with respect to others than on their absolute level of income and wealth. If this is true, and there is plenty of research that says it is, especially in high-income countries,[103] then growth without redistribution can

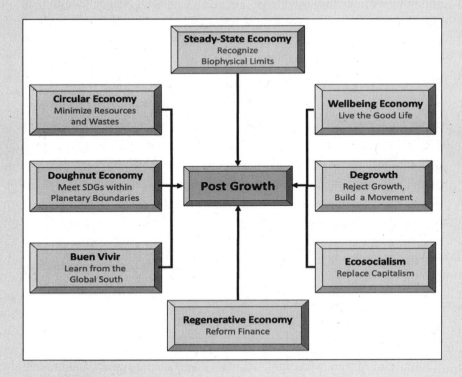

FIGURE 8.2.
Different perspectives on post growth.

reduce wellbeing rather than raise it. Conversely, by reducing inequality, redistribution without growth can increase wellbeing.

If green growth is not the answer to overshoot, then what is? In the previous chapter we considered several contributions to building a post growth world. For the most part they are complementary and mutually supportive, but they differ in what each emphasizes. No single approach has all the answers, but together they provide a body of ideas and practice that are useful for devising an escape from overshoot.

From Local to Global Overshoot

Overshoot happens when the demands of humans on nature exceed the capacity of natural systems to regenerate. This can occur at any scale from the very local, as it has throughout human history, to the global, which is only very recent. Nomadic tribes have long followed the seasons in search of wild plants and game which they harvest and then move on, allowing the populations to recover. Farmers let fields lie fallow so that they can restore organic matter, retain moisture, and disrupt the life cycles of pathogens. Pollution of lakes and rivers from excessive discharges of wastes has been reduced in many places through changes to production processes and adding end-of-pipe water treatment facilities. Urban concentrations of several dangerous air pollutants have been reduced through improved vehicle design and catalytic converters, and greater use of less-polluting technologies such as bicycles. These examples of success in dealing with overshoot at the local level give some hope that global overshoot will also be amenable to change but there are some critical differences between local and global overshoot.

Responses to local overshoot sometimes shift the problem somewhere else. When the tallest chimney in the world was built in Sudbury, Ontario, in 1972 to reduce air pollution from sulphur dioxide, the emissions from the smelter spread far and wide, causing acid rain in Canada and the United States. End-of-pipe effluent treatments often generate solid wastes needing disposal and the energy they use creates other wastes. Shipment of unwanted electronic waste from high- to low-income countries solves a problem in one place but creates health and contamination problems in others. Is this the best that people in high-income countries can do to help those so much poorer and more vulnerable? Typically, those responsible for solving problems of local overshoot are not very concerned with consequences elsewhere, but when it comes to global overshoot shifting the burden to others is not an option. There is no "elsewhere." When manufacturing plants move to areas with lower labor costs, weaker environmental regulations, and older, less efficient technologies, global GHG emissions increase. The widespread use of organochlorine pesticides such as DDT and dieldrin in agriculture and for mosquito control has caused serious and widespread health effects and biodiversity losses. Masses of plastic waste contaminate the world's oceans. It is not a pretty picture.

For most of human history, overshoot was only a local occurrence, but in modern times its severity has become increasingly global, driven by cheap energy from fossil fuels and the expansion of agriculture, forestry, mining, manufacturing, and transportation that this low-cost, convenient source of energy has made possible. Some way and somehow, human demands on what nature can provide must be reduced and brought into line with what nature can provide sustainably. One question is what should be reduced, by how much, and by when? Another is how can this be done in a fair and equitable manner?

Contraction and Convergence

Since the 1990s these questions have been front and center in the ongoing deliberations of countries around the world to prevent catastrophic climate change. The ultimate objective of the United Nations Framework Convention on Climate Change (UNFCCC) is to stabilize "greenhouse gas concentrations in the atmosphere at a level that would prevent dangerous anthropogenic [human-induced] interference with the climate system. Such a level should be achieved within a time-frame sufficient to allow ecosystems to adapt naturally to climate change, to ensure that food production is not threatened, and to enable economic development to proceed in a sustainable manner."[104] The UNFCCC acknowledged "that the global nature of climate change calls for the widest possible cooperation by all countries and their participation in an effective and appropriate international response, in accordance with their common but differentiated responsibilities and respective capabilities and the social and economic conditions."[105] This collaboration called for a commitment by developed countries to assist developing countries in implementing the provisions of the convention through finance and knowledge and technology transfer.

Actually implementing the principles and commitments of the UNFCCC has been the subject of discussion and debate at conferences of the parties (COP) for three decades. Progress in reducing GHG emissions has been frustratingly slow and the atmospheric concentration of GHGs continues to rise. At COP26 in 2021 many countries announced national targets of reaching net zero emissions by 2050, but whether they succeed and do so fast enough to stop and ultimately reverse the increase in the atmospheric concentration of GHGs is a matter of great concern. The record-breaking temperatures in 2022, with 40°C heat in the UK and many parts of Europe bringing forest fires, poisonous air, disease, and premature death is only the beginning of what the experts say is yet to come if global temperatures continue to rise.[106]

In terms of finding an escape from overshoot, the UNFCCC is significant for two reasons. First, it calls for emission reduction targets sufficient to avoid catastrophic climate change that are also equitable, in that they take account of the different circumstances of each country. Second, the UNFCCC calls for transfers of funds, knowledge, and technology from developed to developing countries to reduce their costs and remove obstacles to emissions reduction.

Similar principles can and should apply to all aspects of overshoot that are globally significant and whose causes can be traced, at least in part, to high-income countries.[107] We need reduction targets to avoid

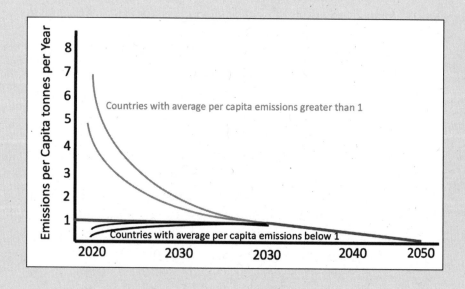

FIGURE 8.3.
Contraction and convergence.

or recover from overshoot—contraction—and we need different paths that converge to some agreed level or levels based on the circumstances of each country. This is the principle of contraction and convergence.

In the case of climate change, where contraction and convergence has been most thoroughly investigated, we can learn from the work led by the Global Commons Institute (GCI). The GCI has enthusiastically promoted contraction and convergence for tackling climate change. The approach has been adopted with variations by many other organizations and some governments though not at the speed and scope that Aubrey Mayer, founder of GCI, had hoped.

In its basic form, contraction and convergence starts with a carbon budget, which is an estimate of the quantity of CO_2 that can be emitted into the atmosphere with a predicted probability of preventing the average global temperature from increasing by a specified amount. (To keep the example as simple as possible we do not distinguish between gross and net emissions.) For example, the IPCC Summary for Policy Makers[108] gives a global carbon budget starting in 2020 of 400 billion tonnes of CO_2 for a 67 percent probability of remaining within 1.5 degrees global warming. The 2021 release of global CO_2 emissions was 36 billion tonnes per year which, if maintained, will exhaust the carbon budget in 2030![109]

The next step in contraction and convergence is to calculate the average annual emissions per person based on the global population, which in 2022 was 4.5 tonnes CO_2 (36 billion tonnes CO_2/8 billion people), assuming no increase in population.

The third step is to establish a path over time to zero CO_2 emissions per person. As a starting point, the per person CO_2 emissions are calculated for each individual country. Some, such as the USA and Canada, have annual per person emissions far greater than 4.5 tonnes and other, poorer countries, much below that. We know that to stay within the carbon budget emissions from all countries must eventually be zero, but they can take very different paths to get there. This is where convergence comes in.

Suppose it is agreed that all countries should reach zero emissions by 2050 and that beyond 2040 they should all have the same per person emissions of one tonne per year. This is the point at which yearly per person emissions converge. Countries having current annual per person CO_2 emissions greater than one tonne per year will have to reduce their emissions while those with current annual per person CO_2 emissions less than one tonne per year can increase their emissions to that level until 2040, the year of convergence. After that, the emissions from all countries must decline to zero by 2050.

This is just one combination of paths to zero emissions. It shows that countries with average per person emissions greater than one tonne per year must cut their emissions sharply. Meanwhile, those with average per person emissions below one tonne per year can let their emissions increase to 2040 before they decline to zero by 2050. Another possibility would be for emissions from this second group of countries to rise above one tonne per year for a few years as they develop to compensate for historical inequities. To stay within the global carbon budget this would have to be balanced by additional emissions reductions from high-emission countries.

Finding emissions paths that contract and converge and keep total emissions within a prescribed budget can be quite complicated. The GCI has developed an online carbon budget accounting tool (CBAT) that simplifies the task. It consists of four domains:

- Domain 1 (contraction and concentration) is where the carbon budget is set taking account of feedback effects, climate sensitivity, atmospheric carbon concentrations, temperature, sea-level rise, and ocean acidification.
- Domain 2 (contraction and convergence) assumes that an equitable distribution of the remaining carbon budget requires countries with high per person carbon emissions to reduce their emissions faster than those with lower emissions.
- Domain 3 (contraction and conversion) shows how the rate of demand for clean sources of energy is tied to different rates of global carbon contraction budgets.

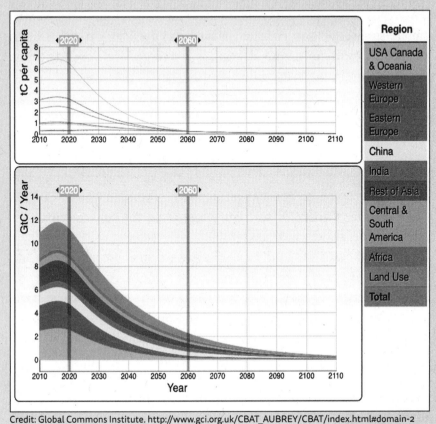

Credit: Global Commons Institute. http://www.gci.org.uk/CBAT_AUBREY/CBAT/index.html#domain-2

FIGURE 8.4.
Contraction and convergence from CBAT (Carbon Budget Accounting Tool).

- Domain 4 (damages and growth) projects climate change loss and damage rates, for a given carbon budget, feedback, and sensitivity levels, in relation to assumed growth in GDP.

Our main interest is in Domain 2, contraction and convergence, which is illustrated here with output from CBAT based on a remaining carbon budget in 2010 of 400 GtC (i.e., 400 billion tonnes of carbon).[110]

The upper graph from CBAT shows emissions per person increasing in all eight regions with slight declines setting in around 2016. From 2020 onwards per person emissions decline most rapidly in the USA

Canada & Oceania region, and at progressively slower rates moving down the list of regions until India and Africa where per person emissions increase to 2040 after which they also decline until 2060 when per person emissions from all regions converge far below one tonne per year, continuing to decline to zero by 2110. [111]

The lower graph shows what happens to total emissions and how these are divided among the regions based on projections of the population in each region and the convergence of per person emissions in the upper graph. This pattern of contraction and convergence in emissions per person is consistent with the specified carbon budget of 400 GtC. If the carbon budget derived in domain one of CBAT is changed, the contraction and convergence pattern of emissions per person automatically adjusts.

As noted earlier, the principle of contraction and convergence has been most assiduously considered and to some degree applied in relation to climate change where it is based on the proposition that the atmosphere is a global commons, belonging to no particular people, groups, or countries. Managing the limited capacity of the atmosphere to assimilate greenhouse gas emissions is complicated by the fact that its use by one generation can affect the climate in which future generations will live. Political philosopher Jörg Tremmel, who has written extensively about these issues and who views contraction and convergence as "currently the concept that is probably the most advanced in ethics,"[112] has reached five main conclusions.

These principles provide useful guidance for considering ways and means of escaping from overshoot beyond just climate change. For example, they can be applied to our ecological footprint, which far exceeds the biocapacity of the planet, and to materials and energy throughput in general, which underlie so many resource and environmental problems, and to food.

Contraction is essential and should be done in ways that are deemed equitable. Even then it will encounter stiff opposition from all sorts of vested interests. But if contraction is not accomplished by design, it

'What is Just with Regard to the Climate?'

1. The notion of a safe emissions budget is a restriction for the current generations' consumption of atmospheric resources, and it limits the leeway for distribution schemes in the present, e.g., between North and South.
2. The cumulative emissions between 1850 and 1990 should not be taken into account for the purpose of considerations of justice [on the grounds that before 1990 when the first report of the IPCC was published people were largely ignorant of the effects of GHG emissions on the climate]. Compensation can (and should) ensue on other grounds though not required by justice.
3. For the sake of justice, countries are accountable for their entire emissions since 1990. This should occur by means of overshooting-rights for a limited time granted to the South from the North [as illustrated in the CBAT illustration of contraction and convergence].
4. For direct damages caused by greenhouse gas emissions between 1990 and the present, the 'polluter pays principle' applies. All damages to the South that came to pass as a result of the actions of the North are to be compensated to the best of one's knowledge and belief.
5. Population changes from 1990 should be taken into account in a climate treaty. 1990 is the year from which climate change – and therewith the contribution of population growth to climate change as well – became known to the global public.

> From a moral point of view, it makes no difference whether the commodity in question is a resource or a sink.
> Principles of distributive justice among individuals can be applied just as well to emission distribution rights as to the sharings of other scarce goods (food, water, living space).

Jörg Chet Tremmel

Credit: J. C. Tremmel, (2013), "Climate Change and Political Philosophy: Who Owes What to Whom?," *Environmental Values*, December (with edits by the author). Photo: https://philpeople.org/profiles/jorg-tremmel

FIGURE 8.5.
What is just with regard to climate?

will be imposed by disaster. What might a planned contraction look like? Later in this chapter we will answer this question based on the author's research about Canada as an example of the possibility of a planned contraction of the physical scale of a developed economy.

FIGURE 8.6. Examples of proposals for contraction and convergence.[113]

	Carbon Dioxide Emissions	Ecological Footprint	Energy	Food	Material Footprint
Units	Annual tonnes per capita	Global hectares per capita	GJ per capita primary energy	Percent of daily requirements for 11 food groups	Tonnes per capita
Geographic Scope	All countries	All countries	All countries	Global and 7 regions	All countries
Starting Date	2020	2018	2019	2016	2020
Starting Value(s)	.03 (Nepal) to 4.71 (USA)	0.5 (Yemen) to 14.3 (Qatar)	79	Varies by region	Varies by country
Convergence Target	1	<1.7 (average)	58-74	100%	10 total abiotic resources 2 total biotic resources 5 raw material consumption
Rationale	Remain with global carbon budget	Per capita footprint if global biocapacity allocated equally	Per capita energy threshold for 95% maximum performance across 9 health, economic, & environmental metrics	Meets dietary requirments for good health and environmental sustainability allowing for cultural differences	Based on environmental and social aspects of safe and fair resource use
Target Date	2060	2050	Not specified	2050	2050

Credit: Author. Based on various sources.

Reprising the Limits to Growth

The year 2022 marked the 50th anniversary of *Limits to Growth*,[114] which presented various simulations of the world system out to 2100. One of the key outcomes of the scenarios in this pathbreaking book was overshoot and collapse occurring sometime in the mid-twenty-first century. As the authors explained in their description of the Standard Run: "All variables follow historical values from 1900 to 1970. Food, industrial output, and population grow exponentially until the rapidly diminishing resource base forces a slow down in industrial output. Because of natural delays in the system, both population and pollution continue to increase for some time after the peak of indus-trialization. Population growth is finally halted by a rise in the death rate due to decreased food and medical services." Other runs of the model showed what happens when obstacles to continued growth are removed. They experimented with a greatly increased resource

FIGURE 8.7. Limits to Growth scenarios.

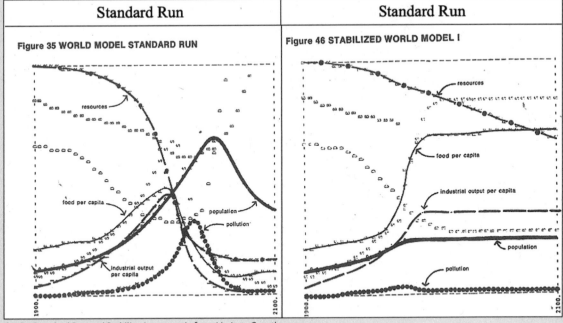

Credit: Standard Run and Stabilization scenario from *Limits to Growth*, (1972), D. Meadows et al., Potomac Associates Press.

base to avoid resource scarcity, technological improvements to avoid resource depletion and pollution problems, increased food yields to feed a growing population, more recycling, and widely accessible birth control. When these changes were introduced one at a time, overshoot and collapse were usually postponed by only a few years. Stabilization of the world system required action on all fronts, which is perhaps the most important message of this seminal contribution to escaping from overshoot.

The authors of *Limits to Growth* certainly did not lack ambition. They sought to understand the world as a single system in terms of its interrelated and interdependent parts and the dynamic relations among them. To do so, they drew on the work of Jay Forrester and other developers of system dynamics. System dynamics is especially useful for analyzing the behavior of systems characterized by positive and negative feedbacks and nonlinear relationships.

FIGURE 8.8. Jay Forrester.

The image of the world around us, which we carry in our head, is just a model. Nobody in his head imagines all the world, government or country. He has only selected concepts, and relationships between them, and uses those to represent the real system.

Jay Forrester 1918-2016

Credit: Photo https://www.technologyreview.com/2015/06/23/167538/the-many -careers-of-jay-forrester/. Quote from J. W. Forrester, (1971), "Counterintuitive behaviour of social systems," *Technological Forecasting and Social Change*, 3, 1–22.

Given the limited availability of global data and the far less powerful computers and software available in the late 1960s and early 1970s, *Limits to Growth* was a remarkable achievement. It gave an unprecedented insight into what might lie ahead at the global level. As noted in Chapter Two, several researchers have since discovered that the experience of the past 50 years has been uncomfortably close to the World Model Standard Run, in which resources are the binding constraint on growth, and even closer to the Double Resources scenario where persistent pollution is the primary cause of overshoot and collapse.

There have been several updates of the original *Limits to Growth*, the most recent being *Earth for All: A Survival Guide for Humanity*.[115]

FIGURE 8.9. Earth4All.

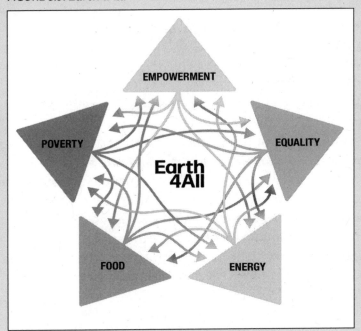

Credit: S. Dixson-Declève et al., (2022), *Earth for All. A Survival Guide for Humanity*, A Report to the Club of Rome, New Society Publishers.

The authors make considerable use of Earth4All, a new global system dynamics simulation model covering the human and natural worlds. "The role of the Earth4All model is to show consistent pictures of possible futures—to help evaluate the potential consequences of various alternative decisions, and to discover which system changes are likely to have a big effect and which are likely to make little impact. The model also gives us an idea of how much these changes will cost and what level of investments are needed to reach a certain level of well-being by a certain time."

The authors of *Earth for All* describe two very different scenarios generated with the Earth4All model: (1) *Too Little, Too Late* and (2) *Giant Leap*. Under *Too Little, Too Late* the economic system is assumed to continue operating much as it has done for the past 50 years. If it does, the model indicates that current trends in reducing poverty, rapid technological innovation, and energy transformation will be insufficient to

FIGURE 8.10.
Five extraordinary
turnarounds in the
Great Leap: key
policy goals.

- **Ending poverty:** *GDP growth rate of at least 5% per year for low- income countries until GDP is greater than $15,000 per person per year; the introduction of new indicators for wellbeing.*
- **Addressing gross inequality:** *The wealthiest 10% take less than 40% of national incomes.*
- **Empowering women:** *Gender equity that will contribute to stabilization of global population below nine billion by 2050.*
- **Making our food system healthy for people and ecosystems:** *Healthy diets for all while protecting soils and ecosystems and not expanding the amount of land, overall, devoted to agriculture; dramatically reducing food waste.*
- **Transitioning to clean energy.** *Halve emissions approximately every decade to reach net-zero emissions by 2050.*

Credit: S. Dixson-Declève et al., (2022), *Earth for All. A Survival Guide for Humanity*, A Report to the Club of Rome, New Society Publishers.

avoid societal collapses and Earth system shocks. "The overall global result is a somewhat slowing population growth and world economic growth to 2050 and beyond, but also declining labour participation rates, declining trust in government, a steady increase in the ecological footprint, and rising loss in biodiversity."

In the *Giant Leap* five "extraordinary turnarounds" are proposed to build a more resilient civilization with a stable global system, more trust, and the elimination of poverty by implementing five key policy goals. These extraordinary turnarounds are all valuable ingredients for an escape from overshoot but are they enough? In *Too Little Too Late*, global average GDP per capita is projected to increase from $6,000 in 1980 (constant 2017 US dollars) to $42,000 per year in 2100, and in *Giant Leap* even higher, to nearly $51,000 per year. In 2020 global average GDP per capita was $16,185 in constant 2017 US dollars. Meanwhile, global population peaks at 8.8 billion in the 2050s in *Too Little Too Late*, and then declines slowly, though to what level is unclear. In *Giant Leap*, global population growth is slower, peaking at around 8.5 billion in 2050 and declining to around six billion in 2100.

The outlook in *Too Little Too Late* is bleak: "The world misses climate targets set out in the Paris agreement. Earth crashes through the 2°C boundary around 2050 and reaches a catastrophic 2.5°C before 2100. It is likely the Earth system will have passed several critical thresholds as a result of the escalating temperature... The losses of the Amazon rainforest get worse every year, as more dries out and becomes savannah. Wildlife is lost, and extinctions of animals and birds accelerate. People have gotten richer, but the natural world is getting grayer year by year through a series of local breakdowns. Civilization has lost its greatest foundation: a stable and resilient earth system."

Giant Leap is more promising. According to the authors it "delivers way more on the sustainable development goals then *Too Little Too Late*, and it does so while bringing the world back within planetary boundaries. The world is far from a utopia, conflicts still erupt, climate disruptions are still causing shocks, and the long-term stability of earth is still deeply uncertain. But much pain and suffering is minimized. Extreme poverty is all but eliminated, and the risk of runaway climate change is diminished."

As an escape from overshoot, the *Giant Leap* falls firmly in the green growth camp. We saw in the previous chapter the implausibility of green growth, especially over the long term. In the *Giant Leap*, global GDP is projected to increase by more than 250 percent between 2020 and 2100. It is hard to see how that could be achieved with a smaller global ecological footprint and lower material and energy throughput than today. Values for the ecological footprint and materials use are not reported in Earth4All, so we cannot tell from the model what happens to the physical scale of the global economy or the constituent ten regional economies in the *Giant Leap* using these measures of scale. But if global economic output is really to increase by such a magnitude to the end of the century, the ecological and material footprints per dollar of output will have to shrink at extraordinarily rapid rates, placing the prospects of a successful escape from overshoot somewhere between possible and preposterous.

The Plausibility and Possibility of a
Planned Contraction of a High-Income Economy

When *Limits to Growth* was published in 1972, people wanted to know what the futures it described would mean for different regions, for individual countries, for sub-national areas, for cities, towns, and villages, and for families and individuals. One of the many improvements in Earth4All compared with the original World3 model used in the *Limits to Growth*, is that it differentiates among regions of the world so that their different circumstances can be considered. But if we want to go into even more detail about national and subnational possibilities for escaping overshoot, then something more is required. For national simulations, two models stand out: LowGrow SFC[116] which has been applied to Canada and EUROGREEN[117] to France. Though designed and implemented independently, they tell rather similar stories about the possible futures for these two high-income economies. Both models include key economic variables and GHG emissions. EUROGREEN represents the economic sectors in more detail than LowGrow SFC, but LowGrow SFC has a more detailed financial sector. The most significant difference between the two models for overshoot is that LowGrow SFC includes material flows and the ecological footprint, making it especially useful for examining possibilities for contraction in high-income economies.[118]

Following in the tradition of *Limits to Growth*, LowGrow SFC is a systems dynamics model. It simulates changes in a wide range of economic, social, and environmental indicators—including GDP, unemployment, public- and private-sector debt, income inequality, work time, GHG emissions, material flows, and the ecological footprint. It does this through the interplay of standard economic factors such as investment in capital, household and government spending, and finance. As well as these demand-side factors, the dynamics of the

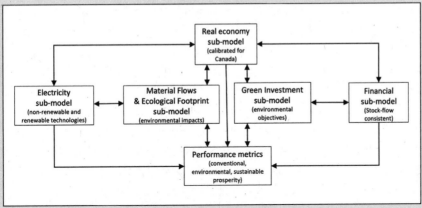

FIGURE 8.11.
LowGrow SFC:
An ecological
macroeconomic
simulation model.

Credit: Author. Based on T. Jackson and P. A. Victor (2020), "The Transition to a Sustainable Prosperity:
A Stock-Flow-Consistent Ecological Macroeconomic Model for Canada," *Ecological Economics*, 177, 106787.

model are determined on the supply side by the relationship between the capital stock and labor productivity.

LowGrow SFC consists of five interconnected sub-models. The *Real Economy* sub-model represents the production of goods and services using labor, capital (buildings, equipment, and infrastructure), materials, and energy. In the *Financial* sub-model, financial flows among the sectors of the economy are tracked, as are their financial assets and financial liabilities. The banking sector creates money by extending loans, subject to capital adequacy requirements set by the central bank. The *Electricity* sub-model captures the shift from fossil fuels to electricity generated from renewable sources to reduce emissions of GHGs. Other sources of GHG emissions are also included in the *Green Investment* sub-model. Green investment is investment in real capital with the primary objective of reducing the environmental impacts of economic activities rather than making a profit. It can be additional or non-additional, and productive or non-productive (see Chapter Six). Finally, the flow of materials through the economy—from extraction to wastes—and the ecological footprint from production are simulated in the *Materials Flows and Ecological Footprint* sub-model.

Models are built for a purpose, and their design is an art as much as a science. Once the purpose is decided, choices must be made about the scope of the model—what to include and what to leave out. Further choices must then be made about what will be determined outside the model (the exogenous variables) and what will be left for the model to determine (the endogenous variables). For example, in LowGrow SFC, population projections published by Statistics Canada are used so population growth is exogenous. Conversely, the rate of economic growth is determined endogenously in the model, based on the ratio of produced capital to labor and other factors. The stock of capital is also determined in the model by investment (endogenous) and the rate of depreciation (exogenous). The structure of LowGrow SFC and relationships among its many variables are informed by theory and statistical analysis taken from a vast literature, and the model is grounded in actual data as far as possible.

To put the LowGrow SFC to work, it is necessary to specify values for key exogenous variables. Different values lead to different scenarios. Here we show the results for two scenarios. The first is a base case, used for comparison with the second, an *Escape* scenario. In the base case, continuing economic growth is combined with existing climate policies by government, such as an escalating carbon price, incentives for emissions reduction from other sources, and progress in switching from fossil fuels to electricity for road and rail transportation. Essentially, the base case retains a commitment to economic growth with the added objective of reducing territorial GHG emissions.

The priority in the *Escape* scenario is to reduce the physical scale of the economy as measured by its material flows and its ecological footprint, and to do so in a fair and equitable manner. There are potentially many combinations of changes that could do this. In the *Escape* scenario described here, GHG emissions are reduced further and faster than in the base case, reaching net zero in 2045 through a higher carbon price, further GHG emissions reduction expenditures by the public and private sectors, and a faster rate of road and rail electrification. To alleviate the burden of adjustment, especially on low-income households, substantial funds are devoted to reducing income

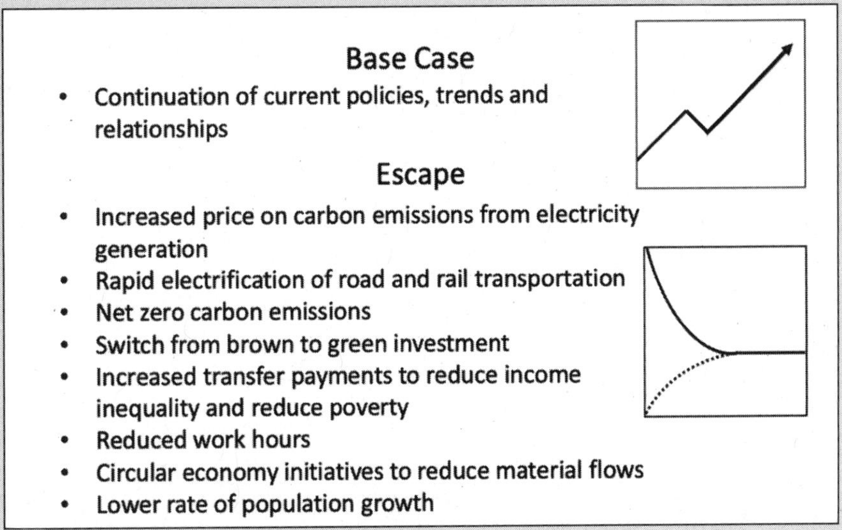

Credit: Author. Based on T. Jackson and P. A. Victor (2020), "The Transition to a Sustainable Prosperity: A Stock-Flow-Consistent Ecological Macroeconomic Model for Canada," *Ecological Economics*, 177, 106787.

FIGURE 8.12.
Two scenarios.

inequality and poverty. A lower rate of population growth is assumed in the *Escape* scenario than in the base case. All changes from the base case begin in 2024 and are phased in over ten years except for the material flow initiatives and reduced work hours which are phased in over 50 years.

The main results of these two scenarios are displayed in a series of graphs for the fifty-year period 2023 to 2073 divided into Figs. 8.13A and B. The six graphs in Fig. 8.13A and first three graphs in Fig. 8.13B show how specific variables are projected to evolve over time under the two scenarios. The bottom two graphs in Fig. 8.13B show the evolution of the net lending positions of the public and private sectors for each scenario.[119] As the last two graphs show, the net lending positions of the private and public sectors in each scenario are mirror images of each other. What one sector lends the other sector borrows, and vice versa.

The differences between the base case and *Escape* scenario in terms of the physical scale of the economy are abundantly clear from the first three graphs. In the base case, material flows and the ecological

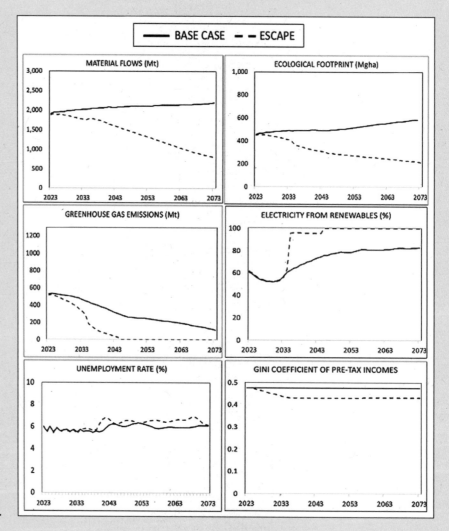

BASE CASE   – – ESCAPE

FIGURE 8.13A.
Two scenarios for
Canada 2023 to 2073.

footprint increase by 15 and 30 percent respectively between 2023 and 2073.[120] If this pattern was to be typical of high-income economies around the world, the environmental and human outcomes would be horrendous, especially for people living in low- and middle-income countries who will be more constrained than ever by materials and ecological scarcities. And although GHG emissions are projected to de-

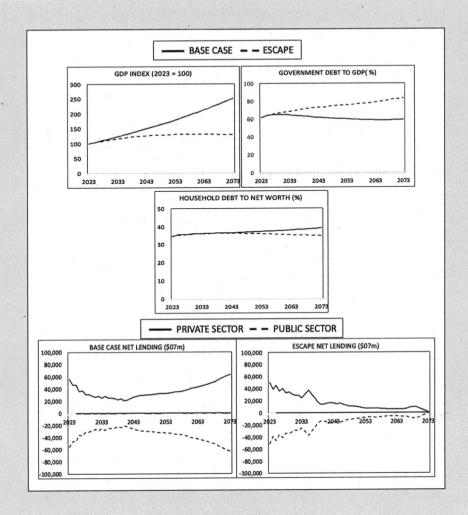

FIGURE 8.13B.
Two scenarios for
Canada 2023 to 2073.

cline in the base case, they do not reach net zero which is required, and soon, if a climate catastrophe is to be avoided. The *Escape* scenario is far superior to the base case on all three of these measures of the physical scale of the economy. The question that naturally follows is, what will contraction mean for the economy and society more generally?

In terms of the futures cone, plausible and possible answers can be found to this question by comparing the base case and *Escape* scenarios. In both, there is a major expansion of electricity production from renewable sources, though only in the *Escape* scenario is there a complete switch to renewables. The unemployment rate in the economy is projected to be similar in both scenarios until about 2050, hovering around six percent. Then the unemployment rate in the *Escape* scenario rises about 0.5% above the base case, a difference that could be moderated by a change in fiscal policy not included in this scenario. One factor that causes differences in the rate of unemployment in the two scenarios is the decline in average work hours in the *Escape* scenario, so that the benefit of increases in labor productivity is reduced working time rather than increased output. This allows work to be shared among a greater number of people, preventing unemployment from increasing very much in the absence of economic growth. In the base case, inequality in the distribution of pre-tax incomes is assumed to be unchanged over the simulation period. In the *Escape* scenario, substantial funds ($60 billion per year in constant 2007 dollars) are allocated to low-income households specifically to reduce income inequality. The difference this makes to the Gini coefficient, a widely used measure of inequality, is considerable, and would hold whatever the actual income distribution turns out to be.

Escape from overshoot is about reducing the physical scale of the economy. What happens to GDP is of secondary importance. In the base case GDP grows steadily, increasing by 150 percent from 2023 to 2073. In the *Escape* scenario, GDP grows at a declining rate until mid-century, after which it stabilizes at about 30 percent higher than in 2023. To be clear, this is not an objective, but simply an outcome of other initiatives included in the *Escape* scenario to reduce material flows, GHG emissions, and the ecological footprint, without significantly affecting employment and reducing inequality. However, the elimination of growth in GDP in the *Escape* scenario increases the ratio of government debt to GDP, even though government borrowing (i.e., negative net lending) is projected to decline to zero by 2073.[121] This compares with the base case, where government borrowing remains substantial through continuous budget deficits, which could be moderated by a change in fiscal policy not included in this scenario. Even so, in the base case, the debt to GDP ratio declines slightly because of the growth in GDP.

There is considerable debate about the significance of the debt to GDP ratio as an indicator of macroeconomic health, especially in countries with their own sovereign currency, and where the national government owns or controls the central bank. Such governments could, if they so wished, provide themselves with funds at no cost.[122] This would make the increased government debt held by the federal government in the *Escape* scenario a problem of little significance. Even so, the absolute level of all government debt is lower in the *Escape* scenario than in the base case, and the debt to GDP ratio is projected to level off at 85 percent, well below levels that have been seen in many countries without serious consequences.

When it comes to household debt and its relation to household net worth (i.e., household assets minus liabilities), in the base case the ratio of household debt to net worth is projected to increase, whereas in the *Escape* scenario it declines. This is largely due to lower consumer spending in the *Escape* scenario and, consequently, reduced credit card and other personal loans, leaving households more financially secure.

The simulation model that generated these scenarios is not detailed enough to reveal implications for various aspects of the economy that a full appraisal of the scenarios would require. For example, some sectors such as waste management will do better than others in the *Escape* scenario in terms of employment opportunities. At the same time, there are likely to be sectors where upskilling will be required for expanded employment opportunities to be realized. We can learn something about these types of issues from related studies of the circular economy and a transition to a net zero carbon economy which are key components of the *Escape* scenario.

Despite their lack of detail, these simulations of alternative paths into the future are useful for assessing the *possibility* of contraction as a way of escaping from overshoot. There is nothing in the *Escape* scenario that suggests that contraction as described here is preposterous. Indeed, all the measures included in LowGrow SFC that define

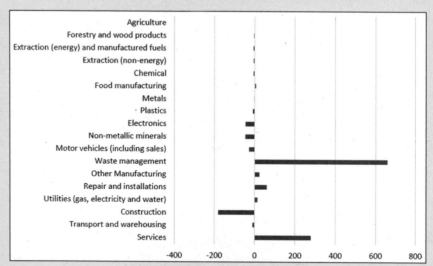

FIGURE 8.14.
Circular economy job impacts across the EU28 sectors in 2030 (thousands).

Credit: European Commission, Directorate-General for Environment, *Impacts of circular economy policies on the labour market: final report and annexes*, Publications Office, 2018 https://data.europa.eu/doi/10.2779/574719.

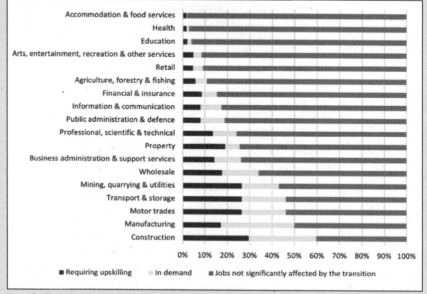

FIGURE 8.15.
Jobs requiring upskilling, jobs in demand, and jobs not significantly affected by the net zero transition, by sector %.

Credit: A. Sudmant, N. Robins, and N.G. Gouldson, (2020), "Tracking Local Employment in the Green Economy: The PCAN Just Transition Jobs Tracker," Place-Based Climate Action Network. https://pcancities.org.uk/tracking-local-employment-green-economy-pcan-just-transition-jobs-tracker

Measure Included In Escape Scenario	Future Cone Rating	Comment
Increased price on carbon emissions from electricity generation	Probable	Carbon price already government policy. Higher levels needed for net zero.
Rapid electrification of road and rail transportation	Probable	Transport electrification underway. Needs accelerating.
Net zero emissions	Plausible	Government target. More measures required.
Switch from brown to green investment	Possible	Financing remains problematic especially on required scale.
Increased transfer payments to reduce income inequality and reduce poverty	Plausible	Increasing inequality is beginning to evoke a response.
Circular economy initiatives to reduce material flows	Probable	Underway but needs acceleration.
Reduced working hours	Plausible	Resumption of long-term trend; likely response to further automation.
Lower rate of population growth	Possible	Fertility rates could decline faster than anticipated.

Complementary Escape Measures	Future Cone Rating	Comment
Better screening of technology	Possible	Difficult to keep up with pace of change.
Education for life, not just work	Plausible	Requires reversal of recent trends.
International debt forgiveness	Possible	Essential for poorest countries to progress.
Limits on materials, energy, wastes, and land use	Plausible	Partially in place, requires considerable expansion.
More efficient capital stock	Probable	Already happening. Will be stimulated by limits on materials, energy, wastes, and land use.
More informative advertising	Possible	Necessary to reduce consumption and increase well-being.
More local, less global	Probable	Being stimulated by rising transport costs and concern about vulnerable supply lines.
More meaningful prices	Plausible	Will come about from the other measures.
New meanings and measures of success	Probable	The focus of work in academia and international organizations. Necessary to divert attention away from GDP growth.
Restructuring of enterprise, work, finance and the money system	Plausible	Necessary for economies focussing on well-being rather than profit.
Stricter controls on the extraction of data from the internet	Plausible	The rise of surveillance capitalism poses a major threat to democracy.

FIGURE 8.16.
Escape scenario measures: a futures cone perspective.

the *Escape* scenario can be reasonably classified as probable, plausible, or possible, and this also applies to a range of complementary escape measures not explicitly included in the model.

Of course, if only one or a few high-income countries pursue this path, global overshoot will only get worse. So, when we look further into contraction and convergence as a possible way of escaping overshoot, we will make the tacit assumption that contraction is being followed in most if not all high-income countries, while poorer countries practice convergence to a level that can be sustained indefinitely on this still wonderful planet. Anything less means failure. So how might we do it? What might life be like in a post growth economy that is escaping from overshoot? These are questions that require a great deal of discussion and debate, and to that end, we offer some initial answers in the final chapter.

9

PLANNING AN ESCAPE
FROM OVERSHOOT

"More than ever, we must face the question: Can the peoples of Earth,
doomed to share a ravaged planet, learn to live together in ways that
encourage our species to flourish in an emergent future?"

— RICHARD FALK[123]

We have the key ingredients for an escape from overshoot, the overall
shape of which needs to be built around some version of contraction
and convergence for environmental and ethical reasons. But a comprehensive plan, should one even be possible given the fractious state of
the world, is beyond us right now. Some look to the UN's Sustainable
Development Goals, endorsed unanimously by 193 countries in 2015, to
provide an overall global framework for ending poverty and pursuing a
sustainable future, but it is far from clear whether they can be reached
simultaneously without a massive realignment of financial and physical resources around the world. That is, without a clear commitment to
contraction and convergence which has yet to be made.

In this chapter I offer some key propositions and policies that might
comprise the beginnings of a plan. We can, of course, learn much from
the various perspectives on post growth described in Chapter Seven
and from other sources too, including this author, who have produced
lists of actions and activities that, while not explicitly about escaping
from overshoot, would, if adopted, move us in the right direction.
Many of these actions and activities have already been implemented
to a varying extent in different countries and jurisdictions, though

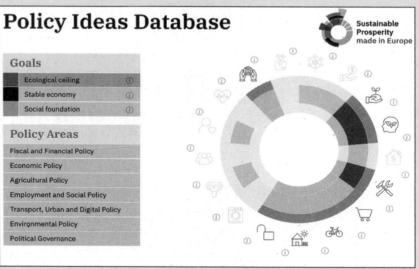

FIGURE 9.1.
Policy ideas
database.

Credit: The Institute for Future-Fit Economies. https://sustainable-prosperity.eu/policy-database/goal/2

not necessarily as part of a post growth agenda. For example: mineral mining and export bans (e.g. El Salvador, Indonesia); oil exploration bans (Greenland, New Zealand, Belize); protected areas (many); managing forests, fishing, agriculture, and groundwater for sustainable yield (many); cap, auction, and trade for GHGs (California and Quebec, EU); ecological tax reform (Germany); progressive taxation (widely used); job guarantee (France, the former Soviet Union); maximum pay differential (Mondragon Corporation, Spain), alternative indicators of progress (Australia, Ecuador, France, Italy, Netherlands, New Zealand, Scotland, Sweden, U.K., United Arab Republics), co-operatives and non-profit businesses (everywhere), universal basic income (many countries and regions); work time reduction (Netherlands, France, Sweden,), and so on.[124]

Policy ideas can be divided into two general categories: reformist and revolutionary. The reformist category takes the basic institutional structure of society as given and offers recommendations for what the institutions that make up this structure—governments, publicly and privately owned businesses, international agencies, labor unions, schools, universities—should do differently. The second category of proposals is more radical. These start from the view that societies as structured today have institutions incapable of being reformed and that other political, social, and economic institutions and arrangements are required to escape from overshoot.

The distinction between reformist and revolutionary approaches should not be overdrawn. What may initially appear to be a reform may have much broader ramifications than originally intended. Even the most revolutionary manifestos include reformist proposals, the Communist Manifesto being a classic example. Its proposals included several measures that have been widely adopted, such as progressive income taxation, free education for all children in public schools, establishment of a central bank, the combination of agriculture with manufacturing industries, the abolition of children's factory labor, the cultivation of waste lands, and the improvement of the soil generally, in accordance with a common plan.

Whether by reformist or revolutionary means, escape from overshoot—if it is to be thoughtfully planned rather than thoughtlessly imposed through failure to change in time—will require a sustained collective effort towards shared objectives at all scales from local to global. Detailed programs of action, which will differ according to time, place, and specific circumstances, will emerge in the process. As a step in this direction, I suggest a set of 14 propositions on which an escape plan could be based. If agreement can be reached on these from local communities to the United Nations, it will make the detailed planning work of who will do what, how, and by when that much easier to accomplish.

Fourteen Propositions for Planning an Escape from Overshoot

1. There is compelling *evidence* that humanity is living in an era of global overshoot.
2. A reduction in the *physical scale* of the human enterprise is essential to escape from overshoot.
3. The historical and current *causes and consequences* of overshoot are extremely unequal within and among countries.

4. Limits on *material and energy throughput* and *land transformation* are critical to an escape from overshoot.

5. *Contraction and convergence* is an appropriate ethical principle for building an escape plan.

6. A planned escape from overshoot requires a *common sense of purpose* such as has been seen in times of war and pandemics.

7. A common sense of purpose should be founded on *principles of justice,* otherwise the escape plan will be compromised by people and institutions seeking their own self-interest rather than working towards shared objectives. These principles of justice should encompass non-human life as well as human.

8. A common sense of purpose is more likely to emerge from forms of *democracy* that combine representation and participation, and which are based on the principle of subsidiarity—that social, political, and environmental issues are best dealt with at the most immediate level consistent with their resolution.

9. Reductions in *population* should be welcomed, planned for, and encouraged through increased measures such as: accessibility to education especially for girls, increased availability of contraception, provision of a basic income and wealth, and better support for the elderly.

10. *Finance* should facilitate the escape from overshoot rather than exacerbate it. To this end, money creation by commercial banks should be curtailed. The *financialization* of nature and the implication that it exists solely to serve human interests, should be halted and reversed.

11. *Technology* does not exist in isolation. It is embodied in materials and requires energy for its production and use. Technologies often have unintended consequences which can be positive and negative. Whether and how technology contributes to the escape from overshoot depends on who owns it and what they seek to obtain from that ownership.

12. *Knowledge and ideas* should be shared as much as possible given that they are non-rival. Exclusion of potential users through intellectual

property rights should be discouraged, especially where it impedes the flow of information, products, and services to low-income countries as happened, for example, during the COVID-19 pandemic.

13. *Capitalism* presents serious obstacles to an escape from overshoot. It serves the interests of the owners of capital, who, through increasingly powerful corporations, are constantly looking for ways to extend their reach, increasing overshoot, and only incidentally serving the interests of other members of society. Experience with *Socialism* has a mixed record in relation to overshoot, having focused on growth almost as much as in capitalism, and it has shown the shortcomings of central planning.

14. *Overshoot will transform economic and political systems.* It is better to choose the transformations we want rather than have them forced upon us by circumstances beyond our control.

Living the Escape from Overshoot

In 1957 John Kenneth Galbraith's *The Affluent Society* caused quite a stir. It showed that, in the immediate post-war period the United States was enjoying unprecedented private wealth at the cost of public squalor. Galbraith illustrated his argument with an account of a family taking a drive in their fancy new car on badly maintained roads, along ugly highways, to camp by a polluted stream. (See Figure 3.9.) A modern version of this might read as follows:

> The parent rises while it is still dark outside to minimize the morning commute, and leaves the children in the care of the foreign nanny whose own children are with their grandmother 3,000 miles away. Ensconced in their self-driving car they join the daily parade of like vehicles, catch up on work, make video calls, then immerse themselves in a virtual world of sunshine and gorgeous landscapes because the real world they are passing through is made ugly by flashing billboards programmed to display ads based on what artificial intelligence has already gleaned from years of surveillance about the occupants of the

FIGURE 9.2.
Autonomous driving.

Credit: Upper image—metamorks/Shutterstock.com. Lower image—Yannick Boussard. https://
gameup24.wordpress.com/2018/01/05/vr-and-self-driving-cars-are-a-fascinating-scary-combo/

cars driving by. Even the views through the windows are synthetic, mere image projections on glass. Arriving at their place
of work they leave the car to park itself and enter a building
where an individual service vehicle whisks them to a cubicle to
spend the day in glorious isolation from any living being, leaving them to wonder if this really is the best of all possible worlds.

Reforms on the Path to Escape

Regulating Emerging Technologies

Galbraith's point, as valid now as when he wrote 65 years ago, is that
modern technology is a mixed blessing. Its environmental impacts
stem from the enormous use of materials that it requires and from the
disruption of time-proven methods without due consideration of prob-

Credits: Morton B/Shutterstock.com, wk1003mike/Shutterstock.com, Aline
Tong/Shutterstock.com, photoagriculture/Shutterstock.com

FIGURE 9.3.
E-waste disposal.

able and possible impacts in advance. For example, the proliferation of electronic equipment in the last few decades brought with it a flood of e-waste that was not anticipated or planned for. Much of this waste is shipped to low-income countries where desperate people are exposed to dangerous contaminants. One feature of the *Escape* scenario is a very substantial increase in reuse, recovery, and recycling so that requirements for virgin materials and waste generation can be reduced absolutely. We know it can be done.

Anticipating the wide range of possible impacts of emerging technologies is not easy. The US attempted it by establishing the Office of Technology Assessment in 1972 for Congress "as an aid in the identification and consideration of existing and probable impacts of technological application..."[125] After producing about 750 reports on a wide range of technology-based issues, the Office was closed in 1995 when Republicans gained majority control of the House of Representatives, on the grounds that major tech decisions should be made by the private

FIGURE 9.4.
Recommendations
for ensuring the
environmental
sustainability
of emerging
technologies.

- Systematize early-stage technology assessments
- Develop methods and tools for prospective life-cycle assessments
- Refine the concept of sustainability-by-design
- Create a value proposition for sustainability
- Work to develop flexible and adaptable regulatory frameworks
- Establish certain guidelines, perhaps in the form of a compass, to indicate the direction to environmental sustainability

Credit: Based on Workshop report of the International Risk Governance Centre (2021), "IRGC Ensuring the Environmental Sustainability of Emerging Technologies Executive Summary."

sector. Now there are calls to restore the Office.[126] In Europe, technology assessment has remained a role for governments, coordinated by the European Parliamentary Technology Assessment network.

Alternative Forms of Provisioning

Much more sharing, both of consumer durables and living quarters catering to entire families, has an important role to play in the escape from overshoot, as do community gardens that provide fresh food and companionship, and makerspaces that give access to tools and training on how to use them. Indeed, these are but components of the broader conception of *provisioning*, which recognizes the much wider range of arrangements that societies use to supply the goods and services on which their members depend. One of the well-known limitations of GDP for measuring the output of goods and services in an economy is the omission of unpaid work. This can be the work undertaken by members of households, still disproportionately women, that is fundamental to the creation and sustenance of the paid work force. It also includes voluntary work, such as that of charities, many of which exist to serve the poorest and weakest members of society when government-funded programs fall short.

Alternative forms of provisioning, especially when combined with a reduced work week, will help shift the work-life balance that, for many in high-income countries, has become too heavily weighted towards

Credits: Monkey Business Images/Shutterstock.com, Zhida Li on unsplash.com

FIGURE 9.5.
Multigenerational housing and community gardening.

work at the expense of life. Increased opportunities for families to spend more time together and for people to participate in community gardens will be important features of the path to Escape.

Local food production, both commercial and voluntary, has much to commend it. It offers improved nutrition, more security of supply, and reduced emissions of GHGs. On a larger scale, the simultaneous existence of obesity, especially in the United States, and

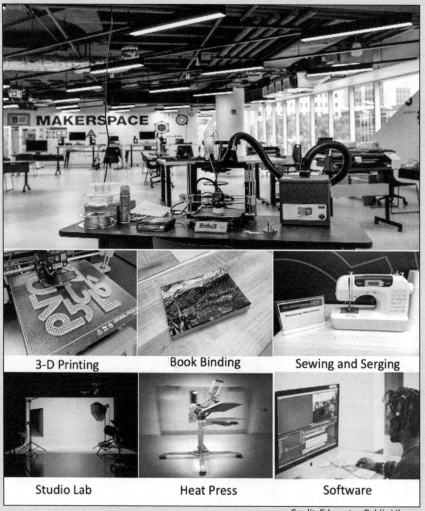

FIGURE 9.6.
Makerspace in a
public library.

under-nourishment in poor countries, notably in Africa, has led to
recommendations for a global diet that is both culturally specific and
environmentally sustainable.[127]

The EAT-Lancet Commission explains that the "planetary health
diet...is largely plant-based but can optionally include modest
amounts of fish, meat and dairy foods."[128] It is designed to optimize

Credit: People Creations.

FIGURE 9.7.
Multigenerational
family picnic.

FIGURE 9.8. Planetary healthy diet.

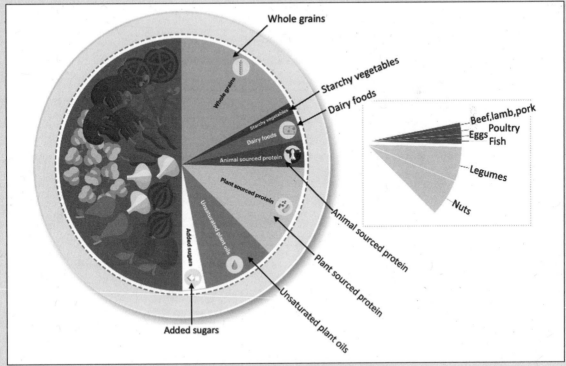

Credit: Summary Report of the EAT-Lancet Commission (2019) available at www.eatforum.org

human health and environmental sustainability on Earth. It will not be easy to transform people's diets and the food systems to support it. The Commission proposes five strategies for a "great food transformation" with a target date of 2050.

Strategy Number	Strategy
1	Seek international and national commitment to shift toward healthy diets
2	Reorient agricultural priorities from producing high quantities of food to producing healthy food
3	Sustainably intensify food production to increase high-quality output
4	Strong and coordinated governance of land and oceans
5	At least halve food losses and waste, in line with the UN Sustainable Development Goals

FIGURE 9.9.
Five strategies for a planetary health diet.

Credit: Summary Report of the EAT-Lancet Commission (2019) available at www.eatforum.org, photo credit-Mollie Katzen

A broader appreciation of how societies provision themselves is important not just as a matter of recognition and fair treatment of those whose contributions to individual and social wellbeing is so important, but also because it opens up possibilities for more resilient communities able to cope with the inevitable stresses and strains of overshoot. Globalization has created an unhealthy overdependence on long, vulnerable supply lines which, when interrupted by harvest failures, pandemics, political and military conflicts, overloaded electrical systems, extreme weather, and the like, can put large numbers of people at risk very quickly. Increased resiliency obtained through a greater variety of provisioning systems involving more localized production, consumption, and distribution via a more balanced combination of market, government, household, and community arrangements, may come at the cost of higher prices and reduced levels of consumption. But it can bring increased security in hard times and a greater sense of wellbeing from people helping each other through direct human relationships that anonymous market transactions make difficult if not impossible. It can also reduce inequality and strengthen democracy, especially at the local level by involving more people in decision making.

FIGURE 9.10. From Earth systems through provisions systems to human wellbeing.

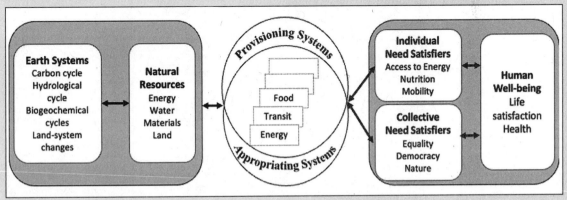

Credit: Based on figure 4 in A. L. Fanning, D. W. O'Neill, and M. Buchs, (2020), "Provisioning systems for a good life within Planetary Boundaries," *Global Environmental Change*, 64, 102135.

Local Currencies

One way of increasing communities' resiliency through increased self-reliance is with the use of local currencies. Local currencies have a long history. They have been introduced in many places around the world with varied success. Typically, they are based in a local area with participating organizations including some or all the farmers, artisans, shops, credit unions, banks, and municipal governments. Local currencies are intended to help meet social and environmental objectives by: democratizing services and organizations (e.g., time credits for volunteer work), supporting small- and medium-sized enterprises by circulating spending power locally, countering inequality and social exclusion by rewarding participation in voluntary programs, and addressing environmental impacts by rewarding changes in behavior.[129]

Local currencies complement the national currency and may not be legal tender. This does not make them illegal. It means only that creditors are not obliged to accept them to settle debts and can insist on being paid in the national currency. Some local currencies, such as

FIGURE 9.11.
Local currencies
around the globe.

Credit: Schumacher Center for a New Economics—Local Currencies Program,
https://centerforneweconomics.org/apply/local-currencies-program/

Berkshares in the USA and Transition Pounds in the UK, are backed by their national currencies, which means that they can be exchanged for the national currency at participating banks and credit unions. This feature increases the willingness of people to accept and use the local currency. Local currencies can also be digital.[130]

In addition to place-based local currencies, there are online community currencies that people sharing a common interest can use to conduct transactions.

Checking the Power of Rentiers

It is a matter of bookkeeping that the GDP of an economy is equal to the sum of incomes paid and received (excluding government-financed transfer payments which move income from one person to another and do not correspond to new production). The system of national accounts, from which both GDP and national income are obtained, makes no judgment about whether a dollar earned or spent by a poor person produces more wellbeing than a dollar spent by a rich person. Likewise, it makes no ethical distinction according to how income is earned, providing it is legal. If it is not it is excluded from the accounts. However, the increasing income and wealth inequities of the past decades have led to a reaction against this agnosticism, especially regarding economic rent. Economic rent is the amount paid to owners of land, capital, information, and labor in excess of the cost of making them available for use. Rent in this sense is "an economic reward which is sustained through control of assets that cannot be quickly and widely replaced, and which exceeds proportionate compensation for the labour of the recipient."[131] Corporations with considerable market power receive economic rent when they charge prices above the level that would prevail under competition. The political economist Beth Stratford argues that "unless we close opportunities for rent extraction, and socialize unavoidable rents, our governments will be compelled to pursue output growth, regardless of its environmental consequences, in order to prevent spiraling inequality and unemployment." Consequently, an escape from overshoot requires not only a

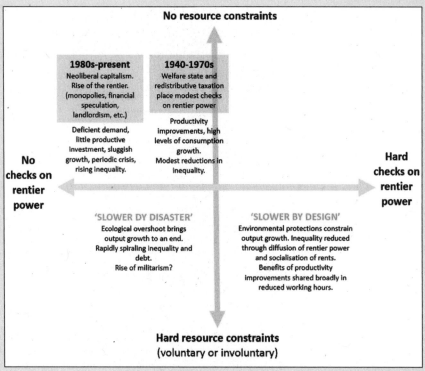

FIGURE 9.12.
Resource constraints and rentier power.

Credit: B. Stratford (2020), "The Threat of Rent Extraction in a Resource Constrained Future," *Ecological Economics*, 169, 106524.

broader conception and rebalancing of provisioning systems; it also requires containment of the appropriating systems that privilege the few at the expense of the many.

Aiming for Satisfaction

How we spend our time has a great bearing on the satisfaction we derive from our lives. It can also have very different impacts on the environment. Amy Isham and Tim Jackson[132] start from the observation that materialistic lifestyles are associated with poor outcomes for personal and planetary wellbeing. Then they use the concept of "flow"— the positive experience of being totally absorbed in an activity—to show that flow experiences are linked to higher levels of human well-

FIGURE 9.13. Finding flow.

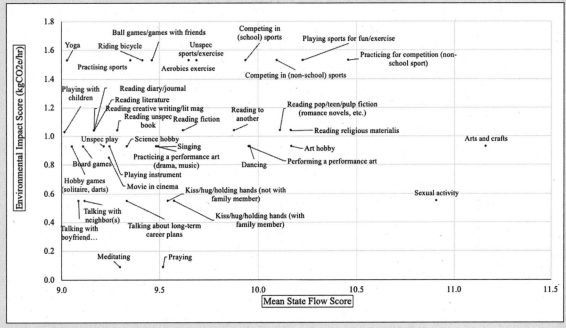

Credit: A. Isham T. Jackson, (2022), "Finding Flow: Exploring the potential for sustainable fulfillment," *Lancet Planet Health*, 6, e66–e74

being and lower levels of environmental costs. This finding, which is consistent with similar observations in the *World Happiness Reports* (see Chapter Five), suggests the very real prospect of improved human wellbeing and much reduced human impacts on the environment. A substantial reduction in material and energy throughput in rich economies is not only possible without economic collapse, but, done well, can enhance the quality of life by strengthening community, increasing security, and expanding the possibilities for a worthwhile and fulfilling life.

All these aspects and more of a successful escape from overshoot will require widespread citizen involvement in the search for solutions. One example of putting this into practice comes from the communities, cities, and governments worldwide that are collaborating with Doughnut Economics Action Lab (DEAL)[133] to transform their local economies. Participants work with change makers and encourage them to adopt and implement concepts from Doughnut Economics. The focus is on action, and on reciprocal learning through experiments in "co-creating a new economy." DEAL's approach to transformative change is to reframe the narrative landscape, influence the policy regime, and collaborate with innovators. In a very short time, DEAL has established a presence in many parts of the world working in five thematic areas: cities and places, communities and art, education and research, business and enterprise, and government and policy.

Conclusion

Finding an escape from overshoot will not be easy, as we can see from the dismal lack of progress in dealing with the excessive and still rising emission of greenhouse gases and the general degradation of the global environment. However, we have outlined some of the main elements of a possible escape plan.

First, we need to understand what we are escaping from. The answer is the multifaceted aspects of overshoot outlined in Chapter

FIGURE 9.14. Doughnut Economy peer-to-peer learning workshop.

Credit: I. Kaur, CIVIC SQUARE, in Raworth (*Doughnut Economics* 2022 edition)

One. As degrowthers and eco-socialists remind us, the imperatives of growth built into capitalism and its institutions may only be overcome by escaping from capitalism itself (though others, such as proponents of the regenerative economy and circular economy, contest this view).

Second, we need to have an idea of our desired destination. In the most general terms, we can describe this as a steady-state economy (defined in physical terms) within planetary boundaries that is conducive to human and non-human wellbeing. This is as much a moral, ethical, social, and political challenge as it is an economic one.

Third, we need a path to get us there. Contraction and convergence is one such path. It calls for substantial and speedy reductions in the physical scale of the economies in high-income countries, allowing for a temporary expansion of the poorest economies, until the human use of biocapacity and human-made artifacts is far more equitable than today.

Fourth, an escape plan needs resources. The efforts of those engaged in post growth work is to be applauded but it is only the beginning and must be multiplied many times. The activities of government leaders such as the members of WEGo,[134] a collaboration of national and regional governments who have adopted the language of wellbeing, and organizations such as the OECD, that have begun working on alternative measures of success, suggest more resources may become available. An acceleration of these efforts is essential as are those of some in the private sector who, aware of overshoot, are looking for business opportunities.

Fifth, obstacles to an escape from overshoot must be understood, confronted, and overcome. This is principally the gross inequality in the distribution of income and wealth within and among nations, and the maldistribution of political power and influence that is both its cause and effect.

In this book I have addressed the pressing problem of overshoot mainly from the perspective of economics. I've done so in the belief that the economy, in all its aspects, is at the heart of the problem. Decisions about what and how to produce and consume are intimately related to material and energy throughput and land transformation.

These decisions must be changed intentionally to escape from overshoot by design, not disaster. In addition to stressing economics over other valuable sources of insight from politics, sociology, and psychology, I have been quite selective in what to include—the focus on rich countries being the most obvious. My justification for this choice, apart from limitations of space and expertise, is that the rich countries are where change is most urgent. Though insufficient on its own for the world to escape from overshoot, if rich countries take the lead, possibilities for poorer countries will open up and they may be induced to rethink their own priorities.

Faced with overshoot, a problem of such magnitude that we may feel helpless before it, the temptation to deny the problem is hard to resist. This has been the record with acid rain, depletion of the ozone layer, and, of course, climate change, plus many other problems. After the initial denial comes the admission there may be a problem, but nothing can be done about it. Then we are told by those responsible for the problem, that something can be done but not by them, or that it is too expensive, or both. Finally, if we are fortunate, the problem is recognized, remedies are found, and action taken, but if this process takes too long and tipping points have been passed, it can bring irreversible, far-reaching, adverse consequences.

If you accept the main line of argument of this book, it raises the question: What can I do about overshoot? There is no one answer. Each of us must decide how best to use our talents, interests, and resources to help find an escape. Individual actions have their place. Changing our diets, shifting transportation modes, growing some of our own food—they can all help, but that can only go so far. We can decide individually whether to drive a private car or take public transit, if that choice is available, but only collectively through government do we decide whether to build highways or transit, hospitals or armaments, protect nature, or phase out fossil fuels altogether. The same is true when it comes to doing something about poverty. We can make individual charitable donations, but a comprehensive anti-poverty program involves changing the tax and transfer system, which requires political decisions. Fortunately, we do not have to choose between acting alone or acting together. Very often, they complement each other. Belonging to a group can strengthen our resolve to change our own behavior. It can be more rewarding too—being part of something bigger than ourselves and knowing that much more can be achieved if we act together.

I bring this book to a close with a reminder that the convenience of treating the economy as an isolated system comes at the cost of neglecting its deep connections to the rest of society, of overlooking the economy's total dependence on the Earth for materials and their disposal and on the life-giving solar energy from the sun. The economy is about much more than a system of markets. Societies provision

FIGURE 9.15.
San Francisco youth climate strike March 15, 2019.

Credit: Intothewoods7, https://commons.wikimedia.org/wiki/File:San _Francisco_Youth_Climate_Strike_-_March_15,_2019_-_33.jpg

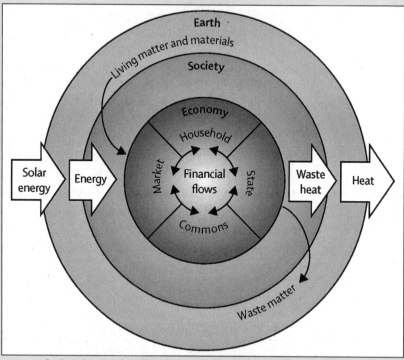

**FIGURE 9.16.
The embedded
economy.**

Credit: K. Raworth, (2017). Original graphic design by M. Mihotich. This version from S. Mair,
(2020), "Neoliberal economics, planetary health, and the COVID-19 pandemic: A Marxist
ecofeminist analysis," *The Lancet Planetary Health* 4, 12, e588–e596, December

themselves through a combination of households, markets, commons, and the state. For the past two centuries these institutions have, to a greater or lesser degree, worked for the common cause of growth. Their respective roles will have to be rethought, reconsidered, and re-evaluated if we and those who come after us are to escape from overshoot.

Notes

1. Rafferty, J. P. "Just How Old Is Homo sapiens?," https://www.britannica
   .com/story/just-how-old-is-homo-sapiens.
2. Roser, M., Ritchie, H., and Ortiz-Ospina, E. (2013), Our World in Data,
   https://ourworldindata.org/world-population-growth.
3. Throughout this book the biosphere is understood as the portion of
   planet Earth that is part of the biological cycle (i.e., biological processes
   that comprise life). The biosphere includes air, land, water, and portions
   of the Earth's crust that contain mineral deposits on which human
   economies depend.
4. George, H. (1879), *Poverty and Progress*, D. Appleton and Company.
5. Speech to the Economic and Social Council of the United Nations,
   Geneva, July 9, 1965.
6. Wackernagel, M. and Rees, W. (1996), *Our Ecological Footprint*, New
   Society Publishers.
7. Global Footprint Network, https://www.footprintnetwork.org/.
8. See, for example, "What is agroecology?" Soil Association. https://
   www.soilassociation.org/causes-campaigns/a-ten-year-transition
   -to-agroecology/what-is-agroecology/ and FAO (nd), *The 10 Elements of
   Agroecology*, https://www.fao.org/3/i9037en/i9037en.pdf.
9. See Global Footprint Network, City and Regional Work, https://www
   .footprintnetwork.org/our-work/cities/.
10. See Global Footprint Network, "What is Your Ecological Footprint?"
    https://www.footprintcalculator.org.
11. Rockström, J. et al. (2009), "Planetary Boundaries: Exploring the Safe
    Operating Space for Humanity," *Energy and Society*, 14, 2.
12. NASA, "The Effects of Climate Change," https://climate.nasa.gov/effects/.
13. Woods Hole Oceanographic Institution, "Ocean Acidification," https://
    www.whoi.edu/know-your-ocean/ocean-topics/how-the-ocean-works
    /-ocean-chemistry/ocean-acidification/.
14. Steffen, W. et al. (2015), "Planetary boundaries: Guiding human develop-
    ment on a changing planet," *Science*, 347 (6223), 1259855. Figures based
    on Persson, L. et al., "Outside the Safe Operating Space of the Planetary
    Boundary for Novel Entities', Environ. Sci. Technol. 56, 1510–1521."

15. Krausmann, F. et al. (2018), "From resource extraction to outflows of wastes and emissions: The socioeconomic metabolism of the global economy, 1900–2015," *Global Environmental Change*, 52, 131–140.

16. Krausmann et al, (2017), 'Global socioeconomic material stocks rise 23-fold over the 20th century and require half of annual resource use', PNAS, 114,8, 1880–1805.

17. FAO and UNEP (2020), The State of the World's Forests 2020. Forests, Bbiodiversity and People. Rome, https://doi.org/10.4060/ca8642en.

18. World Wildlife Fund, "Soil Erosion and Degradation," https://www .worldwildlife.org/threats/soil-erosion-and-degradation.

19. Hasell, J. (2018), "Does population growth lead to hunger and famine?," Our World in Data, April 03, https://ourworldindata.org/population -growth-and-famines.

20. The Associated Press (2022), "Record number of people worldwide are moving toward starvation, U.N. warns," July 7, https://www.npr.org /2022/07/07/1110219180/record-number-of-people-worldwide-are -moving-toward-starvation-u-n-warns.

21. Dasgupta, P. (2021), *The Economics of Biodiversity: The Dasgupta Review*, Abridged Version, London: H.M. Treasury.

22. Kolbert, E. (2014), *The Sixth Extinction: An Unnatural History*, Henry Holt and Company.

23. van der Sluijs, J. P. and Vaage, N. S. (2016), "Pollinators and Global Food Security: the Need for Holistic Global Stewardship," *Food Ethics* 1, 75–91.

24. Clarke, A. C. (1962), *Profiles of the Future*, The Camelot Press.

25. Voros, J. (2017), "The Futures Cone, use and history," The Voroscope, 24 Feb, https://thevoroscope.com/2017/02/24/the-futures-cone-use-and -history/.

26. Meadows, D. et al. (1972), *Limits to Growth*, Potomac Associates Press.

27. Turner, G. (2014), "Is Global Collapse Imminent? An Updated Comparison of The Limits to Growth with Historical Data," Research Paper No. 4, August, Melbourne Sustainable Society Institute.

28. Herrington, G. (2021), "Update to limits to growth," *Journal of Industrial Ecology*, 25, 614–626.

29. Keynes, J. M. (1936), *The General Theory of Employment, Interest, and Money*, Macmillan and Company.

30. Smil, V. (2022), *How the World Really Works*, Viking.

31. Lewis, W. A. (1955), *The Theory of Economic Growth*, Routledge.

32. Mill, J. S. (1848), *Principles of Political Economy*, John W. Parker.

33. Marx, K. (1887), *Capital. A Critique of Political Economy, Volume 1*, Lawrence & Wishart.

34. Jevons, W. S. (1865), *The Coal Question*, Macmillan and Co.

35. Marshall, A. (1920), *Principles of Economics, 8th edition*, Macmillan and Co.

36. Schumacher, E. F. (1973), *Small is Beautiful*, Blond & Briggs.

37. Veblen, T. (1899), *The Theory of the Leisure Class*, Macmillan and Co.

38. Keynes, J. M. (1930), "Economic Possibilities for Our Grandchildren," *Essays in Persuasion*, W.W. Norton & Co.

39. Galbraith, J. K. (1958), *The Affluent Society*, Houghton Mifflin.

40. Pigou, A. C. (1920), *The Economics of Welfare*, Macmillan and Co.

41. Dales, J. (1968), *Pollution, Property, and Prices*, University of Toronto Press.

42. Kapp, K. W. (1950), *The Social Costs of Private Enterprise*, Harvard University Press.

43. Leontief, W. (1970), "Environmental Repercussions and the Economic Structure: An Input-Output Approach," *Review of Economics and Statistics*, II, 262–271.

44. Ayres, R. U. and Kneese, A. V. (1969), "Production, Consumption and Externalities," *The American Economic Review*, 59 (3), 282–297 added materials balance to the theoretical model of a multi-marker economy; Victor, P. A. (1972, 2017) *Pollution: Economy and Environment*, Allen & Unwin, added materials balance to input-output analysis and applied it empirically to a national economy.

45. Soddy, F. (1922), *Cartesian Economics, The Bearing of Physical Science upon State Stewardship*, Hendersons.

46. Boulding K. E. (1966), "Economics of the Coming Spaceship Earth," in *Environmental Quality in a Growing Economy: Essays from the Sixth RFF Forum*. Jarrett H., Ed.: 3–14. Johns Hopkins Press.

47. Georgescu-Roegen, N. (1971), *The Entropy Law and the Economic Process*, Harvard University Press.

48. Daly, H. E. ed. (1973), *Introduction to Toward a Steady-State Economy*, W. H. Freeman. For a comprehensive account of Daly's work see Victor, P. A. (2022), *Herman Daly's Economics for a Full World. His Life and Ideas*, Routledge.

49. Kuznets, S. (1934), National Income, 1929–1932, Senate document no. 124, 73rd Congress, 2nd session.

50. Kennedy, R. F. (1968), Remarks at the University of Kansas, March 8.

51. National Ocean Service, "What is the EEZ?" https://oceanservice.noaa.gov /facts/eez.html.

52. For an accessible, comprehensive account of economic instruments for environmental protection in practice see "Ensuring that polluters pay - toolkit," European Commission https://environment.ec.europa.eu /-economy-and-finance/ensuring-polluters-pay_en.

53. *The Economist.* Economics A-Z terms https://www.economist.com/economics-a-to-z/f#node-21529900.

54. Keynes, J. M. (1936), *The General Theory of Employment, Interest, and Money*, Macmillan.

55. Unless, as in the USA, they are incarcerated. https://www.theguardian.com/us-news/2022/jun/15/us-prison-workers-low-wages-exploited.

56. Zuboff, S. (2019), *The Age of Surveillance Capitalism*, Public Affairs.

57. Real GDP removes inflation (changes in prices) from the measurement of GDP, so that it more accurately measures changes in the output of goods and services over time. Real GDP is shown as GDP in the dollars of a particular year, i.e., what it would have cost in prices prevailing in that year to buy all the goods and services produced in that year.

58. GDP is the total market value of all finished goods and services produced within a country in a set time period. GNI is the total income received by the country from its residents and businesses regardless of whether they are located in the country or abroad...The two number are not significantly different. https://www.investopedia.com/terms/g/gross-national-income-gni.asp.

59. For example, the Breakthrough Institute: https://thebreakthrough.org/es.

60. World Inequality Lab (2018), 4.1 "Global Wealth Inequality: Trends and Projections," World Inequality Report 2018, https://wir2018.wid.world/part-4.html.

61. OECD (2015), "GDP, population and consumption," in Environment at a Glance 2015: OECD Indicators, OECD Publishing. DOI: https://doi.org/10.1787/9789264235199-23-en.

62. Carr, S. (2021), "How Many Ads Do We See A Day in 2022?," LUNIO, 15 February https://ppcprotect.com/blog/strategy/how-many-ads-do-we-see-a-day/.

63. See the New Dream website: "We envision a world in which the values that enhance well-being—relationships, service to others, spending time in nature, community building, and personal growth—are the primary drivers of societal behavior, resulting in reduced consumption and a healthier planet." https://newdream.org/about-us.

64. Helliwell J. et al. (eds), "Measuring and Explaining Differences in Life Evaluations," World Happiness Report 2020, Sustainable Development Solutions Network.

65. Georgiev, D. (2022), "How Much Time Does the Average American Spend on Their Phone in 2022?," techjury, 26 July, https://techjury.net/blog/how-much-time-does-the-average-american-spend-on-their-phone/.

66. Wikipedia contributors (2022), "Transistor count," Wikipedia, https://en.wikipedia.org/wiki/Transistor_count.

67. Carson, R. (1962), *Silent Spring*, Houghton Millflin.

68. Wikipedia contributors (2022), "DDT," Wikipedia, https://en.wikipedia.org/wiki/DDT.

69. Atherton, K. D. (2017), "Mining Monster," May/June, *Popular Science*.

70. Wikipedia contributors (2021), "Universe-class container ship," Wikipedia, https://en.wikipedia.org/wiki/Universe-class_container_ship.

71. Ritchie, H., Roser, M., and Rosado, P. (2020), "Energy," Published online at OurWorldInData.org, https://ourworldindata.org/energy.

72. Smil, V., (2022), *How the World Really Works*, Viking.

73. Total material requirements is a comprehensive measure of materials: direct, indirect, and hidden. See Watarir et al., 2019 for details.

74. Hall, C. A. S., Lambert, J. G., and Balogh, S. B. (2014), "EROI of different fuels and the implications for society," *Energy Policy*, 64, 141–152.

75. Chiraboga, G. et al. (2020), "Energy Return on Investment (EROI) and Life Cycle Analysis (LCA) of biofuels in Ecuador," *Heliyon*, 20 June, e04213.

76. Brockway, P. E. et al. (2019) "Estimation of global final-stage energy-return-on-investment for fossil fuels with comparison to renewable energy sources," *nature energy*, 4, 612–621.

77. Fizaine, F. and Court, C. (2016), "Energy expenditure, economic growth, and the minimum EROI of society," *Energy Policy*, 95, 172–186.

78. Our World In Data, https://ourworldindata.org/search?q=ghg+emissions.

79. Because one rate is less than zero and the other is greater than zero this condition for an absolute reduction in emissions is not quite exact, but at low rates of change the approximation is very close.

80. IPCC (2018), Masson-Delmonte, V. et al, "Summary for Policy Makers," in "Global Warming of 1.5°C. An IPCC Special Report on the impacts of global warming of 1.5°C above pre-industrial levels and related global greenhouse gas emission pathways, in the context of strengthening the global response to the threat of climate change, sustainable development, and efforts to eradicate poverty," Cambridge University Press.

81. IPCC (2021), "Summary for Policymakers," in *Climate Change 2021: The Physical Science Basis*. Contribution of Working Group I to the Sixth Assessment Report of the Intergovernmental Panel on Climate Change, Masson-Delmotte, V. et al. Cambridge University Press. https://www.ipcc.ch/report/ar6/wg1/downloads/report/IPCC_AR6_WGI_SPM.pdf.

82. European Environmental Bureau, "Decoupling Debunked," https://eeb.org/library/decoupling-debunked/.

83. Daly, H. E. (1991), *Steady-State Economics, 2nd edition*, Island Press.

84. Daly, H. E. (2008), "Towards a Steady-State Economy." Essay commissioned by the Sustainable Development Commission, UK (24 April).

85. Ellen MacArthur Foundation (no date), "Circular Economy Introduction," https://ellenmacarthurfoundation.org/topics/circular-economy-introduction/overview.

86. The Expert Panel on the Circular Economy in Canada (2021), *Turning Point*, Canadian Council of Academies, Ottawa, https://cca-reports.ca/-reports/the-circular-economy-in-canada/.

87. Eurostat (2021), "EU'S circular material use rate increased in 2020," https://ec.europa.eu/eurostat/web/products-eurostat-news/-/ddn-20211125-1

88. Janoo, A. et al., (2021), Wellbeing Economy Policy Design Guide, Wellbeing Economy Alliance, https://justeconomyinstitute.org/wp-content/uploads/2021/09/Wellbeing-Economy-Policy-Design-Guide_Mar17_2021.pdf.

89. Wellbeing Economy Alliance, https://weall.org/wego.

90. Daly, H. E. and Cobb, J. (1994), *For the Common Good: Redirecting the Economy Toward Community*, and *A Sustainable Future*, 2nd edition, Beacon Press.

91. https://doughnuteconomics.org/about-doughnut-economics.

92. O'Neill, D. W. et al. (2018), "A Good Life for All within Planetary Boundaries," *Nature Sustainability* 1,2.

93. Hickel, J. (2018), "Is it possible to achieve a good life for all within planetary boundaries?", *Third World Quarterly*, 40, 1, 1–18. Ward, J., et al. (2016) "Is Decoupling GDP Growth from Environmental impact Possible?" *PloS One* 11, 10.

94. The horizontal axis shows the average biophysical impact with respect to planetary boundaries with the boundary as 1. The vertical axis shows the achievement of the resource intensive social indicators (e.g., access to energy), with respect to social thresholds, with achievement shown as 1. No country has a social achievement score of 1 and a biophysical impact score of 1 or less. Some middle-income countries come closest. See Hickel (2018) for more detail.

95. Fullerton, J. (2015), *Regenerative Capitalism: How Universal Principles and Patterns Will Shape Our New Economy*, Capital Institute.

96. Hickel, J. (2020), "What does degrowth mean? A few points of clarification," Globalizations, 18,7,1105–1111.

97. Kallis,G. (2018), *Degrowth*, Agenda Publishing.

98. Trainer, T. (2021), "What does Degrowth mean? Some comments on Jason Hickel's 'A few points of clarification'," *Globalizations*, 18,7,1112–1116.

99. Kovel, J. and Lowy, M., (2001), "An Ecosocialist Manifesto", http://environment-ecology.com/political-ecology/436-an-ecosocialist-manifesto.html.

100. Jackson, T. (2017), *Prosperity without Growth: Foundations for the Economy of Tomorrow*, 2nd edition, Routledge; and Jackson (2021) *Post Growth: Life after Capitalism*, Polity.

101. https://www.postgrowth.org.
102. Ritchie, H. and Roser, M. (2021), "Mammals." https://ourworldindata.org /-mammals.
103. See, for example, Kaiser, C. F. and Vendrik, C. M. (2018), "Different Versions of the Easterlin Paradox: New Evidence for European Countries," Discussion Paper 11994, IZA Institute of Labor Economics.
104. United Nations Commission on Climate Change (1992), United Nations.
105. UNCCC (1992), "United Nations Framework Convention on Climate Change," United Nations.
106. Climate Change 2022: Impacts, Adaptation and Vulnerability. Working Group II Contribution to the IPCC Sixth Assessment Report.
107. Hickel, J. et al., (2022), "Imperialist Appropriation in the World Economy: Drain from the Global South through Unequal Exchange, 1990 to 2015," *Global Environmental Change*, Vol. 73, March 2022.
108. IPCC (2021), Masson-Delmotte, V. et al., "Summary for Policymakers." in Climate Change (2021), "The Physical Science Basis. Contribution of Working Group I to the Sixth Assessment Report of the Intergovernmental Panel on Climate Change," Cambridge University Press.
109. "The term 'carbon budget' refers to the maximum amount of cumulative net global anthropogenic CO_2 emissions that would result in limiting global warming to a given level with a given probability, taking into account the effect of other anthropogenic climate forcers. This is referred to as the total carbon budget when expressed starting from the pre-industrial period, and as the remaining carbon budget when expressed from a recent specified date. Historical cumulative CO_2 emissions determine to a large degree warming to date, while future emissions cause future additional warming. The remaining carbon budget indicates how much CO_2 could still be emitted while keeping warming below a specific temperature level." (IPCC 2021 Summary for Policy Makers, p. 28.)
110. CBAT is calibrated in tonnes of carbon rather than tonnes of CO_2. One tonne of carbon is equivalent to 3.66 tonnes of CO_2.
111. Akenji et al. propose a convergence target of 0.7 tCO_2 per person per year by 2050 to stay within the 1.5-degree temperature increase of the Paris Agreement. See Akenji, L. (2021), *1.5 Degree Lifestyles: Towards a Fair Consumption Space for All*, Hot or Cool Institute, Berlin.
112. Tremmel, J., (2103), "Climate Change and Political Philosophy: Who Owes What to Whom?," *Environmental Values*, 22, December, 725–749.
113. Sources: Carbon dioxide emissions: CBAT (no date). Ecological footprint: Kitzes, J. et al, (2008), "Shrink and share: humanity's present and future Ecological Footprint," *Philosophical Transactions*, R. Soc. B, 363, 467–475 and Global Footprint Network (2002) https://data.footprintnetwork

.org/#/. Energy: Jackson, R. B et al. (2022), "Human well-being and per capita energy use," *Ecosphere*, 13, 4, e3978. Food: Willett, W. et al. (2019), "Food in the Anthropocene: The Eat-Lancet Commission on healthy diets from sustainable food systems," *Lancet*, 393, 447–492. Material footprint: Bingezu, S., "Possible Target Corridor for Sustainable Use of Global Material Resources," Resources, 4.

114. Meadows, D. et al. (1972), *Limits to Growth*, Potomac Associates Press.

115. Dixson-Declève, S. et al. (2022), *Earth for All: A Survival Guide for Humanity*, New Society Publishers.

116. Jackson, T. and Victor, P. A. (2020), "The Transition to a Sustainable Prosperity - A Stock-Flow-Consistent Ecological Macroeconomic Model for Canada," Ecological Economics, 177, 106787. SFC stands for "stock-flow consistent" which is a distinctive feature of the model. It means that all financial transactions among economic sectors are tracked and that all financial liabilities are exactly matched by corresponding financial credits.

117. D'Alessandro, S. et al., (2020), "Feasible alternatives to green growth," *Nature Sustainability*, 3, 329–335.

118. Material throughput and the ecological footprint were added to LowGrow SFC by the author after publication of the paper by Jackson and Victor (2020).

119. Net lending is the difference between what is loaned and borrowed. It is positive if funds loaned exceed funds borrowed, and negative if funds borrowed exceed funds loaned.

120. Material flows are defined as "the total mass of resource flows caused by economic and non-economic activities such as waste rock disposal, as well as direct and indirect flows from economic activities." Watari, T. et al., Supplementary Material for "Total Material Requirement for the Global Energy Transition to 2050: A focus on transport and electricity," *Resources, Conservation & Recycling*, 148, 91–103.

121. Government debt includes the debt of all three levels of government in Canada: federal, provincial, and municipal.

122. Kelton, S. (2020), *The Deficit Myth*, PublicAffairs.

123. Falk, R. (2021), "Global Solidarity: Toward a Politics of Impossibility," opening essay for GTI Forum "Can Human Solidarity Globalize?," Great Transition Initiative (August), https://greattransition.org/gti-forum/global-solidarity-falk.

124. For a comprehensive database of policy ideas directed at overcoming overshoot and supporting the basic foundations of society see the Policy Ideas Database created by Sustainable Prosperity, https://sustainable-prosperity.eu/policy-database/.

125. US PUBLIC LAW 92-484-OCT. 13, 1972.

126. West, D. M. (2021), "It is time to restore the US Office of Technology Assessment," Brookings, Feb. 10, www.brookings.edu/research/it-is -time-to-restore-the-us-office-of-technology-assessment/.

127. Willett, W. et al. (2019), "Food in the Anthropocene: The Eat-Lancet Commission on healthy diets from sustainable food systems," *Lancet*, 393, 447–492. Material footprint: Bingezu, S., "Possible Target Corridor for Sustainable Use of Global Material Resources," *Resources*, 4.

128. Willet et al. (2019), Summary Report p.11.

129. Community Currencies in Action (2015), People Powered Money, https:// neweconomics.org/uploads/files/0dba46d13aa81f0fe3_zhm62ipns.pdf.

130. Brinker, A. (2022), "A local currency in the Berkshires is going digital," *The Boston Globe*, 9 August, www.bostonglobe.com/2022/08/09/business /local-currency-berkshires-is-going-digital/.

131. Stratford, B. (2020), "The Threat of Rent Extraction in a Resource-constrained Future," *Ecological Economics*, 169, 106524.

132. Isham, A. and Jackson, T. (2022), "Finding Flow: exploring the potential for sustainable fulfilment," *Lancet Planet Health*, 6, e66–e74

133. https://doughnuteconomics.org/about.

134. Wellbeing Economy Alliance https://weall.org/wego.

Index

About the Author

PETER A. VICTOR is Professor Emeritus at York University. He was awarded a PhD in economics from the University of British Columbia in 1971 and has worked for 50 years in Canada and abroad as an academic, consultant, and public servant specializing in ecological economics and alternatives to economic growth. Peter sits on the Honorary Board of the David Suzuki Foundation and the Circle of Ecological Economics Elders, is chair of the Science Advisory Committee of the Footprint Data Foundation, and is an elected member of the Royal Society of Canada. He was the recipient of the Molson Prize in the Social Sciences from the Canada Council for the Arts in 2011 and the Boulding Memorial Prize from the International Society for Ecological Economics in 2014. He is the author of six previous books, including *Managing without Growth*. He lives in Toronto, Ontario.

Thank-you for purchasing this print book and supporting the author and independent publishing. To enrich your experience, you can download a free color edition of the ebook at the following link. However we'd kindly ask you not to share this link, thereby continuing to ensure the viability of our publishing as we work together to build a new society.

https://newsociety.com/pages/escape-from-overshoot-colour-ebook

ABOUT NEW SOCIETY PUBLISHERS

New Society Publishers is an activist, solutions-oriented publisher focused on publishing books to build a more just and sustainable future. Our books offer tips, tools, and insights from leading experts in a wide range of areas.

We're proud to hold to the highest environmental and social standards of any publisher in North America. When you buy New Society books, you are part of the solution!

At New Society Publishers, we care deeply about *what* we publish—but also about *how* we do business.

• This book is printed on 100% **post-consumer recycled paper**, processed chlorine-free, with low-VOC vegetable-based inks (since 2002).

• Our corporate structure is an innovative employee shareholder agreement, so we're one-third employee-owned (since 2015)

• We've created a Statement of Ethics (2021). The intent of this Statement is to act as a framework to guide our actions and facilitate feedback for continuous improvement of our work

• We're carbon-neutral (since 2006)

• We're certified as a B Corporation (since 2016)

• We're Signatories to the UN's Sustainable Development Goals (SDG) Publishers Compact (2020–2030, the Decade of Action)

To download our full catalog, sign up for our quarterly newsletter, and to learn more about New Society Publishers, please visit newsociety.com

ENVIRONMENTAL BENEFITS STATEMENT

New Society Publishers saved the following resources by printing the pages of this book on chlorine free paper made with 100% post-consumer waste.

TREES	WATER	ENERGY	SOLID WASTE	GREENHOUSE GASES
56	**4,500**	**24**	**190**	**24,300**
FULLY GROWN	GALLONS	MILLION BTUs	POUNDS	POUNDS

Environmental impact estimates were made using the Environmental Paper Network Paper Calculator 4.0. For more information visit www.papercalculator.org

Certified
B Corporation

new society
PUBLISHERS
www.newsociety.com

FSC
www.fsc.org
MIX
Paper from responsible sources
FSC® C016245

SDG PUBLISHERS COMPACT